MARXIAN SOCIALISM
IN THE
UNITED STATES

MARXIAN
SOCIALISM
IN THE
UNITED
STATES

BY

DANIEL BELL

PRINCETON, NEW JERSEY

PRINCETON UNIVERSITY PRESS

Copyright, 1952, © 1967, by Princeton University Press

L.C. Card: 67:30481

ISBN 0-691-02155-4

First Princeton Paperback Printing, 1967
Second Printing, 1970
Third Printing, 1973

The text of this essay originally appeared in *Socialism and American Life* (Princeton Studies in American Civilization, Number 4), edited by Donald Drew Egbert and Stow Persons, and published by Princeton University Press in 1952. For this Princeton Paperback edition Daniel Bell has written a Preface and a Bibliographical Essay.

Printed in the United States of America
by Princeton University Press, Princeton, New Jersey

For Irving and Bea Kristol

Respice, Adspice, Prospice

Preface

This essay was written in 1949-1950 and published in 1952 in the Princeton compendium, *Socialism and American Life*, edited by Donald Egbert and Stow Persons. Since then about a half-dozen published studies on American socialism have appeared (as well as a dozen unpublished Ph.D. theses), and on American communism ten scholarly volumes have been published in the series edited by Clinton Rossiter for the Fund for the Republic, while a score of other books, historical, analytical, and sensational (see the Bibliographical Essay, pp. 194-201), have increased the bulk of writing on this subject.

This essay is being reprinted unchanged, and the reasons for this are twofold. First, despite the number of books on the Marxian movements in the United States, there is still not a single volume which encompasses, as this sketch does, the history of all the Marxian parties—the Socialist Labor Party, the Socialist Party, the Communist Party—as well as the various splinter and sectarian groups and personalities; and while many details have been added by the more specialized studies, the historical outline as presented in this monograph remains untouched. Second, and perhaps more important, the theoretical and interpretative framework presented in this essay has influenced many of the subsequent studies in the field, and this may be its enduring contribution.

The basic question confronting all the students of American Marxism is the one posed in 1906 by Werner Sombart: "Why is there no socialism in the United States?" In the most advanced capitalist country of the world, there has been no Labor Party, little corporate class consciousness, and feeble intellectual leadership from the Left—though clearly the *ideas* of Marxism and the political proposals of the American Socialist Party are now the common coin of American intellectual life and its polity.

Most of the explanations—one thinks here of those given two generations ago by Sombart or by Selig Perlman, or of the analyses made by such contemporary theorists as Sidney Hook, Louis Hartz, or S. M. Lipset—have stressed the distinctive conditions of American life, which made a barren ground for a socialist movement: the idea of equality, the opportunities for social mobility, the commitment to liberalism, the constraints of a two-party structure, the rising standard of living, the opportunity for labor to realize its demands through economic bargaining, and the like.

The one question which all such explanations eschewed, and the one this essay attempted to answer was: Why did the socialist movement, as an organized political body, fail to adapt to the distinctive conditions of American life and find a place in the society as did, say, the British Labour Party in England (though not the Social Democratic Federation, organized by M. H. Hyndman, which was the first socialist political organization in Great Britain)? The answer explored in this essay—and it is stated baldly in this Preface though the documentation in these pages relates specific times and circumstances—is that a set of ideological blinders prevented the American Socialist Party from understanding the society. To state the paradox most forcefully: the American Socialist Party, though often called reformist or right-wing, was actually too much a Marxist party.

In the language of the Left, reformist or right-wing derives from an attitude towards revolution or the use of force in inducing social change. Yet reformist parties may also be Marxist in that their basic categories for interpreting a society are drawn from a specific canon, and their judgments about the class or social structure are made in Marxist terms; and thus they are sectarian in their own way. What was true about the American Socialist Party was equally true, I would argue, about the German Social Democratic Party or the French Socialist Party, but in a different context. Though also reformist or right-wing, they were equally Marxist; and though they were able to organize large sections of the working class in their countries, at crucial moments their ability to act, or adapt, was paralyzed because of ideological rigidity.

To cite a crucial illustration: In 1930, a Social Democratic government under Herman Müller ruled in Germany; yet when the Socialists were confronted with the deep economic depression and widespread unemployment, they did not know what to do. For them, as Marxists, there was no way of "tinkering" with the capitalist system. As one of the socialist theorists, Fritz Napthali, put it: "The depression simply had to run its course." In fact, the Socialist government followed orthodox deflationary policies, cutting spending and balancing budgets, thus extending the unemployment and deepening the crisis. In retrospect, it seems astonishing that the socialist economists, among them such gifted men as Rudolf Hilferding—whose work *Finanzkapital* served as the basis of the Marxian theory of imperialism, and who served as finance minister in the Müller cabinet—should have been so shortsighted. Yet Marx and Engels had taught that economic crises were endemic in the capitalist system, that imbalances were introduced in the society by chronic "overproduction," and that the system could "start up" again only when such "overproduction" was used up. The thought that unorthodox fiscal policy could tap idle savings or that the state could intervene to redress economic balances—measures introduced by Wigforss in Sweden and Schacht in Germany, and ideas associated with John Maynard Keynes in England—was alien to the Marxist economists.

In the United States, to take a different illustration, the American Socialist Party during the 1930's moved left at a time when the entire labor movement was swinging behind Franklin D. Roosevelt and the New Deal, because of the socialists' ideological judgment that Fascism would necessarily come to the United States and it was necessary to prepare for "revolutionary" activity. Fascism, from this point of view, was the "last stage of monopoly capitalism," and the American capitalist class, like its European brethren, would shed the mask of bourgeois democracy in order to enforce naked repression against the working class. Apart from the misreading of the character of fascism, such ideas as cultural diversity, or the role of value systems in influencing political behavior, were alien to Marxist thought. From the mechanical Marxist point of view, the important source of social change and the root of power are in the economic "substructure" of society, and all politics flow from that source.* Yet England went through as severe an economic crisis as Germany, and barely fumbled its way through to recovery, yet no large-scale fascist movement took root in England because of its distinctive ethos of liberty and its particular structure of civil, not ideological, politics.

At one crucial turning point after another, when the socialist movement could have entered more directly into American life—as did so many individual socialists who played a formative role in liberal political development—it was prevented from doing so by its ideological dogmatism. Why and how this came about is the burden of a large part of this essay.

This historical thesis is rooted in a broader sociological framework which seeks to explain the diverse character of radical social movements, and their particular dilemmas of social action, in a society they seek to change by divers means. The organizing metaphor I used was Martin Luther's phrase describing the character of his church: it was, he said, "in the world, but not of it"; it lived in the society, but transcended it by making a judgment outside of it. I chose the religious metaphor quite deliberately, because the radical movements as secular religions, both as sects and churches, have faced problems similar to the earlier religious movements in confronting an alien world. I felt, too, that the particular tensions of the secular radical movements could be explained by the threefold paradigm implicit in the metaphor itself.

---

* Thus, in the 1920's, Trotsky held that England and America might go to war with each other since they were the victorious economic powers of World War I, and their ensuing and necessary rivalry for the markets of the world inevitably would lead to a clash. (See *Whither England* [International Publishers, 1925].) As late as 1948, in his book *The American Democracy*, Harold Laski argued that fascism would arise in the United States as an inevitable concomitant to capitalism. Such a belief, it should be pointed out, was nourished by Jack London's indigenous and influential novel the fanciful *The Iron Heel*, which predicted the naked and outright repression of the working class by an organized capitalist class using mercenaries.

The Socialist Party, as I saw it, was "in the world, but not of it." It was *in* the world, in that it proposed specific reforms of society and was melioristic in its immediate aims; but it was not *of* society, in that it refused to accept responsibility for the actions of the government itself. Thus, to maintain its purity, the Socialist Party straight-facedly—sixty years ago—expelled a retired Civil War veteran for accepting a minor position in a "capitalist" municipal administration (see the discussion of the Gridley affair, pages 85-86); or, more seriously, during the Spanish Civil War it disapproved of government aid to the Loyalists because it sought only "workers' aid," not "capitalist aid." A religious movement can maintain its divided stance because it is not called upon to prove its ultimate judgment about the nature of God's grace; this is simply a matter of faith. But a secular movement, living in time, cannot escape the liabilities of its political judgments, and when it is rendered politically ineffectual by its contradictory attitude, faith eventually wanes in the light of experience.

The Communist Party, within the metaphor, lived *neither* in the world *nor* of it, but sought to encapsulate itself as a world of its own. It thus faced a peculiar problem of cohesion. Other, earlier alien movements, such as the utopianism or anarchism, had also rejected existing society completely. But the utopians retreated to an Icarian wilderness which was spatially apart from the world, while the anarchists psychologically suspended time while waiting for the magical "deed" that would instantly transform the world. The Communists, living in the society while seeking to promote a revolutionary movement, sought to maintain their zeal by establishing a psychological distance from the society (by nurturing a wholesale distrust of all institutions as "bourgeois" institutions) and by instilling a combat posture in their adherents. But it was that very distance, and the sense of strangeness it created, which allowed individuals to magnify the fear of Communists and make them such ready targets of hostility during the Korean war and the McCarthyite excesses in American life.

The American labor movement, to complete the logic of the metaphor, learned to live in and of the world, and in so doing managed to transform some of the values of the society—most notably in winning the acceptance of collective rights and group action as legitimate norms, as against the older tradition of individualism.

While a full-scale history of American radicalism and a comprehensive sociology of social movements would necessarily add many other elements, fifteen years later I still stand by this organizing metaphor as a useful explanatory model.

Fifteen years later, a New Left has appeared in the United States. This is not the place for an extended analysis of this phenomenon, yet I feel that the scheme used to understand the radical movements of the first half of the century has its analytical utility here as well.

What is striking about the New Left—and I deal here only with its most interesting grouping, namely the Students for a Democratic Society, circa 1962-1965—is its dilemma of being *in* but not *of* the world, in part, for the very reason that placed someone like Norman Thomas in the same position: namely, that its critique of the society (apart from the Vietnam War, which has given a special edge of bitterness to its feelings) is primarily moral, not political. The themes of the New Left are those of alienation and dehumanization. It rejects materialism and competitiveness, and it is horrified by the bureaucratic and hierarchical character of organization. While its manifest focus is on American society, and its rhetoric is directed against "capitalism," the heart of the critique is actually against "industrial society"; and what is so striking in this regard is the similar critiques, in more veiled and abstract philosophical terms, by young "Marxists" in Poland and Yugoslavia against their communist regimes which are also industrial societies organized around the norms of "efficiency" and "production."

What is lacking in the American New Left is any precision of analysis (therefore its reliance on such vague terms as Power Structure, the Establishment, or simply "the system") or any discussion of political philosophy. Some of this lack derives from the emphasis on "gut feeling" and emotion (and a consequent strong anti-intellectualism); some from the inability to locate the sources of power and change in a society where three or more criteria (property, technical skill, and political mobilization) have become the bases of class and social mobility. Their politics thus becomes, on its negative side, simply one of protest or of "confrontation," by which they mean the tearing down of all authority. And to the extent there is a positive proposal, it is an inchoate, primitive Rousseauism, which preaches the virtue of participatory or direct democracy, since in a bureaucratic society "people are unable to control the decisions which affect their lives." (The idea that if individuals could make such decisions they would be progressive ones is an old Populist fallacy. On the theory of participatory democracy, should individuals in a neighborhood have the right to exclude colored people, or those in a work group to refuse a job to a Negro, because such presences would disrupt the existing character of the neighborhood or work group? Few members of the New Left have ever thought through the conflicting nature of group rights or the problems inherent in the tensions between liberty and democracy.)

Whatever one thinks of the criticisms of contemporary society by the New Left—and one can share the apprehensions about bureaucracy while at the same time appreciating the openness of American institutions and their receptiveness to change—the crucial problem is how one translates these concerns into *political* terms and how one confronts, in this regard, the dilemmas of politics and ethics: politics has the virtue of compromise and responsibility, while moralizing has the implicit vice—since it posits a theory of exclusive truth—of total solutions and elimination of dissent as error or falsehood; politics, though, has the vice of opportunism, while moral views have a foundation in conscience. How, then, does one act politically in a moral way, and act morally in politics?

The New Left tends to feel that all such problems—to the extent they perceive them—are being confronted for the first time. And it is at this point that the history of the different Marxian movements—the opportunism of the socialists and the totalitarianism of the Bolsheviks—have relevance for the present. For the New Leftists are in a difficult position: like sons without fathers, they are nihilists without memory. Coming "out of themselves," with no sense of a past, they have a callow vitality, drive, and hubris, uncomplicated by notions of history, complexity, tragedy, or doubt. And yet, though they reject the radicals of the 1930's, the New Leftists are like them in an uncanny way. The radicals of the 1930's also had no "middle generation" between themselves and the pre-World War I radical movement. And, secure in their belief that they were on the express train of History, they were equally heedless of the few small voices that warned them of the wreckages of the past and of those that might lie ahead. (When told of Kronstadt, the episode in 1921 when Lenin and Trotsky shot down the revolutionary Red sailors because they were demanding free elections; the young communists of the Thirties would say, jeeringly, "Who cares about old history?")

While it is too facile to say that a generation which does not know its own past is bound to repeat those errors, it is possible that a generation which knows its past is more likely to make more intelligent decisions about its future. And that is the virtue of History.

For those who have lived through the radical past, T. S. Eliot's elegy in the *Four Quartets* can serve as its epitaph:

> We cannot revive old factions
> We cannot restore old politics
> Or follow an antique drum.
> These men, and those who opposed them,
> And those whom they opposed
> Accept the constitution of silence
> And are folded in a single party.
> Whatever we inherit from the fortunate
> We have taken from the defeated.

What they had to leave us—a symbol:
A symbol perfected in death.*

But an epitaph is not a forgetting; it is a requiem whose echoes can unlock the past: "This is the use of memory / For liberation—not less of love but expanding. . . ."

Daniel Bell

Columbia University
June 1967

---

* From "Little Gidding" in *Four Quartets*, copyright 1943, by T. S. Eliot. Reprinted by permission of Harcourt, Brace & World, Inc. (New York), and Faber and Faber Ltd. (London).

Contents

Preface   vii

I. Socialism: The Dream and the Reality   3

II. The Mirage of Utopia   16

III. 1886—The First Divide   21

IV. Purist and Pure-and-simple   30

V. Fission, Fusion, and Faction   45

VI. The Golden Age of American Socialism   55

VII. The Inner World of American Socialism   81

VIII. The Decline and Fall of American Socialism   90

IX. The Melancholy Intermezzo   117

X. The Caligari World of Underground Communism   122

XI. The Playboys of the Western World   134

XII. In Dubious Battles   157

XIII. The Days of Sere and Yellow Leaf   182

Bibliographical Essay   194

Index   203

MARXIAN SOCIALISM
IN THE
UNITED STATES

I. Socialism: The Dream and the Reality

SOCIALISM was an unbounded dream. Fourier promised that under socialism people would be at least "ten feet tall." Karl Kautsky, the embodiment of didacticism, proclaimed that the average citizen of a socialist society would be a superman. The flamboyant Antonio Labriola told his Italian followers that their socialist-bred children would each be Galileos and Giordano Brunos. And the high-flown, grandiloquent Trotsky described the socialist millennium as one in which "man would become immeasurably stronger, wiser, freer, his body more harmoniously proportioned, his movements more rhythmic, his voice more musical, and the forms of his existence permeated with dramatic dynamism."[1]

America, too, was an unbounded dream. The utopians gamboled in its virgin wilderness. Some immigrants called it the *Goldene Medinah*, the golden land. Here it seemed as if socialism would have its finest hour. Both Marx and Engels felt a boundless optimism. In 1879 Marx wrote, ". . . the United States have at present overtaken England in the rapidity of economical progress, though they lag still behind in the extent of acquired wealth; but at the same time, the masses are quicker, and have greater political means in their hands, to resent the form of a progress accomplished at their expense."[2] Engels, who wrote a score of letters on the American scene in the late 1880's and early '90's, repeated this prediction time and again. In his introduction to the American edition of *The Conditions of the Working Class in England*, written at the height of enthusiasm over the events of 1886—notably the spectacular rise of the Knights of Labor and the Henry George campaign—he exulted: "On the more favored soil of America, where no medieval ruins bar the way, where history begins with the elements of modern bourgeois society, as evolved in the seventeenth century, the working class passed through these two stages of its development [i.e., a national trade-union movement and an independent labor party] within ten months." And five years later, his optimism undiminished by the sorry turn of events, Engels wrote to Schlüter: ". . . continually renewed waves of advance, followed by equally certain set-backs, are inevitable. Only the advancing waves are becoming more powerful, the set-backs less paralyzing. . . . Once the Americans get started it will be with an energy and violence compared with which we in Europe shall be mere children."[3]

But there still hovers the melancholy question, posed by Werner Som-

---

[1] Quoted in Hayim Greenberg, "Socialism Re-examined." *International Socialist Forum* (London), June 1942, p. 2120.

[2] Letter to Danielson, No. 169 in *Karl Marx and Friedrich Engels: Selected Correspondence, 1846-1895* (New York, 1934), p. 360.

[3] Letter to Schlüter, No. 222, *ibid.*, p. 497.

bart at the turn of the century in the title of a book, *Why Is There No Socialism in the United States?* To this Sombart supplied one set of answers. He pointed to the open frontiers, the many opportunities for social ascent through individual effort, and the rising standard of living of the country as factors. Other writers have expanded these considerations. Selig Perlman, in his *Theory of the Labor Movement*, advanced three reasons for the lack of class consciousness in the United States: the absence of a "settled" wage-earner class; the "free gift" of the ballot (workers in other countries, denied such rights—for example, the Chartists—developed political rather than economic motivations); and third, the impact of succeeding waves of immigration. It was immigration, said Perlman, which gave rise to the ethnic, linguistic, religious, and cultural heterogeneity of American labor, and to the heightened ambitions of immigrants' sons to escape their inferior status.

In the end, all such explanations fall back on the naturally-endowed resources and material vastness of America. In awe of the fact that the Yankee worker consumed almost three times as much bread and meat and four times as much sugar as his German counterpart, Sombart finally exclaimed: "On the reefs of roast beef and apple pie socialistic Utopias of every sort are sent to their doom."[4]

Other explanations have indicated equally general, and relevant, facts. Some have stressed the agrarian basis of American life, with the farmer seesawing to radicalism and conservatism in tune to the business cycle. Others have pointed to the basically geographic, rather than functional, organization of the two-party system, with its emphasis on opportunism, vacuity of rhetoric, and patronage as the mode of political discourse; hence, compromise, rather than rigid principle, becomes the prime concern of the interest-seeking political bloc.

Implicit in many of these analyses, however, was the notion that such conditions were but temporary. Capitalism as an evolving social system would of necessity "mature." Crises would follow, and at that time a large, self-conscious wage-earner class and a socialist movement, perhaps on the European pattern, would probably emerge. The great depression was such a crisis—an emotional shock which shook the self-confidence of the entire society. It left permanent scar tissue in the minds of the American workers. It spurred the organization of a giant trade-union movement which in ten years grew from less than three million to over fifteen million

---

[4] Quoted in Goetz A. Briefs, *The Proletariat* (New York, 1937), p. 193. Communist economists deny this material gain. A leading statistician, Jurgen Kuczynski, has stated that the living conditions of American labor in the last hundred years have actually deteriorated. Confronted with his own evidence that real wages had increased from 1790 to 1900, Kuczynski falls back on Lenin's theory that capitalism divided the workers into the labor aristocracy, bribed by higher wages, and the exploited masses. See Jurgen Kuczynski, *A Short History of Labour Conditions under Industrial Capitalism*, Vol. II, *The United States of America, 1789 to the Present Day* (London, 1943).

workers, or one-fourth of the total labor force of the country.[5] It brought in its train the smoking-hot organizing drives and sit-downs in the Ohio industrial valley which gave the country a whiff of class warfare. In the 1940's labor entered national politics with a vigor—in order to safeguard its economic gains. Here at last was the fertile soil which socialist theorists had long awaited. Yet no socialist movement emerged, nor has a coherent socialist ideology taken seed either in the labor movement or in government. So Sombart's question still remains unanswered.

Most of the attempted answers have discussed not *causes* but *conditions*, and these in but general terms. An inquiry into the fate of a social movement has to be pinned in the specific questions of time, place, and opportunity, and framed within a general hypothesis regarding the "why" of its success or failure. The "why" which this essay proposes (with the usual genuflections to *ceteris paribus*), is that the failure of the socialist movement in the United States is rooted in its inability to resolve a basic dilemma of ethics and politics. The socialist movement, by its very statement of goal and in its rejection of the capitalist order as a whole, could not relate itself to the specific problems of social action in the here-and-now, give-and-take political world. It was trapped by the unhappy problem of living *"in* but not *of* the world," so it could only act, and then inadequately, as the moral, but not political, man in immoral society. It could never resolve but only straddle the basic issue of either accepting capitalist society, and seeking to transform it from within as the labor movement did, or becoming the sworn enemy of that society, like the communists. A religious movement can split its allegiances and live *in* but not *of* the world (like Lutheranism); a political movement can not.

In social action there is an irreconcilable tension between ethics and politics. Lord Acton posed the dilemma in a note: "Are politics an attempt to realize ideals, or an endeavour to get advantages, within the limits of ethics?" More succinctly, "are ethics a purpose or a limit?"[6] In the largest sense, society is an organized system for the distribution of tangible rewards and privileges, obligations and duties. Within that frame, ethics deals with the *ought* of distribution, implying a theory of justice. Politics is the concrete *mode* of distribution, involving a power struggle between organized groups to determine the allocation of privilege. In some periods of history, generally in closed societies, ethics and politics have

[5] Actually such a statistic slights the real magnitude of labor's swift rise. The non-agricultural labor force is approximately forty-five million, so that unionization touches one in three. Even here a further breakdown is revealing. Nearly every major manufacturing industry (except chemicals and textiles) is more than 80 per cent unionized.

[6] Cited in Gertrude Himmelfarb, "The American Revolution in the Political Theory of Lord Acton," *Journal of Modern History*, Dec. 1949, p. 312.

gone hand in hand. But a distinguishing feature of modern society is the separation of the two; and ideology—the façade of general interest and universal values which masks a specific self-interest—replaces ethics. The redivision of the rewards and privileges of society can only be accomplished in the political arena. But in that fateful commitment to politics, an ethical goal, stated as "purpose rather than limit," becomes a far-arching goal before which lies a yawning abyss that can be spanned only by a "leap." The alternatives were forcefully posed by Max Weber in his contrast between the "ethics of responsibility" (or the acceptance of limits) and the "ethics of conscience" (or the dedication to absolute ends). Weber, arguing that only the former is applicable in politics, writes: "The matter does not appear to me so desperate if one does not ask exclusively who is morally right and who is morally wrong? But if one rather asks: Given the existing conflict how can I solve it with the least internal and external danger for all concerned?"[7] Such a pragmatic compromise rather than dedication to an absolute (like bolshevism or religious pacifism) is possible, however, only when there is a basic consensus among contending groups about the rules of the game. But this consensus the socialist movement, because of its original rejection of society, while operating within it, could never fully accept.

The distinctive character of "modern" politics is the involvement of *all* strata of society in movements of social change, rather than the fatalistic acceptance of events as they are. Its starting point was, as Karl Mannheim elegantly put it, the "orgiastic chiliasm" of the Anabaptists, their messianic hope, their ecstatic faith in the millennium to come. For the Anabaptism of the sixteenth century, of Thomas Münzer and those who sought to establish at Münster the Kingdom of God on earth, proclaimed not merely that equality of souls stressed by Luther, but also equality of property. Otherworldly religious quietism became transformed into a revolutionary activism in order to realize the millennium in the here and now. Thus the religious frenzy of the chiliasts which burst the bonds of the old religious order threatened to buckle the social order as well; for unlike previous revolutions, chiliasm did not aim against a single oppression, but at the entire existing social order.

The characteristic psychological fact about the chiliast is that for him "there is no inner articulation of time." There is only the "absolute presentness." "Orgiastic energies and ecstatic outbursts began to operate in a worldly setting and tensions previously transcending day to day life became explosive agents within it."[8] The chiliast is neither "in the world

[7] From *Max Weber* (ed. by H. H. Gerth and C. W. Mills; New York, 1946), p. 9. In the same volume see also Weber's "Politics as a Vocation," pp. 119ff.
[8] Karl Mannheim, *Ideology and Utopia* (New York, 1936), pp. 190-93.

[n]or of it." He stands outside of it and against it because salvation, the millennium, is immediately at hand. Where such a hope is possible, where such a social movement can transform society in a cataclysmic flash, the "leap" is made, and in the pillar of fire the fusion of ethics and politics is possible. But where societies are stable, and social change can only come piecemeal, the pure chiliast in despair turns nihilist, rather than make the bitter-tasting compromises with the established hierarchical order. "When this spirit ebbs and deserts these movements," writes Mannheim, "there remains behind in the world a naked mass-frenzy and despiritualized fury." In a later and secularized form, this attitude found its expression in Russian anarchism. So Bakunin could write: "The desire for destruction is at the same time a creative desire."

Yet not only the anarchist, but every socialist, every convert to political messianism, is in the beginning something of a chiliast. In the newly-found enthusiasms, in the identification with an oppressed group, hope flares that the "final conflict" will not be far ahead. ("Socialism in our time," was the affirmative voice of Norman Thomas in the 1930's.) But the "revolution" is not always immediately in sight, and the question of how to discipline this chiliastic zeal and hold it in readiness has been the basic problem of socialist strategy.

The most radical approach was that of Georges Sorel with his concept of the revolutionary myth ("*images de batailles*"), a myth which functions as a bastardized version of the doctrine of salvation. These unifying images, Sorel wrote, can neither be proved nor disproved, thus they are "capable of evoking as an undivided whole" the mass of diverse sentiments which exist in society. "The syndicalists solve this problem perfectly, by concentrating the whole of socialism in the drama of the general strike; thus there is no longer any place for the reconciliation of contraries in the equivocations of the professors; everything is clearly mapped out so that only one interpretation of Socialism is possible." In this "catastrophic conception" of socialism, as Sorel called it, "*it is the myth in its entirety which is alone important*."[9]

But in the here and now, people live "in parts." "History does not work with bottled essences," wrote Acton, "but with active combinations; compromise is the soul if not the whole of politics. Occasional conformity is the nearest practical approach to orthodoxy and progress is along diagonals. . . . Pure dialectics and bilateral dogmas have less control than custom and interest and prejudice."[10] And for the socialist movements, operating on "partial" day-to-day problems, the dilemma remained.

[9] Georges Sorel, *Reflections on Violence* (3rd ed., New York, 1912), pp. 131, 136, emphasis in the original.
[10] Himmelfarb, *op.cit.*, p. 312.

7

Neither nineteenth-century American radicals nor the American social-ists faced up to this problem of social compromise. The utopias that were spun so profusely in the nineteenth century assumed that in the course of evolution "reason" would find its way and the perfect society would emerge. But so mechanical were the mannikin visions of human delights in such utopias that a modern reading of Bellamy, for example, with its plan for conscript armies of labor ("a horrible cockney dream," William Morris called *Looking Backward*) only arouses revulsion.

The "scientific socialist" movement that emerged at the turn of the century mocked these utopian unrealities. Only the organization of the proletariat could bring a better world. But this apparent relatedness to the world was itself a delusion. The socialist dilemma was still how to face the problem of "in the world and of it," and in practice the early socialist movement "rejected" the world; it simply waited for the new. Although the American Socialist Party sought to function politically by raising "im-mediate demands" and pressing for needed social reforms, it rarely took a stand on the actual political problems that emerged from the on-going functioning of the society. "What but meaningless phrases are 'imperial-ism,' 'expansion,' 'free silver,' 'gold standard,' etc., to the wage worker?" asked Eugene V. Debs in 1900. "The large capitalists represented by Mr. McKinley and the small capitalists represented by Mr. Bryan are interested in these 'issues' but they do not concern the working class."[11] These "issues" were beside the point, said Debs, because the worker stood outside society. Thus Debs and the socialist movement as a whole would have no traffic with the capitalist parties. Even on local municipal issues the party would not compromise. The socialist movement could "afford" this purity be-cause of its supreme confidence about the future. "The socialist program is not a theory imposed upon society for its acceptance or rejection. It is but the interpretation of what is, sooner or later, inevitable. Capitalism is already struggling to its destruction," proclaimed the Socialist national platform of 1904, the first issued by the Socialist Party.[12]

But unlike the other-worldly movements toward salvation, which can always postpone the date of the resurrection, the Socialist Party, living in the here and now, had to show results. It was a movement based on a belief in "history"; but it found itself outside of "time." World War I finally broke through the façade. For the first time the party had to face a stand on a realistic issue of the day. And on that issue almost the entire intellectual leadership of the party deserted, and the back of American socialism was broken.

[11] E. V. Debs, "Outlook for Socialism in the U.S.," *International Socialist Review*, Sept. 1900; reprinted in *Writings and Speeches of Eugene V. Debs* (New York, 1948), p. 37.
[12] *Proceedings, National Convention of the Socialist Party, Chicago, Illinois, May 1 to 6, 1904*, p. 308.

The socialist movement of the 1930's, the socialism of Norman Thomas, could not afford the luxury of the earlier belief in the inevitable course of history. It was forced to take stands on the particular issues of the day. But it too rejected completely the premises of the society which shaped these issues. In effect, the Socialist Party acknowledged the fact that it lived "in" the world, but refused the responsibility of becoming a part "of" it. But such a straddle is impossible for a *political* movement. It was as if it consented to a duel, with no choice as to weapons, place, amount of preparation, etc. Politically, the consequences were disastrous. Each issue could only be met by an ambiguous political formula which would satisfy neither the purist, nor the activist who lived with the daily problem of choice. When the Loyalists in Spain demanded arms, for example, the Socialist Party could only respond with a feeble policy of "workers aid," not (capitalist) government aid; but to the Spaniard, arms, not theoretical niceties, were the need of the moment. When the young trade unionists, whom the socialists seeded into the labor movement, faced the necessity of going along politically with Roosevelt and the New Deal in order to safeguard progressive legislative gains, the socialists proposed a "labor party" rather than work with the Democrats, and so the Socialist Party lost almost its entire trade-union base. The threat of fascism and World War II finally proved to be the clashing rocks through which the socialist argonauts could not row safely. How to defeat Hitler without supporting capitalist society? Some socialists raised the slogan of a "third force." The Socialist Party, however, realized the futility of that effort; in characteristic form, it chose abnegation. The best way to stem fascism, it stated, "is to make democracy work at home." But could the issue be resolved other than militarily? The main concern of the anti-Fascist movement had to be with the political center of Fascist power, Hitler's Berlin, and any other concern was peripheral.

In still another way the religious, chiliastic origin of modern socialism revealed itself—the multiplication of splits, the constant formation of sectarian splinter groups each hotly disputing the other regarding the true road to power. Socialism is an eschatological movement; it is sure of its destiny, because "history" leads it to its goal. But though sure of its final ends, there is never a standard of testing the immediate means. The result is a constant fractiousness in socialist life. Each position taken is always open to challenge by those who feel that it would only swerve the movement from its final goal and lead it up some blind alley. And because it is an ideological movement, embracing all the realm of the human polity, the Socialist Party is always challenged to take a stand on every problem from Viet Nam to Finland, from prohibition to pacifism. And, since for every two socialists there are always three political opinions, the consequence has been that in its inner life, the Socialist Party has never, *even for a single year,* been without some issue which threatened to split the party and which forced it to spend much of its time on the problem of reconciliation or rupture. In this fact lies the chief clue to the impotence of American socialism as a political movement, especially in the past twenty years.[13]

But what of the proletariat itself? What is its role in the socialist drama of history? How does the proletariat see through the veils of obscurity and come to self-awareness? Marx could say with Jesus, "I have come to end all mysteries, not to perpetuate them." His role, in his own self-image, was to lay bare the fetishes which enslave modern man and thus confute Hegel's claim that freedom and rationality had already been achieved. But like his old master he could only deal with the "immanent" forces of history, not the mechanics of social action.[14]

All political movements, Marx wrote, have been slaves to the symbols of the past.[15] But history is the process of progressive disenchantment: men are no longer bound to the river gods and anthropomorphic deities of

---

[13] Far beyond the reaches of this essay is the problem of the psychological types who are attracted by such a sectarian existence. Yet one might say here that certainly the illusions of settling the fate of history, the mimetic combat on the plains of destiny, and the vicarious sense of power in demolishing opponents all provide a sure sense of gratification which makes the continuance of sectarian life desirable. The many leadership complexes, the intense aggressiveness through gossip, the strong clique group formations, all attest to a particular set of psychological needs and satisfactions which are fulfilled in these opaque, molecular worlds.

[14] In *The German Ideology* Marx poses the question of how self-interest becomes transformed into ideology. "How does it come about," he asks, "that personal interests continually grow, despite the persons, into class-interests, into common interests which win an independent existence over against the individual persons, in this independence take on the shape of general interests, enter as such into opposition with the real individuals, and in this opposition, according to which they are defined as general interests, can be conceived by the consciousness as ideal, even as religious, sacred interests?" See Karl Marx, *The German Ideology* (New York, 1939), notes, p. 203. But Marx, exasperatingly, never really answered his own question! Sidney Hook, in his article on "Materialism" in the *Encyclopaedia of the Social Sciences* (New York, 1933), x, p. 219, rephrases the problem in these words: "What are the specific mechanisms by which economic conditions influence the habits and motives of classes, granted that individuals are actuated by motives that are not always a function of the individual self-interest? Since classes are composed of individuals, how are class interests furthered by the non-economic motives of individuals?" But he too left it as a question. So far, no Marxist theoretician has yet detailed the crucial psychological and institutional nexus which shows how the "personifications" or mask of class role, is donned by the individual as self-identity.

[15] "Thus Luther donned the mask of the Apostle Paul, the Revolution of 1789 to 1814 draped itself alternately as the Roman Republic and the Roman Empire," Marx wrote in *The Eighteenth Brumaire of Louis Bonaparte.* For an exciting view of the relation of Marx to myths, see the two articles by Harold Rosenberg in the *Kenyon Review,* Autumn 1948, and Autumn 1949, entitled "The Resurrected Romans and the Pathos of the Proletariat."

the agricultural societies; nor need they be bound to the abstract impersonal deity of bourgeois Protestantism. Man himself was potential. But how to realize his potentiality? The intellectual was, in part, capable of self-emancipation because he possessed the imagination to transcend his origins. But the proletariat, as a class, could develop only to the extent that the social relations of society itself revealed to the slave the thongs that bound him. Man is no more free, said Marx in *Das Kapital*, because he can sell his labor power to whom he wishes. Exploitation is implicit in the very structure of capitalist society, which in order to live must constantly expand by extracting surplus value and thus accumulate new capital. In the process, the proletarian would be reduced to the barest minimum of human existence (the law of increasing misery) and thus robbed of any mark of distinction. In the agony of alienation he would realize consciously a sense of identity which would unite him with others and create a cohesive social movement of revolution.[16] In action he would no longer be manipulated but "make" himself.

Thus the scene is set for the grand drama. Out of the immanent, convulsive contradictions of capitalism, conflict would spread. The proletariat, neither in nor of the world, would inherit the world. But History (to use these personifications) confounded Marx's prophecy, at least in the West. The law of increasing misery was refuted by the tremendous advances of technology. The trade union began bettering the worker's lot. And, in the political struggles that followed, it found that it could sustain itself not by becoming a revolutionary instrument against society, but by accepting a place within society.

In the America of the nineteenth century, almost every social movement had involved an effort by the worker to escape his lot as a worker. At times the solution was free land, or cheap money, or producers' cooperatives, or some other chimera from the gaudy bag of utopian dreams. The rise of the American Federation of Labor signaled the end of this drive for some new "northwest passage." Under Gompers, labor's single ambition was to achieve a status on a par with that of business and the church, as a "legitimate" social institution of American life. The socialists within and without the A.F.L. challenged this approach, and lost. As a

---

[16] Actually, in Marx's writings there are three distinct concepts of class, as Raymond Aron has pointed out in "Social Structure and the Ruling Class," *British Journal of Sociology*, Mar. 1950. Marx's historic analysis, as in *The Eighteenth Brumaire*, shows a subtle awareness of the complex shadings of social roles which, in action, give rise to many varied social categories and diverse political interest groups. In the conclusion to *Das Kapital*, however, Marx begins a simplified analysis of "essential" class on the basis of source of income; but the conversion of income groups into congruent categories itself faces the question of what are the mechanisms of self-awareness. Finally, as in the *Communist Manifesto*, there is the eschatological view, in which the *Götterdämmerung* of history polarizes society into two classes and awareness arises from beholding the widening abyss.

11

result, before World War I they found themselves estranged from the labor movement which they regarded as necessary for the fulfillment of socialism. During the New Deal and after, however, the socialists in the unions, faced with a similar dilemma, chose the labor movement. When the Socialist Party refused to go along, it lost its strength as a tangible force in American political life.

But even apart from its presumed relation to socialism, perhaps the most significant fact regarding the "consciousness" of the American proletariat is that in the past thirty years American middle-class mass culture has triumphed over capitalist and worker alike. The America of 1890, the capstone of the Gilded Age, was a society of increasing differentiation in manners and morals, the area, that is, of *visible* distinction and the one that could give rise, as in Europe, to class resentment. It saw the emergence in baroque mansion, elaborate dress, and refined leisure activities of a new *haut* style of life. By the 1920's this style was already gone. Beneath this change was the transformation of entrepreneurial to corporate capitalism, with a corresponding shift in the social type from the self-made man to the smooth, faceless manager. But beyond that it was a change in the very character of society, symbolized in large measure by the adjective which qualified the phrases "mass production" and "mass consumption." Production—apart from war needs—was no longer geared *primarily*, as it had been in the late nineteenth and early twentieth centuries, to turning out capital goods (steel, railroad equipment, tools), but to the output of consumers' durable goods (autos, washing machines, radios, etc.). The mass market became the arbiter of taste, and the style of life was leveled. In another dimension of this vast social revolution that has been taking place during the past quarter of a century, professional skill has been replacing property as the chief means of acquiring and wielding power, and the educational system rather than inheritance has become the chief avenue for social ascent. In short, a new-type, bureaucratic, mass society has been emerging, and with it, new institutions, of which the modern trade union is one. If the worker was "absorbed" culturally into the social structure of this new, bureaucratic mass society, the trade union itself finally achieved its respectability.

World War II brought a social truce and the beginnings of a social merger between the major power blocs in American life. "Labor" was living in and of the capitalist society. It was represented on government boards and was consulted on policy. The rise of totalitarianism and the beginning emergence of a garrison economy here as a response demonstrated that all social groups had a common fate if democracy fell. In this respect all other values have become subordinate. And the emergence of a garrison economy as a response to the threat of a third world war illustrated the need for some defined national interest in the form of government decision to bring the particular self-interest groups to heel.

For the fast-dwindling Socialist Party the answer to this new dilemma was still a "third force," or a "neither-nor" position which sought to stand apart and outside the swirling sandstorm of conflict.[16a] Like the ostrich in the Slavic parable, they put their heads in the sand and thought no one was looking. By 1950, nobody was.

For the twentieth-century communist, however, there are none of these agonizing problems of ethics and politics. He is the perpetual alien living in hostile enemy territory. Any gesture of support, any pressure for social reforms—all of these are simply tactics, a set of Potemkin villages, the façades to be torn down after the necessary moment for deception has passed. His is the ethic of "ultimate ends"; only the goal counts, the means are inconsequential.[17] Bolshevism thus is neither in the world nor of it, but stands outside. It takes no responsibility for the consequences of any act within the society nor does it suffer the tension of acquiescence or rejection. But the socialist, unlike the communist, lacks that fanatical vision, and so faces the daily anguish of participating in and sharing responsibility for the day-to-day problems of the society.

It is this commitment to the "absolute" that gives bolshevism its religious strength. It is this commitment which sustains one of the great political myths of the century, the myth of the iron-willed Bolshevik. Selfless, devoted, resourceful, a man with a cause, he is the modern Hero. He alone, a man of action, a soldier for the future, continues the tradition of courage which is the aristocratic heritage bestowed on Western culture and which has been devitalized by the narrow, monetary calculus of the bourgeoisie. (Can the businessman be the Hero?) Such is the peculiar myth which has taken deep hold among many intellectuals. It is a myth which is also responsible for a deep emotional hatred and almost pathologic resentment felt most keenly by the ex-communist intellectual, the "defrocked priest," toward the party. For the "Bolshevik," through the myth of absolute selflessness, claims to be the "extreme man," the man of no compromise, the man of purity. The intellectual, driven to be moral, fears the comparison and resents the claim. Thus he bears either a sense of guilt or a psychological wound.

In addition to the myth of the Bolshevik as iron-willed Hero, twentieth-century communism has made several other distinctive contributions to the theory and practice of modern politics. Like so many other social doctrines, these were never put down systematically in a fully self-

[16a] The "third-force" position was repudiated by Norman Thomas in 1951. He came out staunchly in favor of America's effort to repel communist aggression in Korea.

[17] "The believer in an ethic of ultimate ends," wrote Max Weber, "feels 'responsible' only for seeing to it that the flame of pure intention is not quelched." Max Weber, "Politics as a Vocation," in Gerth and Mills, eds., *op.cit.*, p. 121.

13

conscious fashion; yet over the years they have emerged as a coherent philosophy. Of these contributions some five can be linked schematically. These are central for understanding the history of the Communist Party in this country and are summarized here.

One of the major innovations of the Bolsheviks is their theory of power. Against the nineteenth-century liberal view which saw social decisions as a reconciliation of diverse interests through compromise and consensus— a theory which social democracy gradually began to accept after World War I when it was called upon to take responsibility for governments and enter coalitions—the Bolsheviks saw politics as a naked struggle for power, power being defined as a monopoly of the means of coercion. Power was thought of almost in the sense of physics, its equation being almost literally mass times force equals power. The individual, central to the liberal theory of a market society, was for the Bolshevik a helpless entity. Only the organized group counted, and only a mass base could exert social leverage in society.

But a mass requires leadership. The great unresolved dilemma of Marxian sociology was the question of how the proletariat achieves the consciousness of its role. To await the immanent development of history was to rely on the fallacy of misplaced abstraction. "Spontaneity" was not for Lenin a reality in mass politics; nor was the trade union an effective instrument. His answer, the most significant addition to revolutionary theory, was the vanguard role of the party.

Against the "economism" which glorified the role of the trade union, Lenin argued that the mere organization of society on a trade-union basis could only lead to wage consciousness, not revolutionary consciousness; against the spontaneity theories of Rosa Luxemburg he argued that the masses, by nature, were backward. Only the vanguard party, aware of the precarious balance of social forces, could assess the play and correctly tip the scales in the revolutionary direction. The classic formulation of revolutionary avant-guardism Lenin outlined in his *What Is to Be Done?* published as early as 1903.

In it he wrote that without the "dozen" tried and talented leaders, and talented men are not born by the hundred, professionally trained, schooled by long experience and working in perfect harmony, no class in modern society is capable of conducting a determined struggle. "I assert," said Lenin, "(1) that no movement can be durable without a stable organization of leaders to maintain continuity; (2) that the more widely the masses are spontaneously drawn into the struggle and form the basis of the movement, the more necessary it is to have such an organization and the more stable must it be (for it is much easier for demagogues to side-track the more backward sections of the masses); (3) that the organization must consist chiefly of persons engaged in revolution as a profession."[17a]

If the party were to become a vanguard, it needed discipline in action, and thus there arose the principle of party hierarchy and "democratic centralism." In theory there was full discussion of policy before decision, and rigid adherence to policy once discussion had been closed. In practice a line was laid down by the leadership which was binding on all. Lenin's promulgation of these doctrines split Russian socialism in 1903 and brought about the emergence of the Bolshevik and Menshevik factions. In the beginning Trotsky opposed Lenin's ideas, but later he capitulated. As he reveals in his autobiography: ". . . there is no doubt that at that time I did not fully realize what an intense and imperious centralism the revolutionary party would need to lead millions of people in a war against the old order. . . . Revolutionary centralism is a harsh, imperative and exacting principle. It often takes the guise of absolute ruthlessness in its relation to individual members, to whole groups of former associates. It is not without significance that the words 'irreconcilable' and 'relentless' are among Lenin's favorites."[18]

From the principle of power and the theory of party organization rose two other key tenets of bolshevism. One was the polarization of classes. Because it looked only toward the "final conflict," bolshevism split society into two classes, the proletariat and the bourgeoisie. But the proletariat could only be emancipated by the vanguard party; hence anyone resisting the party must belong to the enemy. For Lenin, the maxim of the absolute ethic meant that "those who are not for me are against me." Hence, too, a formulation of the theory of "social fascism," which in the early 1930's branded the social democrats rather than Hitler as the chief enemy, and led the communists to unite, in several instances, with the Nazis in order to overthrow the German Republic.

The second tenet, deriving from the backward nature of the masses, was the key psychological tactic of formulating all policy into forceful slogans. Slogans dramatize events, make issues simple, and wipe out the qualifications, nuances, and subtleties which accompany democratic political action. In his chapter on slogans[19] Lenin wrote one of the first manuals on modern mass psychology. During the revolution, the Bolsheviks achieved a flexibility of tactic by using such slogans as "All Power to the Soviets," "Land, Peace, and Bread," etc. The basic political tactic of all Communist parties everywhere is to formulate policy primarily through the use of

---

[17a] V. I. Lenin, *What Is to Be Done?* (New York, 1929), p. 116.

[18] Leon Trotsky, *My Life* (New York, 1930), pp. 161-62.

[19] V. I. Lenin, "On Slogans," in *Toward the Seizure of Power*, Vol. xxi, Book i, *Collected Works* (New York, 1932), pp. 43-50.

key slogans which are transmitted first to the party rank and file and then to the masses.[20]

The consequence of the theory of the vanguard party and its relation to the masses is a system of "two truths," the *consilia evangelica*, or special ethics endowed for those whose lives are so dedicated to the revolutionary ends, and another truth for the masses. Out of this belief grew Lenin's famous admonition—one can lie, steal, or cheat, for the cause itself has a higher truth.

Communism as a social movement did not, with the brief exception of the late nineteen-thirties, achieve any sizable following in the United States. Its main appeal, then, was to the dispossessed intelligentsia of the depression generation and to the "engineers of the future" who were captivated by the type of elitist appeal just described. Within American life, its influence was oblique. It stirred many Americans to action against injustices, and left them with burnt fingers when, for reasons of expediency, the party line changed and the cause was dropped. It provided an unmatched political sophistication to a generation that went through its ranks and gave to an easygoing, tolerant, sprawling America a lesson in organizational manipulation and hard-bitten ideological devotion which this country, because of tradition and temperament, found hard to understand. But most of all, through the seeds of distrust and anxiety it sowed, communism has spawned a reaction, an hysteria and bitterness that democratic America may find difficult to erase in the bitter years ahead.

Thus within the span of a century American socialism passed from those bright and unbounded dreams of social justice which possessed the utopians and early Marxians alike to—in the deeds of one bastard faction at least—a nightmare of distrust and bitterness. The remainder of this essay will be devoted to the history of that transformation.

II. The Mirage of Utopia

When the American colonies broke away from England they inscribed upon the back of the great seal authorized by Congress *Novus Ordo Seclorum*—we are the new order of the ages, the beginning of the American era. The American continent, with its vast lands and mighty riches, was destined to be a great social laboratory. Here the unfolding design of "God, Master Workman," would be manifest. Such a disguised deism, emphasiz-

---

[20] Compare Hitler's use of the idea of slogans: "The great masses' receptive ability is only very limited, their understanding is small, but their forgetfulness is very great. As a consequence of these facts, all effective propaganda has to limit itself only to a very few points and use them like slogans until even the very last man is able to imagine what is intended by such a word. As soon as one sacrifices this basic principle and tries to become versatile, the effect will fritter away as the masses are neither able to digest the material offered nor to retain it." See *Mein Kampf* (New York, 1940; the complete and unabridged Reynal and Hitchcock, ed.), p. 234.

ing the aspect of God as a craftsman rather than a fixed revelation, was congenial to the growth of a pragmatic temper. It was a society which, if it did not welcome, would at least abide without scorn the efforts of small bands to explore the design of the millennium. And if in places the response was hostile, there was the Icarian wilderness, stretching from Texas to Iowa, in which utopian colonies might find refuge, safe from prying eyes, to continue their chiliastic search. Small wonder then that such colonies arose in prodigal number.

Utopian socialism struck many roots in America, but few took hold. One might suppose that this early growth did nourish the later, stronger shoots of political socialism. Yet such a view is denied by Morris Hillquit, American Socialist leader and historian of the movement. "On the whole it is safe to say," Hillquit asserted, "that the early utopian theories and communistic colonies had but little influence on the formation of the modern socialist movement in the United States."[21]

Hillquit, however, viewed the connection only in terms of organizational links between the utopians and the later political movements. Himself an ideologue, he sought to establish a distinctive, "scientific" basis for political socialism. But the Hillquit interpretation is extremely narrow. In the continuing socialist definition of ethical goal, the utopian influence was obdurate. If it failed to take deep root, certainly it affected the character of the soil from which the later movements of social protest emerged. The utopian spirit was largely responsible for a flood of novels, scholarly tracts, semiliterary treatises, and other imaginative bits (catalogued by V. L. Parrington, Jr., in his *American Dreams*) which have fired the minds of millions; these utopias, particularly those of Edward Bellamy and Laurence Gronlund, exercised a strong influence on American socialism. The utopian influence was responsible, too, for the host of dazzling reform schemes which were presented by socialists all through the nineteenth century; these ranged from various money and land panaceas which, by a quick twist of the financial system, promised to change the social structure of the country, to the colonization plans, some of which popped up as late as 1897 and played an important role in the founding—and splitting—of the Debsian Social Democratic Party. Finally the utopian climate shaped the thinking of the early American labor movement and turned it to the espousal of homesteading, producers' cooperatives, and greenbackism. It was in reaction to these futile efforts that Samuel Gompers evolved his own ideas of pure-and-simple unionism. Thus even if only to combat the utopian influence, every section of American political socialism down to World War I had to come to grips with it.

Labor's earliest significant political activity in the United States began

[21] Morris Hillquit, *History of Socialism in the United States* (New York, 1903), p. 149.

in 1829 with the Workingmen's Party of New York. Quite typically, it was organized by middle-class humanitarians. However, it drew labor support and its ticket in 1829 included six workers among eleven candidates for the state assembly. The party's chief aims were the abolition of imprisonment for debt, a lien law which would allow workers to make claim on a bankrupt employer, and free public education. Apart from these immediate demands, however, it had no unified philosophy. Followers of Robert Owen were interested largely in widespread education, while machinist Thomas Skidmore proposed a plan for the renewed division of property in each generation. The party soon split, with the factions cutting across various lines. In part the split was an issue of personalities. A second crossing was between those who insisted on daily "bread-and-butter" issues against those who sought to commit the party to distant political goals, and among the latter there were quarrels over the definition of goals. Finally there were the old-line politicians, ready to step in at the first sign of electoral strength and deal with opportunistic elements. In varying degree these divisions were to recur and split the tens of labor parties that flourished briefly in the latter half of the century.

The political failure of the independent Workingmen's Party inspired some labor people to swear off politics and inspired others, particularly George Henry Evans, a former leader of the party, to a new political tack. Evans had long been convinced that the solution of the labor question lay in opening cheap western lands that would drain off excess and wage-depressing labor supply. In the 1840's Evans shaped a new political strategy—the tactic of the free-floating pressure group. If labor had its own party, he argued, it would have to present a coherent program on a wide variety of fractious issues, e.g., tariff, money, immigration, land, etc. But the Agrarian League could support men of diverse parties, as long as they would sign a preelection pledge to support the free-land plank. Evans' tactic was to become a potent argument in labor's constant debate regarding political action.

Throughout the 1840's the agrarian question and cooperative colonies absorbed the energies of the labor and intellectual groups. At this time almost all discussion of socialism hinged on the distribution of property, and in the specific sense on the land question—so much so, in fact, that in 1848 Webster's *American Dictionary*, as revised by Goodrich, defined both socialism and communism in terms of agrarianism: "SOCIALISM, n. A social state in which there is a community of property among all the citizens; a new term for AGRARIANISM. [See COMMUNISM]."[22]

This emphasis on land was responsible for changing the ideas of many German radicals who flocked here after 1848. One such was Herman

[22] Cited by A. E. Bestor, Jr., in "The Evolution of the Socialist Vocabulary," *Journal of the History of Ideas*, IX, No. 3 (June 1948), p. 263.

Kriege, a leader in Europe of the League of the Just. In the United States the theories of George Henry Evans attracted him and he founded the Social Reform Association to propagate the idea of free land. For his pains he was expelled by Karl Marx from the European socialist group. A better-known figure was Wilhelm Weitling, a magnetic individual who had been active in the secret revolutionary societies in Europe and had been a member of the émigré German workingmen's society of which Marx and Engels were the leaders. In America, his quick eye saw that the abstract theories he once held were meaningless. Here, political rights had been achieved and the problem was one of economic reform. In 1850 Weitling brought forth a plan for a labor exchange bank as a compromise between the existing order and revolution. Since property in this country was widely distributed, he gave up his early faith in the common owner-ship of all property. But because the merchant capitalist was the source of monopoly, exchange alone was to be centralized. To be sure the labor exchange bank was no new idea. It had been tried in London by Robert Owen almost twenty years before and was the favorite theme of Louis Blanc and other French socialists. The idea in simple outline was a socialized marketing plan. The weakness of Owen's scheme had been that any and all commodities were bought by the bank, but only the most use-ful were sold, leaving a huge amount of unwanted items. Weitling thought he could remedy Owen's weakness by linking producers' cooperatives to the exchange.

Weitling called a convention in 1850, the first national convention of German workmen on American soil; but the exchange bank never came to fruition. Weitling's high-handed methods, his refusal to submit to the majority when he disagreed with it, and his self-assertiveness soon antag-onized other members. So, on personal grounds the organization broke up.

In the succeeding decade the socialist "movement" was limited to German working-class centers in the large northern cities. In the early 1850's Joseph Weydemeyer, a personal friend of Marx and Engels, came to New York and sought to introduce their theories to the German workers' groups, but without much success. During the same period vague socialist doctrines were held by various German émigrés who had organized popu-lar sports unions or *Turnvereins*. However, they had little contact with or influence on the labor movement of the time.

In the early sixties unionism again was on the rise. But its course was not clear. Some voices favored straightforward economic bargaining to resist employer wage-cutting; others spoke for broader work reforms (e.g., shortening the work day) through legislative action; some wanted producers' cooperatives; still others demanded reforms in the money and credit system to curb the power of the financier; and some voices, echoing the past, called for new free land as a way of helping reduce the supply of urban labor and give the worker a chance at his own livelihood. In the next forty years, moving almost as regularly as the tides, labor turned first to political action and then to economic organization. A failure in one field would give rise to sentiment for the other and then the tide would turn again.

The first dominant tendency was toward political action, and in 1866 the National Labor Union was organized in Baltimore. (The same year, another organization, the International Workingmen's Association, among whose leaders was Karl Marx, was holding its first meeting in Geneva.) At first, the main objective of the Union, a federation led by William Sylvis of the molders, was the enactment of an eight-hour-day law. A year later, however, this question had been pushed into the background and the new pipe of Pan was money reform. Of the three-thousand-word declaration of principles adopted by the National Labor Union almost two thousand words dealt with financial reform. Labor's interests (in spite of occasional attacks leveled against "producer classes") were still primarily with those of the "producer," the farmer, and the small businessman rather than with wage and hour demands.

In 1869, Sylvis died and shortly thereafter the National Labor Union declined. Whether the organization might have held together if the dynamic Sylvis had lived is an open question. The waters were already running the other way. A labor party in Massachusetts which had scored a smashing success in 1869 foundered badly the following year. A similar loss of political interest was manifest throughout the labor movement. The revival of industry by 1870 and the disastrous failure of almost all the producers' cooperatives brought about a new interest in straightforward trade unionism. By 1872, unionism had grown strong enough to strike successfully in many cases for an eight-hour day. The new leaders of labor—Siney of the miners, Saffin of the molders, and Foran of the coopers—were primarily trade unionists.

When, following the depression of 1873 and the disintegration of a number of national trade unions, the political current came running in again, the Greenback Party was formed, and it included a number of the older leaders of the National Labor Union. The party's platform argued that cheap money would relieve industrial depressions; older references to the exploiting "producer classes," however, disappeared. Peter Cooper was nominated for the presidency in 1876 and received about 82,000 votes, largely from the rural districts.

The depression of 1873 also opened socialism as a possible road for American workers. Although socialist groups had existed for many years they had been confined largely to German émigré circles in the large metropolitan centers. Now new forces were coming in. Greenbackism was still the dominant hope of American trade-union leadership but now socialism began a bid for leadership.

III.   1886—The First Divide

The impetus to socialist political organization in the United States came from three European sources: the International Workingmen's Association (the First International) dominated by Marx; the political ideas of Ferdinand Lassalle, the founder of German social democracy; and the volatile anarchism of Mikhail Bakunin.

The philosophy of the First International was primarily economic. Through the trade-union struggle, Marx felt, the laborer would achieve the consciousness of class that would enable him to act politically and win power; the socialist state would be built on the existing trade unions and cooperative societies. For Lassalle, however, trade unionism implied cooperation between worker and employer and only direct political organization would do; the victorious state would then build a syndicalist structure as the framework of the socialist society. Not only a theoretical but a deep personal enmity existed between Marx and Lassalle, and these wholehearted, venomous hatreds carried over to their followers. In personality, the two men were poles apart. Lassalle was a fashionable dandy, at home in the archly-refined salons of European society; he was a great orator and master of a flaming rhetoric; his escapades and love affairs were notorious over the continent. Marx was not like that. He lived, poverty stricken, harassed, constantly dunned for debts, in a shabby section of London. Sickness forever plagued his large family, particularly the children. But the most galling fact was that the swarthy Lassalle— Marx viciously described him in letters to Wilhelm Liebknecht as that "Jewish nigger"—was gaining a name as the founder of the socialist movement in Germany while Marx lived isolated and ignored in drab and drafty exile.

London in the 1850's and 1860's was the center for Europe's political refugees. There was freedom, but only to study and talk rather than act. This political impotence fed emotional rancor. Marx was the most bitter of all. He feuded constantly both with the German and with the Russian exiles. The most barbed shafts, however, were reserved for the Russians. Marx felt that the Russian populist theories as expressed by Alexander Herzen and the anarchist doctrines espoused by Bakunin were romantic posturings. The chief target was the anarchist. A huge, emotionally-tortured giant, Bakunin spent most of his time dreaming up fantastic schemes to organize underground groups in Russia, where he had been imprisoned and whence he had escaped. Bakunin felt that only a violent revolution, sparked by deeds of terror, could unseat those entrenched in power. His romantic nature made him susceptible to a variety of queer influences, among them that of a young Russian fanatic named Nechayev who soon ran afoul of the Russian secret police, and who in prison betrayed his friends. This episode later gave rise to Marx's scurrilous charge that Bakunin had been a police spy. Although untrue, it was effective enough to cause Bakunin's expulsion from the First International.[23]

These bickerings had their tragi-comic counterpart here in the affairs of the "International." In 1870 the declining National Labor Union had declared its adherence "to the principles of the International Workingmen's Association and expects to join the said association in a short time." It never did. The International then began chartering sections directly in the United States. But its following was only among the established German workingmen's societies. In 1857 a Communist Club had been established in New York, whose leading figure was Friedrich Sorge, a German music teacher. Another German workingmen's society had been formed in New York by some ardent Lassalleans. In 1868, feeling the time ripe for political activity, the two had merged and formed the Social Party of New York. Candidates were nominated for office but the vote was insignificant. In 1869 the Social Party reorganized as the General German Labor Association, or Section 1 of the International. The following year other sections arose and the total membership, according to a report by Sorge, reached 5,000.

But trouble soon boiled up. A group of American intellectuals, many of them Fourierist tinged, had in 1869 formed a group called New Democracy, which two years later disbanded and reorganized as Sections 9 and 12 of the International. Section 12 was dominated by two eccentric sisters, Victoria Woodhull and Tennessee Claflin, who published a weekly bearing their combined names. The two felt superior to the "alien" sections and began issuing manifestoes championing free love, universal language, and other "advanced" ideas. Their activities aroused great antagonism among the sober-minded German workmen. In his autobiography Samuel Gompers recalls his own emotions: "Section 12 of the American group was dominated by a brilliant group of faddists, reformers, and sensation-loving spirits. They were not working people and treated their relationship to the labor movement as a means to a 'career.' They did not realize that labor issues were tied up with the lives of men, women, and children—issues not to be risked lightly. Those pseudo-Communists played with the labor movement. This experience burned itself into my memory so that I never forgot the principle in after years."[24]

These carousings inevitably split the American affiliate of the Inter-

[23] For a picture of this period see the studies by E. H. Carr of the nineteenth-century revolutionists, particularly *The Romantic Exiles* (New York, 1933), and his biographies of Marx and Bakunin.

[24] Samuel Gompers, *Seventy Years of Life and Labor; an Autobiography* (New York, 1925), I, p. 55.

national. In 1872, the Section 12 "intellectuals" called one convention. The Germans led by Sorge called another. Both groups sent delegates to the International's 1872 Hague convention. Marx, who fully controlled the organization, recognized Sorge as the legitimate "Internationalist." At this convention the fight with Bakunin so threatened Marx's power that he transferred the office of the grand council to New York—in order to ditch it—and placed Sorge in charge. Far removed from the center of organized European labor, the International soon disintegrated.

Section 12 went on its merry japes and in due course frittered away. But factionalism was still rampant in the remaining sections. The deepening depression of 1873 brought a demand from some new members led by Adolph Strasser that the American group devote more attention to domestic problems and allow greater cooperation with nonsocialist elements in the labor movement. But Section 1, the German stronghold, stood like a stone wall and the newcomers left in disgust. Together with a number of Lassalleans they formed a new party, the Social Democratic Party of North America, and named Strasser as national secretary. The purified Internationalists (Marxians) denounced this tendency to reformism:

"[We] reject all co-operation and connection," they said, "with the political parties formed by the possessing classes, whether they call themselves Republicans or Democrats, or Independents or Liberals or Patrons of Industry or Patrons of Husbandry (Grangers) or Reformers or whatever name they may adopt."

But factionalism soon developed inside both parties. In the Social Democratic Party a split arose between the dogmatic Lassalleans, who were completely hostile to unions, and those who felt that unions should be brought into the party. In the International, quarrels between Sorge and other members developed on nonpolitical issues; as so often is the case, they devolved largely on questions of power, prestige, and position within the tiny organization. The International was rapidly breaking up. In July 1876 the International Workingmen's Association formally dissolved, an act rare in socialist annals, where an old guard hangs on and rarely surrenders.

The restlessness of the workers, aggravated by years of depression, exploded violently in 1876 and 1877. In the Pennsylvania coal fields, the Molly Maguires, the secret coal unionists, answered employer violence with murder. In 1877 a series of railway strikes swept the country and galvanized the labor movement; it took federal troops to end the disorders. For the socialists these flash fires of violence seemed to signalize the awakening of the American working class. The German Social Democratic Party, only ten years old, had won almost half a million followers. It seemed as if American labor were ready to follow in those steps.

In 1876, an attempt was made, initiated by the fast-growing Knights of Labor, to unite the trade unionists, socialists, and Greenbackers. However, the socialists would not fully accept the money-reform scheme presented by the Greenbackers and withdrew. Those remaining moved into the Greenback Labor Party. Shortly thereafter the old Lassallean (Strasser) and Internationalist (Sorge) groups reunited and formed the Workingmen's Party of the United States. Naturally, old differences were not obliterated. There were still the "trade-union" and the "political" socialists. But in the excitement of the next three years these distinctions were momentarily forgotten.

In 1876 the Workingmen's Party made election gains in Milwaukee, Chicago, and Cincinnati. By the next year, no less than twenty-four newspapers directly or indirectly supporting the party were flourishing, of which eight were in English. These successes strengthened the political faction, and in 1877 the party changed its name to the Socialist Labor Party. The election successes continued: in Chicago, where Albert R. Parsons, a socialist, was secretary of the local trade-union body, the vote in 1879 rose to 11,800, and four men were elected to the legislature. In various other cities (with the exception of Cincinnati, where the socialists and the trade unions were apart), the socialist vote also rose. By the end of the year, the Socialist Labor Party claimed a membership of 10,000 in 100 locals in twenty-five states.[25]

Eighteen hundred and seventy-eight also brought success to the Greenback Labor Party. Peter Cooper's vote in 1876 had been small and the party largely farmer-based, with a sprinkling of Eastern reformers. But the great strikes of 1877 and the open hostility of the federal government to labor brought a resurgence of workingmen's political action. Independent workingmen's parties were formed in New York, Pennsylvania, and Ohio. In several of these states alliances were entered into with the old Greenback Party, and the votes soared. In most of the organizations the active leaders were from the Knights of Labor. These successful electoral alliances, particularly in Ohio and Pennsylvania, naturally gave rise to thought of a national farmer-labor alliance, and in 1878 the National Party was formed. Although a number of veteran labor leaders such as Richard Trevelick, Sylvis' successor (who was made chairman), and Uriah Stephens, founder of the Knights of Labor, were present, the party was largely controlled by farmers, radical small businessmen, and lawyers.

[25] In California, where the Socialist Labor Party refrained from nominating candidates and "dividing the forces of the labor movement," a workingmen's party organized by a popular rabble-rouser, Denis Kearny, had become a power in the state on the basis of the slogans of "Down with the Rich," and "The Chinese Must Go." The socialist-tinged Kearny movement was able to influence the writing of a new liberal state constitution, and even captured San Francisco in 1879, but old-line politicians entered the party and it soon lost its earlier radical characteristics.

In the congressional election that year nearly a million votes were cast for Greenback candidates, and fourteen representatives were elected to Congress.

These astounding successes posed a problem for the Socialist Labor Party. Many members began to agitate for joint action with the money reformers. After much debate the party voted in 1880 to endorse James B. Weaver, the presidential nominee of the Greenbackers. But two dissenting wings formed: one, the trade unionists, argued against dilution of labor issues, the other, the revolutionary elements, protested against truckling to reformist elements. The party compromised, typically, by supporting only the presidential and vice-presidential candidates of the Greenbackers, while nominating candidates of its own for state and municipal offices. In Chicago, however, even such a solution was not good enough for the stiff-necked and anticompromise elements in the party, and they ran candidates against the regular Socialist Labor Party nominees, who were aligned with the Greenbackers.

Socialism's high hopes, however, were soon shattered. "Good times" had returned, and interest in greenbackism and socialism slackened. Weaver's vote fell to a dismal 300,000. Defeatism spread. In his report to the 1880 convention Philip Van Patten, the national secretary of the Socialist Labor Party, stated, "It is especially to be regretted that we had not secured the election of at least a dozen representatives in the legislature of every Northern State, since a party which has elected a number of representatives is considered tolerably permanent, while one who has not, is regarded by the public as transient and uncertain." And when socialist meetings no longer attracted the large crowds they once had, Van Patten remarked bitterly, "The plundered toilers are rapidly being drawn back to their old paths, and are closing their ears to the appeals of reason. They are selling their birthright for a mess of pottage by rejecting the prospect of future emancipation in their greed for the trifling remains of the present."[26]

Party membership fell off rapidly and in the defeat people looked for new roads. The Socialist Labor Party was reduced to an empty shell. Its membership dropped to less than 1,500, of whom perhaps 10 per cent were native Americans. Within the closed, isolated circle of socialists anarchism now burgeoned and political socialism declined. In 1883 Van Patten, discouraged by the tedious quarreling, simply walked out of the party, turning up later in a minor government post.

In 1880 the party split in two. The revolutionary wing organized its own group and in 1881 affiliated with Bakunin's anarchist International Working People's Association, the so-called "Black International." The anarchist movement, also predominantly German, was aided at the time

[26] Cited in Hillquit, *History of Socialism in the United States*, pp. 226-27.

by the arrival in the United States of the German agitator Johann Most. Most, a fiery orator and forceful writer, was noted for his biting wit and sharp, slashing personal polemics. A prolonged sickness in infancy had left him deformed; a cruel childhood and heavy work at an early age deepened his bitterness. He had been imprisoned a number of times in Europe for riotous speeches and had been jailed by an English court for extolling the assassination of Alexander II. Most became the acknowledged leader of anarchism in the United States and wrote most of the Pittsburgh manifesto of 1883, which united the revolutionary splinter of the Socialist Labor Party with preexisting anarchist groups.

In the prosperity of the early 1880's, the workers on the whole were apathetic about revolutionary activity. The beginnings of depression in 1883 marked a reversal of mood. The period of 1883-1885 was hard, not so much because of unemployment as because of a pressure on wages and the tightening of money. Farmers, workers, small businessmen were affected by the squeeze. Hardest hit were the unskilled and the semi-skilled workers who had been brought into the factory, and the farmers who were at the mercy of the railroads. The common outcry of these groups rose against a new Moloch—"monopoly"—and the breakup of monopoly became the great political issue of the next two decades. In this period, the Knights of Labor made sensational gains. In one year, from 1885 to 1886, membership jumped from little more than 100,000 to 700,000. The Socialist Labor Party gained new strength, too, but the anarchist movement gained in even greater proportion.

In 1885, the anarchist movement boasted about eighty organized groups and a total of 7,000 members. Chicago was the center. There the Black International had some 2,000 members, and its leaders, particularly Albert Parsons, had close ties with the local labor movement. Chicago, at the time, was the center also of a widespread agitation for an eight-hour day. By early May 1886 almost 80,000 workers were on strike for that demand. On May 3 the police fired into a large unruly crowd which was struggling with some strikebreakers of the McCormick reaper works, killing four. The anarchists immediately called for a protest meeting in Haymarket Square, a popular meeting place about two miles west of the Loop. A crowd of about 3,000 had patiently listened to long anarchist speeches when, toward the close of the rally, a bomb was hurled, killing one police officer and wounding many others. In the consequent public hysteria, eight anarchists were convicted of conspiracy to throw the bomb. Four, including Albert Parsons, were hanged, one committed suicide, the sentences of two were commuted to life imprisonment, and one was sent to prison for a shorter term. The back of the movement was broken.[27]

[27] In 1893 the three in prison were freed by Governor John Altgeld. Just the previous year, anarchism had again attracted public attention when a young firebrand,

The year 1886 was a momentous one for the Socialist Labor Party, too. The rapid growth of labor organization and an unfavorable court decision on a boycott case had turned the New York unions to political action. In 1886, with socialist support, the Central Labor Union of New York organized an independent labor party and nominated Henry George for mayor. Across the country similar stirrings were felt. The United Labor Party of Chicago, organized by the Central Labor Union, ran up 20,000 votes in the spring elections—before the Haymarket bomb. In eleven other states labor parties of one hue or another, with close cooperation between the labor movement and socialists, Knights, Greenbackers, and other reformers, were organized. The most important effort, however, was the George campaign in New York.

Henry George stands paramount in the authentic tradition of the great agrarian reformers of the United States. Like Henry C. Carey, who disputed Ricardo's theory of rent, he saw land as playing the decisive role in the production and distribution of wealth in the United States, and like George Henry Evans, he saw the solution to our social ills in the public control of land. Born in Philadelphia in 1837, George went to sea as a young lad, roamed the country, learned the printer's trade, and settled for a while in San Francisco, where he became the founder of the San Francisco *Evening Post*. Living on the edge of the economic frontier, George observed that where new areas were opened, land would be gobbled up by speculators, the price would soar, economic enterprise, as a consequence, would contract, and profits and wages drop. The idea of regulating land usage through a tax which would confiscate all speculative gain and allow the land to develop in accord with the needs of industry was for him the means of smoothing out the sharp edges of depression. The single-tax idea had a unique appeal: to the small manufacturer it reduced the high initial costs of starting a business; to the farmer it meant the end

---

Alexander Berkman, shot and wounded the obstinate H. C. Frick, head of the Carnegie Steel Company, during the bloody Homestead strike. But anarchism no longer commanded a following. Johann Most, by that time a bitter old man editing his droning paper *Freiheit* and frequenting the German saloons, met with a mirthless fate. In 1901, while indulging in a protracted "beer session," he thoughtlessly "filled out" an issue of his paper with a hackneyed article entitled "Murder Against Murder," which had been written in 1850 by an old German revolutionist, Karl Heinzen. Unfortunately for Most, the day after the issue appeared President McKinley was shot in Buffalo by a muddled Polish radical, Leon Czolgosz. Most immediately ordered the withdrawal of the paper from circulation, but a copy had fallen into the hands of the New York police. Although there was no discernible connection between the *Freiheit* article and Czolgosz, Most was arrested and convicted in New York courts on the vague charge of outraging public decency. The aging man was sentenced to a year in jail, but this time the strain of prison broke the gnome-like anarchist, and four years later he died. Apart from the flamboyant career of Emma Goldman and some strength in the Jewish labor movement in the early 1900's, anarchism faded away completely as a political force in America.

of the useless land-grabber; to the urban worker it promised jobs and the end of house rent. George published his ideas in two books, the second of which, *Progress and Poverty*, published shortly after the disastrous financial crisis of 1879, caught on in spectacular fashion. In the book George extended his theory and argued that the fertility of land and its desirability as a business location or market were a result of natural and social reasons from which no single individual ought to profit. By taxing all gains from land equal to its full rental value, monopoly would be destroyed and the land thrown open for the use of those who would develop it productively.

For the socialists, the single tax was an old story. Marx had proposed as one of the transition measures included in the *Communist Manifesto* that all ground rents be paid to the state. But his proposal had never been phrased in the striking fashion of *Progress and Poverty*; the single-tax idea, coming at the apt moment it did, gained a sure-fire acceptance, even among the socialists. Marx, fearful of George's influence on the socialists in the United States—where Kriege and Weitling had already been enticed by land theories—sought to demolish the single taxer. In a letter to Sorge, he wrote:

"Theoretically the man [Henry George] is utterly backward! He understands nothing about the nature of *surplus value*. . . . [His] idea originally belonged to the bourgeois economists; it was put forward . . . by the earliest *radical* followers of Ricardo, soon after his death. I said of it in 1847, in my work against Proudhon: 'We can understand that economists like Mill (the elder) . . . Cherbuliez, Hildtich and others have demanded that rent should be paid to the state in order that it may serve as a substitute for taxes. This is a frank expression of the hatred which the *industrial capitalist* dedicates to the *landed proprietor*, who seems to him a useless and superfluous element in the general total of bourgeois production.'" After pointing out that the program had also been offered as a socialist panacea in France, Marx continued: "All these 'socialists' since Colins have this much in common that they leave *wage labour* and therefore *capitalist production* in existence and try to bamboozle themselves or the world into believing that if ground rent were transformed into a state tax *all the evils* of capitalist production would disappear of themselves. The whole thing is therefore simply an attempt, decked out with socialism, *to save capitalist domination* and indeed *to establish it afresh* on *an even wider basis* than its present one. This cloven hoof (at the same time ass's hoof) is also unmistakably revealed in the declamations of Henry George. . . . On the other hand George's book, like the sensation it has made with you, is significant because it is a first, if unsuccessful, attempt at emancipation from the orthodox political economy."[28]

[28] Letter of Marx to Sorge, June 30, 1881, in Marx-Engels Correspondence, *op.cit.*, pp. 394-96.

Despite these cogent criticisms, the Socialist Labor Party supported George because they saw his campaign as a movement of labor against capital. In fact the platform of the United Labor Party as originally drafted contained the "immediate demands" of the socialists. When George accepted the nomination, however, the platform was rewritten to emphasize the single tax, currency reform, and factory legislation.

The campaign was one of the most spectacular in the history of the United States. Pitted against George were Abram S. Hewitt, the son-in-law of Peter Cooper, nominated by Tammany, and Theodore Roosevelt, the nominee of the Republicans. The press of the city was almost unanimously and harshly aligned against George. He had the support, however, of various liberal leaders and professionals including Daniel De Leon and the famous Catholic priest Father McGlynn. McGlynn, a great hero of the Irish workers, rallied so much Catholic support for George that Tammany obtained a statement from the vicar-general of the church in which he declared that the majority of the Catholic clergy would "deeply regret the election of Mr. George to any position of influence."

Hewitt won with 90,000 votes. But George ran ahead of Roosevelt, garnering 68,000 votes to T. R.'s 60,000. The United Labor Party was now in a position to make great advances, but two events typical of the fate of labor parties occurred, robbing it of that opportunity. First, the old-line parties at the next legislature passed a series of labor laws which embodied a number of the immediate demands of the laborites. Secondly, the fissure between the incompatible single taxers and the socialists cracked open. The single taxers sought to turn the party into an all-inclusive movement, uniting all producing classes against the landlords, thus answering such critics as Hewitt, who claimed that the Labor Party was setting class against class. The socialists wanted a more radical party.

The struggle between the two continued for a year, splitting almost every club in the state. The break came when the call for the state convention in 1887 omitted all labor demands and concentrated instead on land and currency reforms. Then, on the demand of George, who charged dual alliances, the socialists were expelled. Still hoping to rally the unions, the socialists next organized a Progressive Labor Party. But the elections of 1887 proved a disappointment to all. George's total in New York City fell to 37,000; the Progressive Labor Party received 5,000 votes. Prosperity was returning and the radical voters were proving fickle, so that the labor parties in other cities shared the same fate. A year later George left his own party and supported Democratic Grover Cleveland for president. Father McGlynn, who had been excommunicated from the church for criticizing his archbishop, conducted a final campaign of the United Labor Party in 1888 and then laid it to rest.[29]

[29] Arthur Nichols Young, *The Single Tax Movement in the United States* ('Princeton, N.J., 1916).

For the socialists, the experience was the beginning of a decisive new phase in policy and tactics. The Henry George campaign had given them new life but had also demonstrated to their minds the futility of fusion politics. Henceforth, they were committed unswervingly to a straight class approach and a socialist ticket. It was a decision which was reinforced in the ascendancy of a new and decisive leader, Daniel De Leon.

That fateful year 1886 also marked the emergence of the American Federation of Labor. Trade unionism was being established on a new and permanent basis in American life. With the lesson of the foundering Knights of Labor in mind, it rejected the old utopian mirages; its aims were limited and practical. The relationship between the American Federation of Labor and the new socialist movement was to be crucial for the development of socialist strength in America.

On the national scene, a new industrial plutocracy was flexing its muscles in a crude and powerful way. Economically, it was exerting powerful leverage against the farmer while heavily squeezing the worker; politically, it was buying up state legislatures and exercising a dominant influence in the Republican Party; culturally, it was spawning the gilded architectural monstrosities and displaying a grossness of taste that was to turn against it both the scions of the older upper-middle classes, such as Brooks and Henry Adams, and the rising intellectual class. The consolidation of industrial capitalist power was beginning. With it, said Engels, would come the emergence of a class-conscious proletariat ready to take up the struggle. With that perspective, the socialists entered the next two decades.

IV. Purist and Pure-and-Simple

In 1893, said Oliver Wendell Holmes, "a vague terror went over the earth and the word socialism began to be heard." This was a year of violence.

In Homestead, Pennsylvania, Henry C. Frick locked out the workers of the Carnegie Steel plant and brought in the Pinkertons. Seven strikers and three strikebreakers were killed in the ensuing gunfire before the militia smashed the strike. At Homestead a craft union for the first time had faced not just an employer, but the modern industrial corporation, and had lost. It was an important symbol for American labor. On the same day that the state troops arrived at Homestead, a running battle was being fought in Idaho's Coeur d'Alene district between silver miners and company strikebreakers. The federal troops sent in by Grover Cleveland broke that strike. A year later, the workers in the "model" village of Pullman struck, and 40,000 railway men west of Chicago refused to haul the Pullman cars, virtually halting all rail traffic. It took a federal injunction and federal troops to start the trains rolling again.

These were the jungle years. The Supreme Court had written Herbert Spencer's social statics into the law of the land, and the iron-jawed capitalists prepared to demonstrate that the philosophy of natural rights meant their God-given authority to rule untrammeled. Social Darwinism was a congenial doctrine for the new plutocracy.

Not only did labor feel oppressed but the dirt farmer likewise felt that this was now the last-ditch stand against the money power in the East. Six months after the Chicago World's Fair the border farmers met in the windy city to organize for free silver and populism.[30] The costumes were garish, but the talk was earnest. Present at the sessions were William Jennings Bryan, Ignatius Donnelly—former congressman, adventurer, and author of a fabulous utopian novel about the lost continent of Atlantis— Jacob Coxey, James B. Weaver, and "Bloody Bridles" Waite, the populist governor of Colorado, who presided. They demanded that the government act to break the money power of Wall Street. A year later, Coxey's army was to symbolize this demand with the famous petition to Washington "with boots on."

The "masses were in motion." This seemed to be the moment that Marx had prophesied in one of his last letters, written in 1879.[31] But if the masses were growing restless, nowhere was there a movement to assume the initiative. The American Federation of Labor was cautiously skirting any radical commitments. In the West a native radicalism was beginning to congeal, but it lacked a theory and a sense of direction. In the East the sectarian and disputatious Socialist Labor Party was coming under the inflexible and iron hand of Daniel De Leon, who would only divert it further from the main stream of American labor.

In 1888, the Socialist Labor Party, exhausted by the battles of 1886, was largely an old soldiers' home, its hoary veterans bitterly disputing the tactics of past campaigns. Following the Henry George debacle, the S.L.P. again split into its two tiresomely familiar factions. The minority, around the New York *Volkszeitung*, favored abandoning political action; the majority, however, decided to run pure socialist candidates. The minute socialist vote in the New York municipal elections in 1888, however, plus the renewed emphasis of the American Federation of Labor on the need for an eight-hour day, helped the trade-union faction. In a

[30] Unnoticed amidst the hubbub of the fair, Frederick Jackson Turner quietly read before the sessions of the American Historical Association a paper entitled "The Significance of the Frontier in American History." The frontier was passing, said Turner. The primary pioneer stage and the second phase of pastoral life were already past. Random crop method was giving way to intensive individual farming. But beyond these loomed the factory farm and centralized production. It is doubtful whether the populists, the actors in Turner's drama, knew of his words, although to them the portents were painfully clear.

[31] See the letter to Danielson cited in footnote 2.

stealthily organized *Putsch* they ousted the political action leadership and eliminated all "Lassallean" theory from the party platform. The deposed group seceded and organized the Socialist Labor Party of the "Cincinnati persuasion," as it was called (taking the name of its head-quarters city), a group which led a cursory existence until its amalgamation with the Social Democracy of America, the party formed by Debs and Victor Berger in 1897.

Engels, who maintained close interest in the United States, arising out of a trip to America in 1888, sorely wished the entire *"alte Genossen"* (old comrades) would disappear. To the faithful Sorge, he wrote acidly: ". . . If the whole *German* Socialist Labour Party went to pieces as a result, it would be a gain, but we can hardly expect anything as good as that. . . . I consider the decay of the specifically German party, with its absurd theoretical confusion, its corresponding arrogance and its Lassalleanism, a real piece of good fortune. . . . The Socialist laws were a misfortune not for Germany, but for America to which they consigned the last *Knoten*. I often used to marvel at the many *Knoten* faces one met with over there; these have died out in Germany, but are flourishing over yonder."[32]

Two events tended to change the character of the party. One was the immigration in the late eighties, especially from Russia and eastern Europe, which supplied new recruits to the party. These immigrants, particularly the younger Jewish intellectuals, were eager to learn American ways. They built up strong unions in a short time and became a factor in New York labor life. The United Hebrew Trades, organized in those lines of work in which Jewish workers predominated, started in 1888 with one union and two years later had 13,500 members in forty affiliates. Its organizers, among them Morris Hillquit, joined the Socialist Labor Party.[33] The second event was the advent of Daniel De Leon, who joined the party in 1890, and within a year was its undisputed leader and master.

Daniel De Leon, the most controversial figure in American socialism, was born in 1852 in Curaçao, Dutch West Indies. Although often considered Jewish, he referred to himself as a "respectable Venezuelan Catholic."[34] Sickly as a boy, he was sent to school in the European mountains and then to the University of Leyden. He entered Columbia Law

[32] *Knote* was a favorite term of derision of Marx. The word meant a diehard philistine, and derived from the old handicraftsmen of narrow and backward mentality. See Marx-Engels Correspondence, *op.cit.*, pp. 467 and 87.

[33] "When I joined the party, the net result of its Americanization efforts was represented by the publication of one English weekly," wrote Hillquit in his autobiography. "Subsequently, an 'American Section' of the party was formed in New York. In our zeal for the cause, we did not even appreciate the exquisite humor of a political party of the United States establishing a solitary 'American section' in the metropolis of the country." See Morris Hillquit, *Loose Leaves from a Busy Life* (New York, 1934), p. 44.

[34] Waldo Frank in *Commentary*, July 1947, p. 44.

School in 1872, practiced in Texas, and returned to teach international law at Columbia for six years. But the excitement of politics attracted him. He became active in the Henry George campaign, joined the Knights of Labor two years later, passed through Edward Bellamy's Nationalist clubs, and, attracted by the rigorous logic of Marxist theory, joined the Socialist Labor Party. There, his status among the German workingmen as a *Gelehrte*, a "professor," his intelligence and his ruthlessness, quickly won him the leadership of the party and the editorship of its English-language paper.

De Leon was intensely personal and his forthright ways provoked either immediate loyalty or bitter hatred. Slight-bodied and of small stature, he had a large head which, with his piercing black eyes, fine-etched features, and carefully modeled beard, gave him a commanding presence. He had a remarkable talent for elucidating simply the vagaries of abstract theory; he was also a debater with a decided flair and love for picturesque invective—a necessary talent, in those days, for political success. Under De Leon's initiative, the Socialist Labor Party nominated a national presidential ticket in 1892 which received 21,000 votes, a feeble total compared to the over one million received by General Weaver, the Populist candidate that year. Yet for the Socialist Labor Party there now was at least the exhilaration of activity.

De Leon's first political objective was to capture the trade unions. Within the American Federation of Labor the socialists persistently sought to win endorsement of socialist aims, and almost succeeded in doing so. De Leon, however, wanted to capture the declining Knights of Labor, which would be a more malleable instrument. He infiltrated the New York assembly and made a deal with the western elements to oust Terence V. Powderly, grand master of the Knights. But he failed to gain national power when the new grand master reneged on his bargain of giving the Socialist Labor Party the editorship of the Knights' *Journal*, and added insult to injury by refusing even to seat De Leon as a delegate. De Leon's answer to these failures was to create a new organization, the Socialist Trades and Labor Alliance. For him it was to be an instrument of social change, but for the half-million organized workers in the United States such a move, coming after the fratricidal war between the Knights and the American Federation of Labor, spelled dual unionism and danger. Trade unionists within the party, especially from the Jewish unions, opened attack on De Leon, but his policy was endorsed in a resolution which condemned the Knights and the A.F.L. as "buffers of capitalism against whom every intelligent effort of the working class for emancipation has hitherto gone to pieces." De Leon's trade-union policy plus his high-handed application of party discipline caused a revolt. In 1899 the faction led by Morris Hillquit and Job Harriman, known as the "Kangaroos," jumped the party and joined with Debs in forming the Socialist Party. Thereafter, the Socialist Labor Party declined. De Leon went on *in vacuo* developing his powerful theoretical schemes, jibed at and mocked, until his death in 1914.

Daniel De Leon was a mechanical giant in a doll's house. Although the political drama passed him by, he continued setting the scene in immaculate fashion for the revolution that never came. His devotion to his cause was deep and abiding. He lived in a tenement on New York's lower east side, barely meeting his needs from the small and irregular salary as editor of the Socialist Labor Party's paper, yet refusing, on moral grounds, to supplement his income by writing for the capitalist press. Despite this personal attitude, he feared the role of sentiment and moral indignation as a motive force in socialist organizations. It was a quality which he shared with Lenin.[35] "The more feeling you put into them, the surer they are to capsize and go down," he wrote. He considered his job the creation of the "scientific" principle (it was the word most employed in his vocabulary), and he prided himself that his propositions were as neat as the theorems of trigonometry. "His peculiar traits and methods," reflected Hillquit in his autobiography, "were not due entirely to his personal temperament and character. In part at least they were the logical expression of his social philosophy."[36] The modern psychological temper, however, would reverse the emphasis of the two statements.

De Leon had carefully studied Marx and had set himself the task of extending the unfinished portion of the Marxist analysis—the road to power. With a rigor unsurpassed in Marxist exegetical writing, he drew a schema that, abstractly, was a cleanly-thought-through progression from a number of Marxist premises. He argued, first, the futility of seeking higher wages and shorter hours within the capitalist system, and therefore the chimerical quality of gains through "reformist" unions. In a sharp attack on the Fabians, he pointed out that partial gains won by the workers would be eroded by the corrupting nature of bourgeois values, and in an acid metaphor drawn from the Roman struggles of the Gracchi, he predicted that the trade-union leaders, as they became established, would be absorbed into the capitalist system as "labor lieutenants." In a fully developed capitalist country, said De Leon, the concern of the

[35] The Russian Bolshevik leader held a high opinion of the American Marxist, and there is in their works a striking parallelism. Lenin's theory of "economism"—the doctrine that the workers without vanguard communist leadership would only develop trade-union, not revolutionary, consciousness—contained in *What Is to Be Done?* written in 1903, is quite similar to De Leon's harsh condemnation of the "labor lieutenants" of capitalism in his *Two Pages from Roman History*, written in 1902. De Leon's specific image of the revolutionary industrial union as the functional unit of the socialist society was given definite expression in Lenin's theory of soviets two decades later.

[36] Hillquit, *Loose Leaves from a Busy Life*, p 46.

Marxist must be entirely with the program of revolution: "A political party that sets up 'immediate demands,'" he wrote, "by so much blurs its 'constant demand' or goal. The presence of 'immediate demands' in a Socialist platform reveals pure and simple politicianism—corruption, or the invitation to corruption."[37]

For De Leon, the political and economic revolution had to proceed *simultaneously*, because the victory of one without the other would invite corruption. "Suppose that at some election, the class conscious political arm of labor were to sweep the field . . . what would there be for them to do? *Simply to adjourn on the spot sine die* . . . it would be . . . a signal for social catastrophe if the political triumph did not find the working class of the land industrially organized, that is, in full possession of the plants of production and distribution, capable, accordingly, to assume the integral conduct of the productive powers of the land . . . the plants of production and distribution having remained in capitalist hands production would be immediately blocked."[38] The key to worker's emancipation was the industrial union in which the workers in each industry would combine. Production and administration would be guided by industrial-union government. All the workers who use "the identical tool" would join trade and shop branches (i.e., a craft unit). The crafts making the same product would be combined into a local industrial union and pyramided into a national industrial union. At the peak would be the industrial council of national industrial unions.

The operation of the socialist state, which Marx never attempted to describe, was envisaged by De Leon in this lulling fashion: "The parliament of civilization in America will consist, not of Congressmen from geographic districts, but of representatives of trades throughout the land, and their legislative work will not be the complicated one which a society of conflicting interests, such as capitalism, requires but the easy one which can be summed up in the statistics of the wealth needed, the wealth producible, and the work required—and that any average set of workingmen's representatives are fully able to ascertain, infinitely better than our modern rhetoricians in Congress."[39] Lenin's *State and Revolution* more than a decade later repeated this simple, functional scheme, even to the claim that the ordinary worker would be as able an administrator as any professional.

Although De Leon insisted on the radical overthrow of the existing

[37] Daniel De Leon, "Demands, Immediate and Constant," cited in *Platform of the Socialist Labor Party* (New York, 1932), a leaflet published by the New York Labor News Company.

[38] Daniel De Leon, *Socialist Reconstruction of Society* (New York, 1905), a pamphlet published by the New York Labor News Company.

[39] Daniel De Leon, cited in Arnold Petersen, *Proletarian Democracy vs. Dictatorships and Despotism* (4th ed., New York, 1937), p. 29.

capitalist institutions, he was against force. "The ballot is the weapon of civilization,"[40] he wrote, and the working class should not adopt the methods of class war, which is provoked by the capitalist, but "place itself upon the highest plane civilization has reached. . . . It must insist upon the enforcement of civilized methods."

For a number of years after the 1899 split, efforts were made to reunite the Socialist Labor Party and the Socialist Party. The Amsterdam congress of the Second International in 1904 called for the fusion of both parties. In 1908 De Leon took the initiative and suggested unity but was turned down unceremoniously by the Socialist Party executive. In January 1917, three years after De Leon's death, the last futile effort was made. Through the years, the Socialist Labor Party has remained firm and unyielding, the most consistent Marxist organization in America, a bleak cenotaph to the cold genius of Daniel De Leon.

De Leon had rigorously outlined one pole of American labor—doctrinal purity and sectarian isolation. Sam Gompers evolved another—*ad hoc* pragmatism and continual compromise. If socialism as an historically organized movement has not achieved a permanency in American life, it is largely due to the role of the American Federation of Labor.

For years Engels had warned against the isolation of the Socialist Labor Party. In a letter to Sorge in 1891, he said, "it proves how useless is a platform—for the most part theoretically correct—if it is unable to get into contact with the actual needs of the people." Yet when the American Federation of Labor was formed, the socialists for the most part were hostile to it, or sought to divert it from trade-union policies. The official leadership of the A.F.L. returned the hostility. In the heat of conflict both sides were driven to positions more extreme than either had intended.

The socialist attitude derived in large measure from a consistent misreading of the tempo of development of the American working class. Marxian theory had predicted that in the "logic of events" the working class would arrive at a self-conscious evaluation of its own position and become socialist. Every fresh stirring of labor from the National Labor Union on was hailed as a demonstration of that rising class-consciousness. The campaign of 1886, the frenetic activity of the Knights of Labor, and the burgeoning labor parties were each hailed as starting points. In that context, the formation of the American Federation of Labor, with an emphasis on the skilled worker and narrow craft organizations, which in effect were largely beneficiary societies, could only be seen as a retrogression. What the socialists failed to perceive was the crucial fact that the American Federation of Labor was the first labor group to accept its role as a permanent class within American society and to create an

[40] De Leon, *Socialist Reconstruction of Society*, p. 59.

institutional framework for its continued existence. The earlier labor movements sought to build enclaves within the structure of capitalist society—in producers' cooperatives, land reform, money reform, and other straws from the land of Prester John. But they did not want to be unions and accept the singular condition of unionism—the day-to-day acceptance of capitalist society.

The early leaders of the American Federation of Labor, Adolph Strasser, P. J. McGuire, and Samuel Gompers, had gone through the sectarian schools of socialist dogmatics. The interminable theoretical wranglings which constituted the curriculum had left them with a skepticism of Marxian politics as applied to the American scene, and helped to shape the here-and-now, pure-and-simple trade unionism of the A.F.L. Because the aims of the Federation were limited to the immediate problem of wages and hours, two important consequences followed. One of these was the decisive rejection, after tentative flirting, of the farmers, Green-backers, small businessmen, and the various "antimonopoly" political campaigns; such alliances, which proved the undoing of the National Labor Union and the Knights of Labor, merely sucked the worker into the vortex of a swiftly rising political whirlwind, lifted him high, and dumped him unceremoniously when its force was spent. The second consequence was the open acceptance of the concentration of economic power as an inevitable fact of industrial capitalism. Labor could try to hedge in, but not challenge, the power of the rising new class. On the "trust issue," thus, the new trade-union movement broke with the middle-class and agrarian reformers. These two basic assumptions meant that labor would not stand outside capitalist society and challenge it, but would seek a secure place within it, and, when powerful enough, slowly transform it by demanding a share of power.

These attitudes gain vividness only when interpreted through the life history of Sam Gompers, the man who enunciated them and who, with driving force, created the American labor movement in his own stubborn and pragmatic image. Samuel Gompers is the great totem of the American labor movement, and the rules of endogamy and other taboos he set down have become the prescribed rituals of American labor. A forbidding and stubborn father, the "sons" were reared in his image, retaining all the ritual forms but, except for John L. Lewis, little of the vitality.

Born in 1850, the son of Dutch-Jewish parents, Gompers grew up in London working-class quarters, where he absorbed a sense of his own class; and at the age of thirteen came to the United States. When Gompers was twenty-three he went to work in the cigar shop of David Hirsch, a German revolutionary exile whose factory was the center of many burning theoretical controversies. Cigarmaking at that time was an easy and gregarious operation. The men sat around large tables, talking volubly as their fingers swiftly and mechanically shaped the cigars. In the shop Gompers came under the influence of Karl Ferdinand Laurrell, an ardent Marxist who had been active in the First International. Marxism then meant, however, a fierce trade unionism, as against the political biases of the Lassalleans, and Gompers was quickly won to the trade-union viewpoint. But it was the obstinate manner in which the sectarians ignored the bread-and-butter concerns of the union that soured him completely on the political socialists. At that time the cigarmakers' union faced competition from cheap, low-paid "homeworkers" who made the cigars in their tenement homes. Gompers, as the head of the union, sought legislation outlawing the production of cigars in homes. He marked for reprisal those legislators who voted against the measure and called for support of those who worked for the bill. These men were running on old-line party tickets. But the political socialists were dead-set against voting for old-party candidates, even the prolabor ones, charging that such a move might provide temporary gains for the cigarmakers but corrupt the labor movement and destroy political socialism. Even when the first tenement-house bill was enacted, the socialists refused to support for reelection Gompers' man, Edward Grosse, who had been instrumental in pushing through the measure.

But the Marxist influences left indelible traces in Gompers' philosophy. This was particularly true of the crude "economic determinism" which was characteristic of his view of society. In his autobiography, Gompers wrote sententiously, "Economic power is the basis upon which may be developed power in other fields. It is the foundation of organized society . . . economic organization and control over economic power [are] the fulcrum which made possible influence and power in all other fields. . . . This fundamental concept upon which the A.F. of L. was later developed was at that time not formulated in men's minds."[41]

This conviction underlay Gompers' philosophy of "voluntarism," which consisted, essentially, in a fear of the state. Since the state was a reflection of dominant economic power groups, any state intervention could only lead to domination by big business. Gompers, like the old Manchester liberals, wanted a "negative state." At the 1914 convention of the American Federation of Labor, one delegate asked: "Why, if you are opposed to the eight-hour work day for men by law, did you ask for a law regulating and limiting injunctions?" Gompers replied: "In the law to limit and regulate injunctions we propose to clip the power of the courts insofar as labor is concerned, and in an eight-hour law for men it is to give courts still greater power than they now have. Is there no difference?"[42]

It is an old axiom that men develop loyalties to the institutions they

[41] Gompers, op.cit., I, pp. 286-87, 223.
[42] David J. Saposs, Readings in Trade Unionism (New York, 1927), p. 397.

build, and tend to see events from those particular vantage points. In Gompers, we have a case study of the socialist who entered the union movement, began to see the American scene from that perspective, and changed his viewpoints as unionism in the course of its development found a respectable place in American society. For the socialists, however, life was still a triumph of dogma over experience.

Within the Socialist Labor Party, the influence of Sorge, acting as Engels' emissary, had been thrown consistently on the side of the trade-union faction. The defeat of the politicos in 1890 raised hopes that peaceful cooperation between the socialists and Gompers might be reached. But they could not agree. The issue was too fundamental. It arose out of the demand of the socialists within the A.F.L. for the revival of a separate central trades charter in New York City, for they charged the Central Labor Union with insidious Tammany Hall connections. Gompers refused, stating that the constitution of the American Federation of Labor permitted only labor unions and forbade political representation. At the 1890 convention Lucien Sanial, the socialist spokesman, argued that the Socialist Labor Party was a "bona fide" labor body, and that in Europe the socialists had organized the first trade unions and kept them free of capitalist interference. Gompers stated his case with impressive logic: if the Socialist Labor Party were admitted, he asked, why not such other parties as single taxers, anarchists, and Greenbackers? Partisan politics, he added, was a source of disruption and would split the Federation. If the Socialist Labor Party were admitted, it would be the wedge to independent political activity through the S.L.P. or a party dominated by it. Such an action would be construed as an endorsement of socialism and split the American Federation of Labor. It would keep many unions, such as the railroad unions and bricklayers, who were considering joining, from affiliating.

During this debate Gompers used a phrase which has since become famous as descriptive of the intention of the A.F.L. "Unions, pure and simple," he said, "are the natural organization of wage workers to secure their present material and practical improvement and to achieve their final emancipation." Gompers denied in the debate that he was unsympathetic to socialism, but, he said, "the working people are in too great need of immediate improvement[s] in their condition to allow them to forego them in the endeavor to devote their entire energies to an end however beautiful to contemplate. . . . The way out of the wage system is through higher wages."[43]

When Gompers was upheld by a vote of 1,574 to 496, Lucien Sanial, the

---

[43] Gompers, *op.cit.*, I, p. 385. See also *An Interesting Discussion at the Tenth Annual Convention of the American Federation of Labor* (1891), a pamphlet published by the American Federation of Labor.

S.L.P. representative, declared war against the "fakirs" and said that the "Socialists would cram Socialism down the throats of the American workingman."[44]

In the next three years the debate raged fiercely. De Leon argued that the rapid growth of industrial concentration would bring with it the corollary of Marx's law, the increasing misery of the working class. The American Federation of Labor was attacked as seeking to make the workers contented. In turn Gompers charged that the Socialist Labor Party cared less for the strike than for a few more votes and for newspaper circulation. The attacks became personal. De Leon wrote in the *People*: "From this fear of ruining individual prospects arises the slander of socialism on the part of such men as McGuire and Gompers . . . and all other advocates of pure and simple trade union fakism who are secretly plotting for personal advancement with either capitalism or capitalistic politicians."[45]

In 1893, the socialists came within a hair of capturing the American Federation of Labor. Led by Thomas J. Morgan, the secretary of the machinists' union, and J. Mahlon Barnes of the cigarmakers, they introduced a series of planks which demanded compulsory education and the nationalization of mines, railroads, and utilities. Plank ten called for "the collective ownership by the people of all means of production and distribution." They asked that these planks be submitted for "favorable consideration" to the A.F.L. affiliates. After a hectic debate, the phrase "favorable consideration" was deleted by 1,253 to 1,182 but the entire resolution of submission was carried overwhelmingly. The convention also voted to endorse free silver and instructed the executive council to bring about an alliance with the farmers' organizations.

During the year, a large number of unions within the American Federation of Labor voted to endorse the socialist program, and local affiliates were active in politics. But political activity proved fruitless. A report in the A.F.L.'s *Federationist* in November 1894 listed 300 members of the A.F.L. who had been candidates for office, but of whom only a half dozen had been elected. Strasser, Gompers, and McGuire came out unequivocally against plank ten of the program. They charged it would prevent the growth of the organization and discourage many unions from joining. At the 1894 convention, plank ten was defeated through a parliamentary maneuver by 1,217 to 913. The socialists took revenge on Gompers by voting for and electing the miner John McBride for president. The year that followed was the only one during the rest of his life that Gompers

---

[44] Quoted from N. I. Stone, "Attitude of the Socialists toward the Trade Unions" (New York, Volkszeitung Library, 1900), p. 4, in Louis S. Reed, *Labor Philosophy of Samuel Gompers* (New York, 1930), p. 80.

[45] De Leon in the *People*, August 13, 1893; October 8, 1893.

was out of office in the American Federation of Labor; and in 1895 he was returned to office once more.

Gompers had now grown quite bitter against the socialists. When De Leon launched the dual Socialist Trades and Labor Alliance—and in Gompers' lexicon dual unionism was the worst of all crimes—Gompers, who was himself no mean polemicist, poured out some vitriol of his own. In an editorial in the *Federationist*, he wrote:

"We note . . . that the work of union wrecking is being taken up by a wing of the so-called socialist party of New York, headed by a professor without a professorship, a shyster lawyer without a brief, and a statistician who furnished figures to the republican, democratic and socialist parties. These three mountebanks, aided by a few unthinking but duped workers, recently launched, from a beer saloon a brand new national organization, with the avowed purpose of crushing every trade union in the country."[46]

A few years later, when De Leon's dual unionism had split the Socialist Labor Party and his union movement was failing, Gompers wrote, ". . . this moribund concern, conceived in iniquity and brutal concubinage with labor's double enemy, greed and ignorance, fashioned into an embryonic phthisical dwarf, born in corruption and filth; and now dying, surrounded by the vultures of its progeny ready to pounce on the emaciated carcass of the corpse."[47]

By 1900 Gompers had shed the socialist influence and even most of its rhetoric. He had no ultimate aim for labor nor was he in favor of replacing private enterprise. He wanted ten cents an hour more and a half hour a day less. At first Gompers fought the socialists on differences in tactics and organizational strategy, later he fought them on the grounds of principle.

It was shortly after this that the A.F.L. took the much debated step of entering the National Civic Federation, an organization of employers, labor, and the public whose chief officers were, in seeming anomaly, Mark Hanna, the Republican political boss and McKinley kingmaker, as president, and Samuel Gompers as first vice-president.[48] Gompers' own explanation of the move indicated his new concerns. "It helped to establish the practice," he wrote, "of accepting labor unions as an integral social element and logically of including their representatives in groups to

---

[46] Gompers in the *American Federationist*, April 1896, p. 33.

[47] Gompers in the *American Federationist*, August 1898, p. 115.

[48] Although Gompers at this point mingled freely with the political and business greats, he would refuse dining invitations at the homes of the wealthy. In his autobiography he relates that he would often go to dinner parties at the homes of industrialists and explain to them labor's viewpoints. But he never dined there, waiting until the end of the discussion to leave and eat outside. It is unlikely that such behavior arose out of a fear of being corrupted. More likely, Gompers, self-conscious of his proletarian origins, used this device to shock his audience pleasurably and to reinforce his own arrogance.

discuss policies."[49] This was now labor's single ambition: to win acceptance as a "legitimate" social group, equal with business and the church as an established institution of American life. For Gompers, the immigrant boy, it was a personal crusade as well. He sought to win recognition for labor in all civic aspects of American life: an entry and a hearing at the White House; an official voice in the government, i.e., the Department of Labor; respectful relations with employers; representation in community agencies; etc. To become respectable—this was Gompers', and labor's, aim.

The socialist opposition to Gompers consistently iterated two themes: one, the charge of class collaboration; second, the failure to organize the unskilled into industrial unions. In 1897 the Western Federation of Miners, under left-wing socialist leadership, withdrew from the American Federation of Labor and helped form the Western Labor Union, later the American Labor Union, which sought to organize the unskilled along industrial lines and endorsed socialism. To the jealous Gompers this was another instance of the treacherous "dual unionism" of the socialists. In 1902, Max S. Hayes, a socialist leader, introduced a resolution at the A.F.L. convention fully endorsing socialism. After heated debate, the resolution was just barely defeated 4,897 to 4,171, with 387 not voting.

In the fluctuations of socialist power within the American Federation of Labor, 1902 was the peak year, after which the socialist strength declined. This is an incongruous fact, for 1902 was the beginning of rising socialist political influence in the United States. The answer to this paradox is that the socialist vote was never drawn primarily from organized labor—a fact that was one of its fundamental weaknesses.

In 1905 the revolutionary elements in the labor movement launched the I.W.W. (Industrial Workers of the World). Gompers' retort was characteristic. "The Socialists have called another convention to smash the American trade union movement. This is the sixth 'concentrated' effort in this direction in the past decade. . . ."[50] The literal charge was unfair. Although Debs was present at the founding of the I.W.W., the organization was never socialist nor did it have party endorsement—but Gompers no longer made simple distinctions. In the large, however, the charge was true. Socialism was "dual" to the A.F.L. and suffered the consequences. For Marx and Engels, the need for close kinship between socialism and the working class was integral to their theory. In America, the practice was deficient. In later years a significant wing of the Socialist Party, led by Morris Hillquit, sought to modify the party's harsh attitude toward the leadership of the A.F.L., but the differences arising from the contradictory conceptions of labor's course were too strong. The needed unity was impossible to achieve. Since this lack of unity is the basis for

[49] Gompers, *Seventy Years of Life and Labor*, II, p. 105.
[50] Gompers in the *American Federationist*, March 1905, p. 139.

one of the crucial questions to be asked regarding the failure of socialism in the United States, the problems in connection with it are worth exploring in more systematic detail.

The first problem was the socialist characterization of the policies of the A.F.L. as "class collaborationist." Shaw once remarked that trade unionism is not socialism, but the capitalism of the proletariat. In one sense this is true. But the corollary that the trade-union leader must become the "labor lieutenant" and "lackey" of the capitalist class is not the literal sequitur. The basis of this charge was that the A.F.L. sought to benefit the skilled workers at the expense of the other sections of the working class by refusing to admit industrial unions. While the socialists may have been correct in the abstract, it was Gompers who showed the keener insight into working-class psychology. In a clumsy manner, he sought to indicate his theoretical differences with the socialists in respect to class attitudes. They only had an intellectual and he a living knowledge of the workers, he felt. "I told [the socialists]," Gompers wrote, "that the *Klassen Bewusztsein* (class consciousness) of which they made so much was not either a fundamental or inherent element, for class consciousness was a mental process shared by all who had imagination."[51] The real social cement, he said, "was *Klassengefühl* (class feeling) . . . that primitive force that had its origin in experience only." And these experiences, for the average workingman, were of a *limiting* nature: the desire for better wages, shorter hours, etc. The skilled workers had accepted their role, had a "commodity" of their own, and were in a position to bargain. Most of the unskilled, many of them immigrants, had no thought of staying in an especially low-paying job, and drifted. They constituted a large reservoir which the capitalist could always use to break strikes or depress wages. Thus it was difficult to build a permanent organization of men with no particular stake in their jobs. In behalf of the skilled worker, the American Federation of Labor forged the trade agreement as the instrument for exacting a higher price for his commodity, i.e., his skill. Control of the job supply became the prime means of giving the wage worker protection. It also meant that the union became involved in the market problems of the industry. "Business unionism," is inevitable in the maintenance of the union as a stable organization. The necessity of "business unionism"—living in and of the market—is one that the early Socialist Party could not adequately understand.

A second issue was monopoly. Every major American movement of social protest in the last two decades of the nineteenth century and the first decade of the twentieth had been organized around the antimonopoly motif. Gompers felt that monopoly as an outcome of economic growth was unavoidable. Nor did he feel that it could be controlled by the state,

[51] Gompers, *Seventy Years of Life and Labor*, i, p. 383.

which itself was subservient to the powerful economic interests. "The great wrongs attributable to the trusts," he wrote, "are their corrupting influence on the politics of the country, but as the state has always been the representative of the wealthy persons, we shall be compelled to endure its evils until the toilers are organized and educated to the degree that they shall know that the state is by right theirs, and finally and justly shall come into their own while never relaxing in their efforts to secure the very best economic, social and material improvements in their conditions."[52] This statement by Gompers, before the conservative mold finally jelled, was actually in line with socialist economic theory later developed by Rudolf Hilferding in his *Finanzkapital*. The theory saw the growth of monopoly as inevitable under capitalism. It condemned antimonopoly programs as out of keeping with historical development, and in many instances approved the development of monopoly because such concentration of productive prices would make the transformation to socialism easier. The major concern of the Marxists, therefore, was political. By winning state power they would expropriate the monopolies and take over a fully developed "socialized" mode of production. Only the "social relations" had to be changed. The German unions acquiesced in the cartelization program of German industry, and the English unions early abetted the monopoly devices of British industry. In the United States, however, socialist attention was riveted largely on the trade-agreement policy and Gompers was attacked for "class collaboration." On the monopoly issue in general, the party never defined its stand squarely. In theory and in its arguments with middle-class elements, it prophesied the inevitable concentration of industry. In its politics, however, the party, largely under the influence of agrarian elements in the West, raised political slogans of an antimonopoly nature.

The third dilemma arose out of the limited program of the American Federation of Labor. To the socialists the demand for a shorter work-day and more wages was no solution to the capitalist crisis. Some ultimate goal had to be fixed lest the workers gain illusions that the trade union was a sufficient instrument for melioration. If one accepts the viewpoint that the union, by its own nature, becomes an end in itself and an integral part of capitalist society, then such a socialist theory makes sense. If, however, one regards unionism as a social force which by its own position in an industrial hierarchy becomes a challenge to managerial power and changes the locus of power in capitalism, then Gompers' strategy of focusing on the day-to-day issues was undeniably correct. This is the very problem which unionism, now an established and powerful force in the economy, faces today.

[52] Gompers in the *American Federation of Labor Convention Proceedings*, 1899, p. 15.

V. Fission, Fusion, and Faction

Out of the European dogmatism of De Leon and the native evangelicism of Debs arose the American Socialist Party—and it combined some of the backward features of both. Hillquit, although stemming from the German tradition, was intellectually flexible; but ultimately his Marxism was too constricting a yoke; Debs, who emerged from the rich American soil, was unstable temperamentally and too rigid intellectually to allow his experiences to modify his prejudices. If one adds to this the boyish romanticism of a Jack London, the pale Christian piety of a George Herron and of the large number of Protestant ministers who flocked into the Socialist Party, the reckless braggadocio of a "Wild Bill" Haywood, and the tepid social-work impulse of do-gooders interested in prison reform, vegetarianism, birth control, woman's suffrage, and other advanced notions of the day, you have as unstable a compound as was ever mixed in the modern history of political chemistry.[53]

Formally the American Socialist Party was a fusion of two schismatic groups: an eastern wing came as a faction of the De Leonite Socialist Labor Party; a western wing as a faction from the Debsian Social Democracy of America.[54] From 1895 on, the splits in the Socialist Labor Party were as regular as binary fission among the amoebas. First to go were the Jewish socialists, who under the urging of Meyer London voted to join the Debsian movement out West. Next to go was the section in Haverhill, Massachusetts. James F. Carey, local leader of the party, had been elected a member of the city council on the Socialist Labor Party ticket, but when he voted for a new armory in town, he was attacked by De Leon and joined the Social Democracy. In St. Louis, another section of the party shook loose. The final *Götterdämmerung* took place in New York. The De Leon faction was supported by the official party papers, the *People* in English, and the *Vorwärts* in German. The Hillquit group

[53] Nor is this list of the varied types that abounded in the party meant to be exhaustive. One could add puritan consciences of millionaire socialists such as Joseph Medill Patterson (once a member of the national executive committee of the Socialist Party and in later years the Roosevelt-hating publisher of the New York *Daily News*) and J. G. Phelps Stokes; the burning Jewish intensity of Meyer London; the flaming discontent of the dispossessed farmers; the inarticulate and amorphous desire to "belong" of the immigrant workers; the iconoclastic idol-breaking of the literary radicals; the rebellious free-love addicts of Greenwich Village Bohemia; the old and broken workers; and the angry, idealistic college-student generation. And more.

[54] The geographical identifications are important in Socialist Party history. The westerners, like the American public generally, feared the "New York" influence; the easterners were afraid to put the party headquarters in Chicago, where it might be subject to the vagaries of native quack-reform doctrine. In the early years of the Socialist Party, the national headquarters were first located in Springfield, Mass., and St. Louis, Mo., because of these considerations. Although the headquarters were finally placed in Chicago, these suspicions lingered, and flared again when the "New York" influence became a factor in the party split of 1935.

rallied around the daily *Volkszeitung*. In the elections to party office each side, De Leon and Hillquit, accused the other of stuffing ballots, organizing bogus clubs, and, in general, behaving in rowdy Tammany fashion. Both claimed victory and prepared to take over the party headquarters, printing presses, and offices. When each faction came to claim possession, the two arrived head-on and came to blows. The action is described in a contemporary account: "[An] act of violence on the part of Keep [a De Leon follower] was the signal for an outburst of passion seldom witnessed in any political meeting, much less in a meeting of Socialists. The delegates pummelled each other until blood was seen flowing from many wounds. Men were sprawling on the floor, others were fighting in the corners, upon the tables, chairs and upon the piano, Hugo Vogt [another De Leon stalwart] having climbed upon the latter, yelling and fairly foaming from the mouth. . . ."[55]

Two days later another pitched battle erupted. The *Volkszeitung* (Hillquit) faction, claiming legal sanction, sent a delegation of able-bodied men upstairs to the office of the *People* to claim the party property. The De Leonites, however, in good revolutionary fashion barricaded themselves in the office and stood armed with clubs, bottles, and other weapons. "Fierce did the conflict rage for fully ten minutes; blood flowed freely," reported the *People*.[56] More blood might have flowed but for the salutary intervention of the gendarmerie. Since the De Leonites held possession, the police ordered the insurrectionists to "move on," a dramatic illustration of the old revolutionary adage that property is theft. As a result of the conflict, there appeared two Socialist Labor Parties and two *Peoples*. The case was finally decided in the capitalist courts, which awarded both the name of the organization and the title of the newspaper to De Leon. The Hillquit faction, dubbed the "Kangaroos," withdrew and opened negotiations with the Debs-Berger Social Democratic Party of America, negotiations leading to the formation of the Socialist Party of America.[57]

[55] Quoted in Social Democracy of America, *Social Democracy Red Book* (Terre Haute, Ind., 1900), p. 72.

[56] Nathan Fine, *Labor and Farmer Parties in the United States, 1828-1928* (New York, 1928), p. 175.

[57] As for De Leon's Socialist Labor Party, the natural law of evolutionary fratricide continued with remorseless logic. Even after the withdrawal of the Hillquit group, split after split continued. One group of thirty-one members issued a statement charging De Leon, the national editor, with being a Robespierre. "Every member of Section New York," they stated, continuing the metaphor, "has been declared a suspect and the Jacobin Club recently issued a decree for the establishment of a Revolutionary Tribunal variously styled Committee of Inquiry, or Spying Committee or the Holy Inquisition." Heads did roll, ideologically, and in the short period of three years a number of prominent S.L.P.ers had been vicariously executed. Among these were the former editors of the *People* and *Vorwärts*, Lucien Sanial and Hugo Vogt, two of De Leon's cohorts on the famous ruling triumvirate, Herman Simpson, chief

If American socialism thus imported its quarrelsome sectarianism from European-flavored Marxism, it more than redressed the balance with a loose evangelical fervor and moralistic tone drawn from the native West. Two men, J. A. Wayland and Eugene Victor Debs, were largely responsible for that leathery "Yankeefying" flavor. Wayland, the "one hoss philosopher," published the *Appeal to Reason*, socialism's cracker-barrel weekly, which, at its height, had a Bible Belt circulation of more than 500,000 believing readers. Debs, whom Sinclair Lewis once called the John the Baptist of American socialism, was the man whose gentleness and sweet, passionate anguish touched a chord of goodness in more Americans than probably any other figure in American life after Lincoln. Both Debs and Wayland came to socialism not through Marx, but via utopianism and dizzy cooperative-colony schemes.

Wayland, a restless and shrewd Indiana businessman, had made a sizable fortune in the printing business and Colorado real estate, but, about 1891, when already middle-aged, he became a socialist by reading Laurence Gronlund and other socialist writers of the period. Wayland felt his conversion triumphantly confirmed when, as a result of his readings, he predicted a panic in 1893, and by quickly liquidating his real-estate holdings, found his fortune increasing. In 1893 he returned to Indiana and started the *Coming Nation*. Its rambling anecdotal style ("simply Ruskin turned into the language of the common people") attracted a large readership and Wayland felt bold enough to start a socialist colony at Ruskin, Tennessee, which would serve as a practical example of the cooperative ideal. A contemporary account records his cheery disillusionment. "He sent money down to a few people who were first to arrive on the ground, and one of them who was a sort of self-constituted agent kept writing for more, alleging that various work was under way. . . . When Wayland appeared on the scene he found nothing had been done, but that the pioneers were quartered at a hotel at Tennessee City, living in luxury on the money he forwarded. . . ." Before going to Ruskin, Wayland had read none of the books on the history of the American communities. But even reading of their failures would not have deterred him, he said. He had to find out by actual experience the impossibility of all-around success in such undertakings.[58]

In 1895 Wayland began the publication of the socialist *Appeal to Reason*, which, after an initial setback during the Bryan campaign of 1896, soon caught on, and in little more than three years rose to a circula-

---

editor of the Jewish *Abendblatt*, Benjamin F. Keinard, the party's candidate for mayor, Arthur Keep, and various other former De Leonite stalwarts of the 1899 battle. The membership finally shriven and doctrinal purity achieved, the Socialist Labor Party retired into a political lamasery to await the collapse of society.

[58] "A Trip to Girard," by Wayfarer, in *Social Democracy Red Book*, p. 91.

tion of almost 100,000. In 1896, the saving remnants of the Ruskin Colony group sent out a call for a nationwide convention of socialists. Out of that convention emerged a new group, socialist in goal but utopian in orientation, the Brotherhood of the Co-operative Commonwealth. With an ambitious program ("Mutualism or the Kingdom of God Here and Now") the Brotherhood divided its work into various departments: the teaching of socialism, the settlement of colonies, the establishment of industries by building and operating factories and mills, and political action.[59] A year later, the program unrealized, the Brotherhood joined with the remnants of the American Railway Union, led by Eugene Debs, to form the Social Democracy of America.

The American Railway Union, an all-inclusive organization of railway workers organized in 1893, was Debs's break with traditional unionism. Eugene Victor Debs, born in 1855 in the dusty town of Terre Haute, Indiana, had railroading in his blood from his early youth. During the transport boom created by the Civil War, Terre Haute had zoomed into a railroad town, and young Debs roamed the switching yards soaking in the romance of rail adventure. Young Eugene Victor had absorbed his romanticism from his father, Jean Daniel Debs. His two given names, in fact, were in honor of Eugene Sue and Victor Hugo, "a tradition of reason and justice," father Daniel felt, "by which men should live."[60] At the age of fifteen, with a smattering of high-school learning but with the deep imprint of Schiller's poetry and Victor Hugo's *Les Miserables* in mind, the young Debs went to work as a wiper on the railroad. A year later, a lean, six-foot lad, he became a fireman on the short but cold run between Terre Haute and Indianapolis.

Debs worked only three years as a fireman, for on the insistence of his mother he left the hazardous occupation and took a job as a clerk in a wholesale grocery. In all, Debs worked less than five years on the railroad, but the hardships of the toil remained vivid in his impressionable mind. When the struggling Brotherhood of Locomotive Firemen organized a lodge in Terre Haute, Debs, though no longer a railroad man, joined it. In a short while, Debs became a national officer of the union. At the same time he entered local politics, being twice elected city clerk of the town. As the Brotherhood grew more powerful, Debs felt that the ultimate security of the union lay in an industrial federation which would also include the unorganized semiskilled and unskilled road workers. (In this same period, Debs was reading Gronlund's *The Co-operative Commonwealth* and Edward Bellamy's *Looking Backward*.) However, the dream of a unified railway federation collapsed under the weight of jurisdictional

---

[59] James Dombrowski, *The Early Days of Christian Socialism in America* (New York, 1936), p. 75.
[60] Ray Ginger, *The Bending Cross* (New Brunswick, N.J., 1949), p. 6.

disputes and petty rivalries, and Debs retired from the firemen's union, devoting his energies to a publishing company and to the editing of the *Locomotive Firemen's Magazine*, a forum whose pages were open to every dissonant voice of the day.

In 1893, in the wake of the labor turmoil that had boiled over at Coeur d'Alene, Debs returned and organized the American Railway Union on an industrial-union basis. Within a year, the new union had won a sensational strike against James J. Hill's Great Northern railway, and the membership had risen to more than 150,000. In that year the total membership of the three old-line brotherhoods was about 70,000 while the American Federation of Labor had little more than 260,000.

The panic of 1893 gave rise to the discontent and national hysteria of 1894. The threatening armies of the commonwealth—Coxey's army, Fry's army, Kelly's army—had marched grimly on Washington to demand relief for the unemployed, only to end as a ludicrous tatterdemalion mob, their leaders arrested for trampling on the grass of the Capitol.[61] But on the heels of Coxeyism came the more serious Pullman strike at Chicago, a strike that catapulted Debs to national fame. It was obvious at the time that the conservatives had the jitters. A week before the strike, an "anarchist plot" to blow up the national Capitol had been exposed by the New York *Tribune*; in Paris, the French stateman Carnot had just been assassinated. The echoes of Coxey's tramping army were still reverberating. When the American Railway Union declared a boycott on Pullman cars, within three days 40,000 railroaders had walked out in a sympathy strike, bringing traffic west of Chicago to a halt. The capitalists felt that the revolution was knocking at the door. Attorney General Richard Olney, the strong man in Cleveland's cabinet, acted swiftly to break the strike. Two federal judges granted his application for "the most sweeping injunction ever issued from a Federal Court." "A Gatling gun on paper," declared the joyful General Managers Association.[62] Under the cover of the blanket injunction, the strike slipped away fast, leaving in its wake a trail of violence and destruction.

The Pullman strike made Eugene Debs a national figure, and by his own account converted him to socialism. For violating the government injunction, Debs was sentenced to six months in prison. In Woodstock jail, he was visited by noted socialists, including Keir Hardie, the founder of the British Labour Party, and Victor Berger. In this period of enforced idleness Debs read a great deal, and, according to legend, found his Damascan road. The story is told by Debs himself in an essay, "How I Became a Socialist."[63] Debs wrote: "... it was here that Socialism gradually

[62] Matthew Josephson, *The Politicos* (New York, 1938), p. 578.
[61] Donald L. McMurry, *Coxey's Army* (Boston, 1929), p. 119.
[63] New York *Comrade*, April 1902; reprinted in *Writings and Speeches of Eugene*

laid hold of me in its own irresistible fashion. Books and pamphlets and letters from Socialists came by every mail and I began to read and think and dissect the anatomy of the system in which workingmen, however organized, could be shattered and battered and splintered at a single stroke. The writings of Bellamy and Blatchford early appealed to me. The Co-operative Commonwealth of Gronlund also impressed me, but the writings of [the German Marxist] Kautsky were so clear and conclusive that I readily grasped, not merely his argument, but also caught the spirit of his socialist utterance—and I thank him and all who helped me out of darkness into light."

Actually, these recollections, written in 1902 many years after the fact, obscure the backsliding and involutions of Debs's march to socialism. In 1894 and 1896, after his release from jail, Debs still considered himself a populist and figured prominently in the speculations of various populists for nomination to high office. The American Railway Union, at its 1894 convention, had endorsed the People's Party and free silver. In 1896, Henry Demarest Lloyd sought to swing the People's (Populist) Party behind Debs for president instead of Bryan. Debs, however, now vacillated on the importance of the money question. In his magazine, *Railway Times*, Debs wrote that the railroads were using the currency issue in order to divert attention from the real threat of government by injunction. During the campaign, however, he declared that free silver "afforded common ground upon which the common people could unite against the trusts."[64] Debs was active in the populist campaign and worked tirelessly for Bryan, Altgeld, and Darrow. "If Bryan had been elected President in 1896," writes Ginger, "Eugene Debs might never have become a socialist."

In 1897, Debs came around to declaring that "the issue is socialism versus capitalism. . . . We have been cursed with the reign of gold long enough." Yet the same year, Debs proposed a mass migration of unemployed to the western states in order to form cooperative colonies; and, in the most politically naive fashion imaginable, he wrote to John D. Rockefeller, of all people, for help in financing the colonization scheme. "The purpose of the organization, briefly speaking," Debs wrote to Rockefeller, "is to establish in place of the present cruel, immoral and decadent system, a co-operative commonwealth, where millionaires and beggars . . . will completely disappear, and human brotherhood will be inaugurated to bless and make the world more beautiful. . . . Then the strong will help the weak, the weak will love the strong, and the Human Brotherhood

---

V. *Debs* (New York, 1948). This version is accepted without question by a number of early biographers. See David Karsner, *Debs: His Authorized Life and Letters* (New York, 1919), p. 178; McAlister Coleman, *Pioneers of Freedom* (New York, 1929), p. 151; Fine, *op.cit.*, p. 188.

[64] Ginger, *op.cit.*, p. 190.

will transform the days to come into a virtual Paradise."[65] There is no record that Mr. Rockefeller ever replied.

Debs had announced his conversion to socialism, but his thinking was still colored by colonization and western schemes. He did not join the Socialist Labor Party, feeling that De Leon's party was too narrow and boss-ridden ever to attract a popular following. Instead, under the urging of friends, particularly Victor Berger, Debs moved toward the formation of a new political party. The contrast between Debs and Berger symbolizes, in part, two dimensions of the future Socialist Party. The core of Debs's character was a deep emotionality streaked with a homely sentimentalism; his politics derived from a romantic conception of the underdog and his commitments flowed quickly to those who also subscribed to this conception. Berger, stocky and assertive, had a shrewd sense of the practical, and had the political trick, within the Socialist Party, of clothing his ideas in revolutionary phrases and his actions in the practicalities of ward and precinct politics. His métier was organization, and in tight, almost bullying fashion, he built a machine in Milwaukee which was to be the solidest rock of the socialist achievement in America. Yet his devotion to socialism was unquestionable. Born in Austria-Hungary in 1860, Berger received a university education in Vienna and soon after came to the United States. For a while he tramped through the West doing odd jobs before settling finally in Milwaukee, where he became a school teacher. In 1892 Berger became the editor of the German-language paper *Milwaukee Vorwärts* and embarked on a political career. Berger was a Marxist and convinced, therefore, that the various colonizing and utopian schemes could not succeed. He felt that a socialist movement would develop in the United States as industrialization proceeded, but that its tempo might be different from that of the movement in Europe. In 1896, the Milwaukee socialists organized a branch of the People's (Populist) Party in an effort to capture the party's convention. When that attempt failed, Berger took a leading role in the creation of a new party.

On June 15, 1897, the skeleton of the American Railway Union met in Chicago and with the tattered remnants of the Brotherhood of the Cooperative Commonwealth formed the Social Democracy of America. The convention adopted a socialist platform calling for public ownership of all monopolies and utilities, and also public works for the unemployed. But the party could not shake the ghost of colonization. Christian socialists, footloose rebels, and middle-class romantics still made up the core of the native dissident left in the United States. As the rapid industrialism brutalized the American character, these elements saw colonization as the only "practical" implementation of their need to escape from the

[65] *Ibid.*, p. 201.

aggressive, egotistical, competitive individual nurtured by capitalist society.[66]

The Social Democracy of America never even rode out one year of life. The schism was there from the start. The executive board of the new party was dominated by the "old-guard" leaders of the American Railway Union, a fact which from the beginning created hostility among other elements in the organization. This leading group, augmented by some anarchist adherents, plumped hard for colonization. The "political" faction was led by Berger. He argued that the party could win offices, and pointed to such success as the election of two aldermen in Sheboygan, Wisconsin, and the quintupling of the vote in Milwaukee. By the second convention, in 1898, the issue of colonization could no longer be avoided. During the year, a colonization commission had explored sites in Tennessee, Washington, and Colorado. Just before the convention, it announced that it had purchased 560 acres in Cripple Creek, Colorado, on which was a gold mine of "the deeper you go the richer the ore" variety. (Later the gullible commission discovered that it had bought a gold brick.)[67] The fight during the convention was bitter, the comrades reviling each other unmercifully. The political faction charged, with merit, that the colonizers had chartered "fake" locals in order to capture the convention; in turn the colonizers charged, unfairly, that the secretary of the party had mishandled party funds. When the issue finally came to a vote after three days of wretched wrangling, the colonizers won, 52 to 37. At 2:30 in the morning, the minority bolted and at that ghostly hour formed the Social Democratic Party, its leaders being Eugene Debs, Victor Berger and Frederic Heath of Milwaukee.[68] At the final voting, Debs was absent in bed in his hotel

[66] Perhaps the last great pathetic attempt in this direction was the Christian Commonwealth colony at Commonwealth, Georgia, in 1896. "They were resolved to follow an absolute love ethic of complete sharing. Their success would be a vindication of the efficacy of Christianity for solving social problems; their failure would be the failure of love." (See Dombrowski, op.cit., p. 133.) Unfortunately they failed.

During its four-year lifetime, the colony attracted between 300 and 400 persons, and in the pages of its magazine, the Social Gospel, could be found the works of Bliss, George D. Herron, Bellamy, and other leading thinkers of the Christian socialist movement in the United States.

Since this was a Christian colony, it was almost fated that it recapitulate the eternal drama of sin and betrayal. Following a heavy freeze in 1899 and subsequent damage to crops, grumbling arose over the slim rations. A member of the colony who had been cast out for falsely accusing it of favoring "free love" began to sow the seeds of dissension. Finally, twelve backsliders from apostledom sought to throw the colony into bankruptcy hoping, through the subsequent liquidation of assets, to benefit greatly. Reluctantly, the colony decided to fight the issue in the courts. "This was regarded by many as the final surrender of the principle of love, the acknowledgment after several compromises that the ethic of nonresistance was not an adequate standard for meeting the issue of a complex social situation." (Dombrowski, op.cit., p. 165.)

[67] Social Democracy Red Book, p. 67.

[68] Theodore Debs, "The Birth of the Socialist Party," New Leader, April 28, 1934.

room with a fierce headache. It was a pattern to be constantly repeated. With no stomach for the quarrelsome factionalism and angry invective that accompanied party conventions, Debs was to remain away during his lifetime from almost every national convention of the Socialist Party.

The new party declared itself a "class-conscious, revolutionary social organization"; its motto: Pure Socialism and No Compromise.[69] Soon after its start, it met with some local success. In Massachusetts, in 1898, it elected a mayor in Haverhill and sent two men to the state legislature. The following year, independent socialist groups in Texas and Iowa joined the party. When the Social Democratic Party met in first national convention in March 1900 at Indianapolis, it had more than 4,500 members with 226 branches in twenty-five states.

The formation of the Social Democratic Party as a purely political party, using political methods and formulating political demands, was an important turning point in the development of a socialist movement in the United States. Perhaps the most significant aspect of its platform and outlook was the inclusion of a set of "immediate issues" as the basis for the party's agitation and educational program. It was at this time that Daniel De Leon's Socialist Labor Party had scrapped all specific resolutions and planks, retaining only the statement of principles in its public declarations. "The whole string of planks," said De Leon, ". . . remind us of the infancy of Socialists, when Socialists were still impressed with the idea that we must do something immediately for the working class."[70] The Socialist Labor Party action could only narrow the party membership, since the condition of joining was agreement on a specific doctrinal view. The inclusion by the Social Democrats, on the other hand, of meliorative appeals tended to encourage almost any variety of dissident to join, and extended the basis of consequent factionalism.

The platform of the Social Democratic Party of America, adopted at Chicago in June 1898, is interesting in the light of later New Deal legislation. It declared conventionally for a system of "co-operative production and distribution." In addition, the platform demanded "national insurance of working people against accidents, lack of employment and want in old age," a "system of public works and improvements for the employment . . . of unemployed," the "reduction of the hours of labor in proportion to the increasing facilities of production," "equal civil and political rights for

[69] The colonizers, on the other hand, moved in the opposite direction, rejecting the viewpoint of class struggle and broadening their appeal to "all men." Shortly after this, their group dwindled to only a few. A small colony with 110 settlers eventually was established at the head of Henderson Bay in the State of Washington, but it soon petered out.

[70] *Proceedings of the Tenth National (1900) Convention of the Socialist Labor Party*; cited in Joseph Dorfman, *The Economic Mind in American Civilization*, III (New York, 1949), p. 236.

men and women," "the adoption of the initiative and the referendum," the "abolition of war as far as the United States are concerned and the introduction of international arbitration instead."[71]

Two omissions should be noted. One was a plank on farmers. The original statement called for the leasing of public land to farmers in parcels not greater than 640 acres, and the construction of grain elevators and cold-storage buildings to be used by the farmer at cost. Doctrinaire socialists, however, charged that this program was "reactionary" (i.e., populist). The supporters of the plank pointed out that concentration of land ownership was not taking place in the rural districts as the early theorists of socialism had predicted, and that steps to aid small private farmers were necessary. After considerable debate the plank was dropped, with the result that no section on agriculture appeared at all in the party platform. The farm issue was to plague the party for the next twelve years and never was satisfactorily resolved.

The second omission was the absence of any reference to Negroes. The lack of a policy on ethnic questions—other than the vacuous statement that socialism would solve the problem—was also to play a debilitating role in the political development of the party.

It is important to note that while the Social Democratic Party (and later the Socialist Party, which took over the platform virtually intact) focused attention on *immediate demands*, it did not take stands on the *current* issues agitating the American body politic. These "immediate demands" (or palliatives, as De Leon sneeringly called them) were measures to relieve the economic want of the workers and steps to the attainment of socialism. As such they were more politically relevant than the vague promise of a socialist industrial republic which the Socialist Labor Party held out. But the party's failure to commit itself on the actual immediate issues that had to be solved in the here and now tended to isolate it from the labor movement and from the farmers. The party failed to discuss the money issue, which was a shining panacea of previous socialist and labor parties. Nor did it consider tariff and immigration, two issues which vitally affected the interests of the trade-union movement. But perhaps most curious was the fact that the party did not take a stand on the Spanish-American war and the "paramount issue" of imperialism which was to loom so large in Bryan's campaign of 1900. Senator Albert Beveridge had proclaimed his doctrine of "Manifest Destiny." "The question is elemental," he cried out. "It is racial. God has not been preparing the English-speaking and Teutonic peoples for a thousand years for nothing but self-administration. No! He has made us the master organizers of the world. He has made us adepts in government that we may administer government among savage and senile people. And of all our race He has

[71] *Social Democracy Red Book*, pp. 132, 133.

5 4

marked the American people as His chosen Nation to finally lead in the regeneration of the world."

However, the Socialists would not take up this challenge. Debs wrote in 1900: "The campaign this year will be unusually spectacular. The Republican party 'points with pride' to the 'prosperity' of the country, the beneficent results of the 'gold standard' and the 'war record' of the administration. The Democratic Party declares that 'imperialism' is the 'paramount' issue and that the country is certain to go to the 'demnition bow-wows' if Democratic officeholders are not elected instead of the Republicans. The Democratic slogan is 'The Republic vs. the Empire' accompanied in a very minor key by 16 to 1 and 'direct legislation where practical.' . . ." And then he wrote, as mentioned earlier herein, "What but meaningless phrases are 'imperialism,' 'expansionism,' 'free silver,' 'gold standard,' etc., to the wage worker? The large capitalists represented by Mr. McKinley and the small capitalists represented by Mr. Bryan are interested in these 'issues,' but they do not concern the working class."[72]

But were these actually "meaningless phrases" and side issues?

VI. The Golden Age of American Socialism

Every society and every social movement has its "golden age"—its period of muscularity and vigor—where the sense of growth is sure, the surge to power seemingly irresistible, and the crest of victory the only point in the line of vision. The years from 1902 to 1912 were the "golden age" of American socialism. In that shiny decade the voice of socialism was being heard in the land. The dabbler in cold statistical facts may find this picture puzzling. At its peak, the socialist vote never reached the heights of the Greenbackers and populists. The latter even elected a large number of congressmen and some governors, while the socialists were never able to elect more than two representatives. Yet the name of Debs is historically secure in American life, while few know the name of James B. Weaver, who as a Populist candidate in 1892 received over a million votes, a total higher than any ever achieved by Debs. The salient fact was that socialism was seen as a danger to the system in a way that populism never could be. Bryan, a moralist, never challenged the fundamental intellectual creeds of capitalism. Nor did Henry George, whose single-tax scheme was perhaps the boldest attempt to reinstate an individualist America. Neither of them threatened the power position of the rising industrial capitalist, nor could the single tax or the utopian colonization schemes ever challenge the economic power of the market system. Bryan and George, when they were radical, attacked particular *groups* of privileged men; socialism threw down the gauntlet to the system of power itself.

[72] "Outlook for Socialism in the United States," *International Socialist Review*, 1900; reprinted in *Writings and Speeches of Eugene V. Debs*, p. 37.

However, for fully half a century socialism as an intellectual system had sought to gain converts in America. Yet it was only at the turn of the century that it gained force and strength. It did so for a variety of reasons: the inheritance of the populist remnants; the existence of a stable labor movement, and above all the emergence of a rising social class whose members felt themselves outside the pecuniary values of business and who found in socialism a justification of their own social position and values. This was the intelligentsia.

In his day Herman Melville saw in a melancholy way that the individual man was trapped. But the sense of evil he felt was some vague diffuse force which enveloped the spirit. At the turn of the century, the villain was tangible and real—the industrial capitalist. He became the target of all whose values were being trampled. The Jeffersonians awoke to find that the country was no longer agrarian, that private property was now monopoly, and that freedom of contract was largely a means of achieving giant combinations, which, like an octopus, reached into every nook of economic life. These men, Brandeis, Weyl, Croly, Wilson, raised anew the cry of "bigness." Others, like Henry and Brooks Adams, who had sought to achieve a sense of tradition in American life, were outraged that money alone was becoming the basis of power and status, and wept in anger at the rising plutocracy. The self-conscious emergence of a gaudy "style" of upper-class living lent bite to the mordant satire of a Veblen. At the same time, the naked self-interest displayed by the industrial capitalists gave weight to the economic interpretations of American politics being written by Charles Beard, Gustavus Myers, and J. Allen Smith. The muckrakers were finding a richly fallow field in exposing the machinations of the corporations and the corruption of the cities.

The sense of an American past was emerging in consciousness, not in the triumphant way of justifying a manifest destiny, but in the angry response of a man whose inheritance was being squandered by others. The "wine of the Puritans" had gone sour, and the rationale of god-fearing piety had become the justification of the god-posturing exploiters. At a time when "Protestant ethic" was crumbling in the area of manners and morals, it was reaching its peak in the compulsive Methodist fervor of an acquisitive Daniel Drew. The period was marked by such an explosive burst of anger and criticism as to produce perhaps the most concentrated flowering of criticism in the history of American ideas. A whole new literary generation was to mock at its pretensions and exhaust itself in aesthetic revolt.

In this fervid onslaught against American capitalism, sympathy with socialism and its aims was easy and natural. The tremendous industrial expansion had produced a new race of wealthy, and the chasm between rich and poor was deep and visible, and growing wider. It was no accident that many of the early intellectual converts to socialism were ministers and charity workers who came into contact with the poor. The ethic of Protestant individualism charged these "failures" with being responsible for their own defeats, and denied them help on the self-righteous Malthusian grounds that such charity would sap their moral fibre; to the socialists, however, these people were victims of "the system," and the system would have to be changed.

The awareness of class sharpened the *historical* sense. A class had emerged, but, as with all life, it would also pass. The theory of evolution held marked sway at this time and contributed to the impact of socialist ideas. Followers of Spencer, or Comte, or Ward might dispute as to where society was heading. But the appeal of the socialists was simple: society was heading in a rational direction because men in the nature of their social evolution were becoming more rational, were mastering nature and harnessing it to men's purposes; they would also, in the course of events, harness society and turn it to the common good rather than to the profit of a few.

Although the socialism of the early twentieth century was "scientific," people were rarely attracted to it merely by the cold, rational analysis of society. What gave socialism its impact was the moral indignation at poverty and the evangelical promise of a better world. Therefore, in the pantheon of socialist messiahs, a forward place in the American contingent must be reserved for Edward Bellamy. For it was the "indigenous, homespun made-in-Chicopee-Falls" vision of that religiously-minded New England journalist rather than the Marxian dogmatics of organized socialism which introduced the idea of socialism to millions. Bellamy's *Looking Backward*, published in 1888, preached a simple message in an engaging, lullaby style. Julian West, a young Bostonian, is mesmerized and awakens in the year 2000. Here he finds the rational life. For twenty-five years each individual is called on to serve in the "industrial army." "All persons choose their occupations in the army of industry according to natural tastes and gifts. . . . In order to equalize the attractiveness of different occupations, the hours of work in those which are more laborious or otherwise unattractive are shortened as compared with the easier and more attractive trades . . . all alike, whether men or women, strong or weak, able-bodied or defective, share in the wealth produced by the industrial army and the share of all is equal." Acquisitiveness and aggression would vanish when men had enough for all. "Soon was fully revealed what the divines and philosophers of the old world never would have believed, that human nature in its essential qualities is good, not bad, that men by their natural intention and structure are generous, not selfish." The new society was instituted not by a moral new birth of humanity but by the "reaction of a changed environment upon human nature." As Bellamy naively pictured this soft regimentation—no one questioned the image of an "army" as an ideal—no decent individual could object to these simple and obvious truths.

Bellamy's book was not unique in that time. In 1884 Laurence Gronlund's *The Co-operative Commonwealth* had outlined a society based on cooperation rather than competition which would be reached by the gradual extension of state activity. And in the decade following the publication of Bellamy's book, variants on its utopian pattern were supplied by no less than nineteen other novels, the most famous of which was William Dean Howells' *Traveler from Altruria*, published in 1894.

Bellamy's new version of utopia was a staggering success. In a few years the novel sold more than 600,000 copies. The political credo of the book, the nationalization of industry, spurred the organization of a new political movement, the Nationalist clubs. By 1891 some 162 had been organized in order to spread the "principle of association," i.e., the substitution of cooperation for competition. The movement attracted almost all the socialist-minded men of the period and became in effect a way station on the road to socialism. Daniel De Leon was a Nationalist for a short period before arriving at the hardier and tougher logical doctrines of Marxism. The organized labor movement of the period was friendly and Nationalism received the endorsement of both T. V. Powderly, head of the Knights of Labor, and Samuel Gompers. P. J. McGuire, the secretary of the American Federation of Labor, formed a Nationalist club in Philadelphia. Eugene Debs, whose political views had been strongly affected by Gronlund's *The Co-operative Commonwealth*, was an enthusiastic reader of Bellamy, and in a lengthy review of Bellamy's book concluded: "Labor is organizing for such work, and those who relish good reading should read *Looking Backward*."[73] J. A. Wayland, whose famous *Appeal to Reason* was to become the most fabulous publishing venture in socialist journalism, in 1893 founded the *Coming Nation*, which fought "for a government of, by and for the people as outlined in Bellamy's *Looking Backward*."

However, it was perhaps among the clergy that the ideas of Bellamy had the most direct influence. In 1889, the famous economist and Christian socialist Richard T. Ely wrote: "We have in this country the American type of socialism, the New Nationalism. . . ."[74] A later historian of Christian socialism, James Dombrowski, wrote: "The [Nationalist] movement quickened the social consciences of multitudes within and without the Church. It gave an impetus to the cooperative movement and provided

---

[73] Cited in Ginger, *op.cit.*, p. 72.
[74] Richard T. Ely, *Social Aspects of Christianity* (New York, 1889), p. 143; cited in Dombrowski, *op.cit.*, p. 93.

the inspiration for the founding of many cooperative colonies. It was an important factor in the founding of the first Christian Socialist group in the United States."[75] In Boston, the Rev. W. D. P. Bliss, one of the leaders of Christian socialism, organized an American Fabian Society in 1895 and began the publication of the *American Fabian*, whose contributors included Edward Bellamy and Henry Demarest Lloyd, to spread the ideas of Christian socialism. Closer at hand, the socialists themselves acknowledged the strong influence of Bellamy. In the *Social Democracy Red Book* of January 1900, the handbook of the Debsian Social Democratic Party of America, Frederic Heath, tracing the history of socialist thought in America, wrote: "The American awakening to Socialism began with the appearance of Edward Bellamy's *Looking Backward* in 1888."

If Bellamy and other utopian messiahs had proclaimed the vision of the new society, it was the muckrakers who exposed the corruption of the old. Though the influence of these exposés may not have been so great as the extravagant claims of John Chamberlain ("Muckraking, indeed, provided the basis for the entire movement toward Social Democracy that came to its head in the first Wilson administration. . . ."), these exposés did provide a set of tangible and simplified symbols, large identifiable targets for those who had suffered reverses, lost their jobs, or had in some way been crushed by the ruthless competition for reward. In short, muckraking supplied a devil theory of history for those who could not master the complicated algebra of political economy.

The badge "muckrakers" was pinned on the magazine writers by Theodore Roosevelt.[76] Roosevelt used the term in opprobrium, but its import was deeper than he realized. Although the later sensationalism and flamboyance of the exposés, especially those by Hearst, eventually brought muckraking into disrepute, the impulse to muckraking in the writings of Henry Demarest Lloyd grew out of a deep religious quest to rake up and cast out the corruption which prevented man from donning the "celestial crown." Lloyd, a famous magazine editor and writer of his day, wrote *Wealth against Commonwealth*, published in 1894, the first comprehensive examination of a great trust in action. The son of an orthodox Calvinist minister, he was deeply interested in "social Christianity" throughout his life. During the 1890's Lloyd became interested in cooperative colonies as an ethical solution to capitalist immorality; their failures convinced him that the good society could not be achieved piecemeal. In his last years he regarded himself as a socialist and was, when he died in 1903,

[75] Dombrowski, *op.cit.*, pp. 94-95.
[76] From a passage in Bunyan's *Pilgrim's Progress*: "The man with the Muck-Rake, the man who could look no way but downward with the muck-rake in his hand; who was offered a celestial crown for his muck-rake but who would neither look up nor regard the crown he was offered but continued to rake to himself the filth of the floor."

on the verge of openly identifying himself as such. In his last notebook he wrote, "Christianity is the religion that was, socialism is the religion that is to be."

Wealth against Commonwealth consists largely of a "transcript of the record" taken from legislative proceedings and flavored with such tart epigrams as "Standard [Oil] has done everything with the Pennsylvania Legislature except to refine it." While the book had a solid impact on sections of the clergy and other groups interested in social reform, it never reached a mass audience. However, a technological revolution in the art of printing—the use of glazed paper from woodpulp rather than rag, and the invention of the photoengraving process—was making possible the cheap magazine and a mass audience. And a mass audience needs excitement. The formula was supplied by S. S. McClure, who found in business practices and municipal corruption the raw meat of scandal. In a few years *McClure's* had published Ida Tarbell's *History of Standard Oil*, Lincoln Steffens' series on the shame of the cities, and later, on the shame of the states. Burton J. Hendrick exposed the life-insurance companies, and other writers related the existence of prostitution and other vices to the needs of "the system." Other magazines followed the scent. Almost no industry in American life was exempt from scrutiny. In 1905 Thomas Lawson wrote his lurid stories of stock-market manipulation in *Frenzied Finance*, Charles Edward Russell pointed to the existence of a monopolistic beef trust, Ray Stannard Baker put "the railroads on trial," leading to remedial legislation in the Hepburn Act of 1906. Perhaps the largest explosion was made by Upton Sinclair's *The Jungle*. Although written as fiction, the sickening details regarding the sale of putrid and decayed meat galvanized public opinion. But Sinclair's novel went beyond the usual peeking under stones. His hero, Jurgis, exploited by the meat-packers, fleeced by unscrupulous real-estate interests, and cast out as a hobo, finds, in a modern Pilgrim's Progress, his redemption in socialism.

In a few years the muckrakers faced the same problem, because a mirror had been held up to American society and it showed a picture of Dorian Gray. The problem was: What was to be done? Many of the muckrakers themselves as well as thousands of others came to feel that the socialists possessed the answers to this question. Upton Sinclair was a socialist even when he started. Charles Edward Russell joined the Socialist Party and became one of its leaders. Steffens, more romantic and attracted to strong power figures, became interested in Christian socialism; later, attracted by the romance and power of the Russian Revolution, he became a Bolshevik sympathizer. As a muckraker, Steffens had talked of "the system," but the socialists showed him that "the system" encompassed all of society.

In general, it can be said that four factors go far to explain the rising tide of socialism in the United States at the time we are considering. One was the absorption of populist strength, especially in the West. Most of the populist elements had been folded into the Democratic Party when Bryan became its candidate in 1896, but large unassimilable blocs found their way in and later out of the Socialist Party, a fact which goes far to explain the uneven striations of the socialist vote in the decade. A second factor was the spread of factory work and the rising demand for social legislation to guard against the attendant hazards. This issue was of great appeal to socially minded and reform elements among the middle class and especially among women. Third, was the growth of socialism in Europe, particularly in Germany, the great model in those days of culture and education. This particularly influenced intellectual opinion for it seemed to confirm the Marxist prediction of the inevitable world rise of the working class. And fourth was the newly articulated American idiom in which the socialist movement spoke, at least publicly, although inner-party debates were still conducted in the private patois of socialist dialectic.

In addition to these general reasons, a structural factor played a significant role in party growth—the loose organizational and ideological make-up of the Socialist Party, which permitted the party to be different things to different men. The iron hand of De Leon had left a deep mark. Out of a deep fear of centralized control, the new Socialist Party was so organized that the individual state organizations maintained complete control of party affairs, subject only to the national constitution. And, to avoid any one paper becoming a dominant voice, the party refused until 1914 to designate an official party press which would speak authoritatively on immediate issues of the day. The same looseness prevailed on doctrine. "The international socialist program is broad enough for the widest variety of opinion as to detail, and as to the working out of principle," wrote the Reverend George D. Herron, one of the leading figures of the party, in 1900.[77] Thus agnostic and Christian, Bohemian and Puritan, could and did join the party and seek to mold it in their image. These discordant elements could only be held together by the sure promise of victory. And without victory the loosely-tied party structure would collapse.

The Socialist Party was born in a "bloomin', buzzin', confusion." In early February 1900, the dissident members of the Socialist Labor Party led by Morris Hillquit assembled in a first national convention in Rochester and tentatively nominated Job Harriman, a California lawyer, for president, and Max S. Hayes, a Cleveland printer and editor, for vice-president.

[77] George D. Herron, "A Plea for the Unity of American Socialists," *International Socialist Review*, Dec. 1900; cited in Dorfman, *op.cit.*, III, p. 236.

Actually, the Hillquit group wanted a united ticket with the Social Democratic Party. The Social Democratic leaders were hesitant, but finally a joint ticket of Debs and Harriman was named. One disputed point, the name of the combined party, remained to be settled; otherwise everything was harmonious, or so it seemed. But soon, the "buzzin'" began. In reality, each side was still too touchy and suspicious of the other's motives. At one point, the Social Democrats accused the "Kangaroos" on the provisional national committee of violating the interim agreement on the use of name. Other charges were hurled. Actually, the real fear of the Social Democrats, smarting before the fancied contempt of the didactic S.L.P.ers who would quote Marx at the drop of a resolution, was that they would lose control of the organization. Debs wrote: "For years the official organ of the Socialist Labor Party had drilled it into their members that the Social Democratic Party consisted of a lot of freaks, frauds and fakers without a redeeming feature. . . . Hundreds of them, members of the anti-De Leon party, and I speak advisedly, still rankle with that feeling. . . ."[78] The attacks became mean and personal, and almost no one, with the exception of Debs, escaped the free-flowing invective. The confusion started blooming when the Hillquit faction, meeting with a dissident (anti-Debs) section of the Social Democrats, publicly announced that unity had been achieved, took over the name Social Democratic Party, and opened an office in Springfield, Massachusetts. Throughout the 1900 campaign there was thus one ticket, but two parties.

As public interest stirred in Debs's campaign, the rivalry began to die down. Jubilation grew when Debs received nearly 97,000 votes against 34,000 for the De Leon S.L.P. ticket. Both sides now expressed a willingness to work together, and another unity convention was called at Indianapolis. But factional lines developed at this convention before the party could be fully stabilized.[79] The new divisive issue was the old problem of "immediate demands." One faction, led by A. M. Simons of Chicago, dubbed the "impossibilists" (as against the "opportunists"), argued against the inclusion of such planks in the platform because no immediate relief was possible for the working class under capitalism. Since the social revolution was only a few years away, attention to these problems would only "sidetrack" the socialist movement. The impossibilists were defeated 82 to 30 (representing a party membership of 5,358 to 1,325), but the issue was renewed at subsequent national conventions.[80] On the second issue—a resolution on farmers—the factional lines crossed in weird fashion. In the debate, a number of so-called "opportunists," including James Carey and Job Harriman, argued for a rigid class stand against the "mid-

[78] Cited in Fine, op.cit., pp. 199-200.
[79] John M. Work, "The Birth of the Socialist Party," (Socialist) Call, March 5, 1948.
[80] Fine, op.cit., pp. 204-9.

dle-class" farmer, while Simons, the impossibilist, joined Hillquit in calling for an appeal to the farmer. Finally, because farmers were not considered as members of the working class, the delegates voted to drop all reference to meliorative demands for them from the platform and to refer the problem for study to the next convention. Eugene Debs, as was to become his habit, was absent from the convention.

Debates such as these must have been bewildering to the party novitiate. And for the historian they involved schismatic niceties in relating internal party problems to the general scene. Certainly from 1901 to 1919 the public and private doctrines of American socialism often seemed to bear little relation to each other. Publicly, the socialist message was simple and compelling: economic crises were endemic in the system because the worker was not paid the full return of his labor and the capitalist could not find markets for his goods or investment; the centralization of industry, occasioned by the need to control markets, was insistently eliminating the small entrepreneur and the middle class; the growth of trusts presaged the necessary next stage in social evolution, socialism. Internally, however, the new recruit would find himself in a morass of competing factions, each talking a special jargon, each claiming to point to the correct road to socialism. He would be assaulted by "impossibilists" who told him that a fight on taxes as a political issue was meaningless because the workers did not pay taxes.[81] He would find himself involved in detailed arguments concerning industrial versus craft unionism. And, as is typical in sectarian milieus, he would be regaled with detailed bits of gossip and innuendo about the various party leaders.

Since a party's ability to meet the various challenges of the political environment depends on its internal cohesion, the flexibility of its leadership, and the responsiveness of a mature rank and file, the tortuous internal history of the Socialist Party is worth studying in some detail.

The trade-union issue was the main axis around which the major factional groupings in the Socialist Party revolved. There was the "right wing" which sought to work within the American Federation of Labor because the bulk of organized labor was in the Federation. But the right-wingers were constantly getting caught in the cross fire from Gompers on the one side, who accused them of seeking to capture the Federation for socialism, and from Debs and the left-wingers on the other, who accused them of kowtowing to the reactionary labor leaders. The left wing itself had no consistent and unifying viewpoint. It was a

---

[81] This was a favorite intellectual tartar of the Socialist Labor Party. Through a complicated analysis of surplus value (i.e., the extra profit gained by the capitalists), De Leon always "proved" that the practical effect of fighting taxes would only "champion the interests of the little cockroach businessman." Why worry then about taxes? the S.L.P.ers would taunt.

varying mélange, made up in part of those who were against *all* immediate reforms, of those who were for syndicalism but against political action, and of those who favored industrial unions and militant tactics instead of the "class collaborationist" policies of the American Federation of Labor. The dilemma of the leftist wing, however, was that the militant unions it created either fell apart because it didn't know how to settle down, or became "conservative" when it did. These contradictions were reflected sharply in Debs. Of a romantic nature, he would promptly fly to any strike situation that needed his impassioned prompting to sustain its willingness and morale. Yet Debs could never accept the routine and plodding course of a day-to-day trade-union situation.

One of the earliest and important fights centered about the formation of the American Labor Union. For many years, the unions in the West, particularly the strong Western Federation of Miners, had felt that they were being ignored by the American Federation of Labor. In 1898 these groups banded together and formed the Western Labor Union, which would function west of the Mississippi River. In 1901, under the prompting of Debs, the organization changed its name in order to span the continent. Against the charge of dual unionism, Debs stingingly declared: "When the American Federation of Labor . . . relegates leaders to the rear who secure fat offices for themselves in reward for keeping the rank-and-file in political ignorance and industrial slavery, when it shall cease to rely upon cringing lobbying committees, it shall have the right to object."[82] The American Labor Union endorsed socialism. "On the practical side, however," write Perlman and Taft, "it was like any other American union. The right to strike was strictly circumscribed and controlled by central authority. Likewise, its socialism notwithstanding, the temper of the West showed itself in the advocacy of Oriental exclusion as a measure of wage protection."[83] Two years after its start, the American Labor Union began to wobble; and it finally was submerged in the Industrial Workers of the World.

Within the American Federation of Labor, meanwhile, the socialists had demonstrated some continued following. At its 1902 convention a resolution urging "the working people to organize their economic and political power to secure for labor the full product of its toil and the overthrow of the wage system and the establishment of an industrial cooperative commonwealth" was defeated by 4,897 to 4,171. The socialists, however, obtained the support of the miners, carpenters, and brewery workers, and if, as the miners had urged, the resolution had ended with the word "toil," the motion probably would have passed.[84]

[82] McAlister Coleman, *Eugene V. Debs* (New York, 1930), p. 219.

[83] Selig Perlman and Philip Taft, *History of Labor in the United States, 1896-1932* (New York, 1935), IV, p. 217.

[84] J. W. Sullivan, *Socialism as an Incubus on the American Labor Movement* (New York, 1909), pp. 18-19.

This promising show of strength in the A.F.L. on the one hand, and the formation of the American Labor Union on the other, sharpened the factionalism within the Socialist Party. The resident "action committee" of the party issued a statement attacking the founders of the American Labor Union as "compromising" the party. In reply, Debs charged that certain socialist politicians "were perhaps advised that it was wiser policy to curry favor with numbers than to stand by principles."[85] The battle was carried to the executive committee, where Debs and Berger engaged in acrimonious exchanges. Debs won this first skirmish, and the national secretary of the party who had issued the statement was replaced.

The feuding carried over into the Socialist Party national convention of 1904, the first since the unity convention of 1901. In the intervening years, party membership had grown steadily, and more than 20,000 were now enrolled. This was the first convention in which major policy decisions could be assessed in the light of practical experience as a political party. But no such assessments were made. The one thing the convention did show was that factionalism and sectarian spirit had permeated so deep that some split was inevitable in the future.

At the convention the "impossibilists," concentrated in Chicago, fought against the adoption of a state or municipal program by the party. "We have [in Chicago]," said delegate Stedman, "a question of municipal transportation, and there [are] members of this party in that city who [take] the position that they would vote in favor of granting franchises to the corporations until we controlled the entire country. . . . Some members are in favor of nothing until we have recognized Socialism which would come in by a grand cataclysm."[86]

But it was the trade-union issue which produced the sharpest strain. A resolution introduced by a Wyoming delegate called for support of industrial unions and denounced the leaders of the A.F.L. for working with the businessmen in the National Civic Federation. The resolution also had the support of a dozen or so delegates, largely from the agricultural states of the West, although, or perhaps because, they opposed unions altogether. One delegate, Irene Smith of Oregon, declared in strident fashion: "The Trades Unionist is leaning upon his little crutch and until that crutch is broken entirely under him, he will have to lean upon it, whether we preach Socialism or not. . . . the moment that the Socialist Party of the United States steps out upon a clear class-conscious platform of its own and frees its skirts from all these petty movements, then we will begin to move forward and grow."[87] The majority itself had no unified view on industrial unionism, but felt that such a flat statement would amount to interference in internal union affairs. That issue, "inter-

---

[85] Ginger, *op.cit.*, p. 220.   [86] *Proceedings*, 1904, p. 23.
[87] *Ibid.*, pp. 178-79.

vention," was to recur constantly in socialist debates. The minority lost 52 to 107. However, as a concession to the left wing the immediate demands of the party were condensed into a single paragraph and buried in the platform. Since the Socialist Party was not a disciplined movement, the Chicago organization, dominated by the "impossibilists," was able to repudiate the national platform and conduct its own type of campaign.

Debs was again nominated in 1904, together with Ben Hanford, an ardent New York printer who created the character of "Jimmie Higgins."[88] The growth of trusts was the main campaign issue in 1904. In previous years, capitalism had been attacked for the evils of competition; now the attack had shifted to the evils of monopoly. Debs toured the country from Maine to Oregon, drawing huge crowds wherever he went, and calling up an impressive 409,230 votes, a figure which quadrupled the previous presidential total of 96,931.

Notable as the gain was, it failed to unite the party. In fact the rift between the proponents of revolutionary unionism and the supporters of the American Federation of Labor grew deeper. The rupture deepened still further when in December 1904 Debs and five others sent a secret letter to thirty radical leaders over the country inviting them to meet in Chicago in January 1905 "to discuss ways and means of uniting the working people of America on correct revolutionary principles."[89] The conference in turn called a convention out of which arose the Industrial Workers of the World.

Like a meeting of *Meistersingers*, almost every major radical voice in America was represented at the founding convention of the I.W.W. in June 1905. Present were Debs, De Leon, Lucy Parsons, the widow of the famed anarchist Haymarket martyr, and syndicalist Big Bill Haywood. However, except for the Western Federation of Miners with its 27,000 members, no major established unions were represented. The first year's results were disappointing. No unions seceded from the American Federation of Labor and even the few within the I.W.W. were dubious of its effectiveness. The socialist press, including the *Social Democratic Herald* of Victor Berger, the Cleveland *Citizen* of Max Hayes, and the *Jewish Daily Forward* in New York, all attacked the I.W.W. When Debs took steps toward a rapprochement with De Leon, his column in the Milwaukee socialist paper was dropped.

In the midst of this fierce intramural quarreling, the Moyer-Haywood-Pettibone case broke with the sharpness of a thunderclap, and during the

---

[88] "Jimmie Higgins," a mythical rank-and-file member, was the "common man" of the party, the unsung hero who, through rain, snow, and sleet trudged from house to house selling party newspapers, passed out leaflets on the street corner, set up the soap-box, and performed the other laborious and menial jobs of party work uncomplainingly.

[89] Ginger, *op.cit.*, p. 237.

subsequent excitement all labor factions momentarily forgot their own concerns. Governor Frank Steunenberg of Idaho, who had been elected as a populist but had turned against the miners and small farmers during the Coeur d'Alene riots of 1899, was assassinated by a bomb on December 30, 1905. On the sworn confession of a suspect, Charles H. Moyer and Big Bill Haywood, heads of the Western Federation of Miners, and George Pettibone, a Denver businessman, were charged with plotting the murder. Although the three lived in Colorado, they were whisked across the state line without extradition hearings. The kidnapping roused the entire labor and socialist movement. Samuel Gompers at the A.F.L. convention denounced the act. Debs, with flaming passion, began a nation-wide campaign to arouse support of the three. The case made Bill Haywood a national figure.

In the midst of the Moyer-Haywood-Pettibone agitation, the I.W.W. opened its second convention. In this there arose the first split. The question was on the technique of unionism. The "conservatives," domi-nated by the Western Federation of Miners, wanted to build stable industrial unions. The opposition, led by Daniel De Leon, Vincent St. John, and William Trautmann, called for "revolutionary activity."

"It is true," writes Paul Brissenden, "that principles and policies were involved in the feud of 1906, but they lurked obscurely in the background, while personal antagonisms—charges and counter-charges of graft, cor-ruption and malfeasance in office—held the center of the stage. From the inception of the movement the year before a smoldering dissension developed between the poorer and less skilled groups of workers—largely migratory and casual laborers, the 'revolutionists' or the 'wage-slave delegates' as they were called in the second convention . . . and the more highly skilled and strongly organized groups called (by the other side) the 'reactionaries' or the 'political fakirs.' It might be remarked in passing that, in this ultra-revolutionary I.W.W., the 'conservatism' of the 'reaction-aries' ought to be heavily discounted and the radicalism of the 'revolution-ists' raised to the *nth* degree to get the true perspective. Involved with this group hostility was the trouble stirred up by various members of the two Socialist political parties."[90]

The Western Federation of Miners, without Haywood, withdrew from the I.W.W. and began slowly to set up orderly collective-bargaining contracts. "Furthermore," as Perlman and Taft point out, "the leaders had become aware that the whole social topography of the arena of their activity was undergoing a radical transformation. . . . Into this altered environment, with a 'public' of farmers and urban middle classes, Win-chester rifles and dynamite no longer fitted. Their own best fighting days

[90] Paul Brissenden, *The I.W.W.: a Study of American Syndicalism* (New York, 1919), p. 136.

over with advancing middle age, the leaders, although still nominally socialists, were moving toward a conception of the role of their organization not far apart from the American Federation of Labor. . . ."[91] In 1909, the Western Federation of Miners, under Moyer's leadership, moved to rejoin the A.F.L.

Members of the Socialist Party were less prominent at the I.W.W.'s second convention. Neither Debs nor A. M. Simons, the leaders of the left wing, attended. So the dominant role was played by De Leon, and his attitude alienated those socialists who were present. But more than De Leon's attitude, the growing syndicalist antipolitical view of the organization gave the socialists pause.

After 1906, and still more after 1908, the I.W.W. became an organization of the unskilled, and conspicuously of the migratory and frequently jobless unskilled. This transformation of the I.W.W. became complete in 1908, when De Leon himself was eliminated. De Leon wanted to fight capitalism on the "civilized plane" of political action. He charged the opposition—"slum proletarians" he called them—with "veiled dynamitism." The "Overall Brigade" ousted De Leon by the simple act of denying the validity of his credentials, a stunning blow to a man who prided himself on his organizational astuteness. De Leon then formed his own group, also using the name I.W.W. (or the Detroit faction), against the "beggars" (or Chicago faction).

The Chicago I.W.W. (i.e., the St. John and Haywood group, or the "Wobblies")[92] were unconditionally opposed to political action and favored direct action and sabotage. This anarcho-syndicalist viewpoint led to the complete break with the socialists. But although Debs himself resigned from the I.W.W., he could not bring himself to attack it: instead of issuing a public statement of disavowal, as in other instances of disagreement, he simply permitted his dues to lapse.[93]

The Socialist Party's 1908 convention opened in a spirit of optimism. In four years' time the party had doubled its membership.[94] The number of locals had grown to 2,500. Yet a basic cleavage still dominated the party. Although "impossibilist" overtones were still present, the differences had crystallized again on the union issue. The imminence of a presidential

[91] Perlman and Taft, *op.cit.*, p. 253.

[92] The origin of the name "Wobblies" is shrouded. Brissenden says the I.W.W. was so christened by Harrison Grey Otis, the editor of the *Los Angeles Times*, although no reason for the peculiar nomenclature is given. Mencken, in his *The American Language* (4th ed., New York, 1949), pp. 190-91, ascribes the name to the garbled pronunciation of the initials I.W.W. by a Chinese cook in Seattle who, unable to say W, would say I, Wobble, Wobble. From that, the name was shortened to Wobblies.

[93] Ginger, *op.cit.*, p. 256.

[94] 20,763 in 1904, and 41,751 in 1908. Data from *American Labor Year Book* (1916), p. 94.

campaign worked for unity. A resolution opposing immediate demands was snowed under, and the trade-union resolution counseled a "hands off" policy. In view of the I.W.W. stand, the socialists put the party squarely behind political action. On the farm issue, the convention continued, quixotically enough, an "impossibilist" position. The resolutions committee called for the collectivization of the agricultural trusts (i.e., farm machinery, beet sugar, oil, etc.), but said, "as for the ownership of the land by the small farmers, it is not essential to a Socialist program that any farmer shall be dispossessed of the land which he occupies and tills." However, the convention rejected this report. A variety of divergent opinions commingled in opposition. Some "right-wingers" for dogmatic Marxist reasons insisted that title to land be held in the nation; others insisted that farms, as well as industry, were being trustified so that an approach favoring small owners was false. The minority report, which stated, "we insist that any attempt to pledge to the farmer anything but a complete socialization of the industries of the nation to be unsocialistic," was passed 99 to 51.[95]

The platform finally adopted was interpreted in various ways. To Haywood, "the convention . . . adopted a platform that rang clear. The class struggle was its foundation. This was the most revolutionary period of the Socialist Party in America."[96] Actually the platform was a subtle compromise written with an eye to harmonizing the clearly defined factions. The statement of principles strongly emphasized the class struggle. But the specific demands strongly emphasized reform measures, and, unlike the 1904 platform, were not incorporated in the general text but stood out independently and could be propagated independently. Each side, therefore, was free to emphasize its own slants.

Debs was named the presidential candidate again in 1908. But now for the first time other names had been placed in opposition. No reasons were given publicly and the anti-Debs campaign was uncoordinated, but it was clear that a number of elements, particularly the strongly right-wing Wisconsin party, felt that Debs was too "left." His magnetic name, however, still swayed the convention and Debs was nominated overwhelmingly.

The Socialist Party entered the 1908 campaign fully confident of a swelling vote. In a magnificent propaganda gesture, national secretary J. Mahlon Barnes proposed that the party outfit a railroad car, to be called the "Red Special," which would tour the country and carry Debs to every corner of the land. The money was raised and the Red Special set off on its run. Debs himself carried the brunt of the campaign. Ill and subject to racking bodily pains from rheumatism and lumbago, he

[95] *Proceedings*, 1908, pp. 178-91.
[96] *Bill Haywood's Book* (New York, 1929), p. 230.

spoke from five to twenty times a day for sixty-five consecutive days. Everywhere he went great crowds jammed the meeting halls: in New York more than 10,000 persons jammed the old Hippodrome to hear him. A St. Louis paper predicted that Debs would poll more than a million and a half votes and that the 1912 election would be fought on the issue of capitalism versus socialism.[97]

When the votes were counted, the Socialist Party had 420,973—almost no increase in the four-year period. The most obvious explanation was the counterappeal of William Jennings Bryan, the Democratic candidate in 1908. In 1904, the Democrats had nominated a conservative lawyer, Alton B. Parker, and Debs had been the only outlet for a protest vote. Four years later the "Great Commoner," basing his campaign on his hoarse old battle cry of monopoly and privilege, had garnered the protesters.

The disappointing vote set the party back on its heels and started the various factions quarreling among themselves to determine who was responsible for the fall. Different reasons were adduced: lack of contact with workers, lack of militancy, domination by intellectual and middle-class elements, etc.

The fight broke out into the open when A. M. Simons, now a right-winger and editor of the *Chicago Daily Socialist*, privately raised the question of the advisability of a labor party "on the English model" to supplant the Socialist Party. The letter written to William English Walling and released by him raised a storm in the party. The most galling sections of Simons' letter were his disdainful opinions of the "left." "On the one side," he wrote, "are a bunch of intellectuals like myself, Spargo, Hunter and Hillquit; on the other side a bunch of never-works, demagogues and would-be intellectuals, a veritable 'Lumpen-Proletariat'. . . . The present executive committee is more than willing to surrender their positions if real workingmen are to take their places. They do not propose to surrender to those who have never worked save with their jaws and are tearing down every organization to which they belong."[98]

For months the socialist welkin rang with denunciations and denials of the labor-party proposition. To the left wing, a labor party, taking in diverse elements, meant a dilution of the socialist program and political compromise; to the right wing, it meant a bridge to large masses of trade unionists who were still not socialist. In the midst of the controversy, the *International Socialist Review*, a voice of the left wing, queried prominent members of the party asking: "If elected to the National Executive Committee will you favor or oppose merging the Socialist Party into a Labor Party?"

[97] Ginger, *op.cit.*, p. 283.
[98] Cited by Thomas J. Morgan, in *Who's Who and What's What in the Socialist Party*, No. 2 (January 1911).

Debs's answer to the question was immediate. He wrote: "The Socialist Party has already catered far too much to the American Federation of Labor and there is no doubt that a halt will have to be called. . . . If the trimmers had their way, we should degenerate into mere bourgeois reform."[99]

Hillquit's reply was guarded. He pointed out that no labor party existed, but if ". . . independent of our desires and theories [the workers] should form . . . a *bona fide* and uncompromising working class political party . . . the logical thing for our party to do would be cooperate with such a party," although not merging, in order for the socialists to continue their propaganda work.[100]

Although the issue had threatened to disrupt the party, it soon subsided. No labor party was in sight, and the debate had been a convenient occasion for the left wing to blow off steam. But even among the right-wingers the idea did not meet full support. Many right-wingers, even Fabian-minded evolutionists, wanted a pure Socialist Party as their instrument in politics; for some the reasons were sentimental; for others doctrinaire ideological reasons were involved; for still others a stake in jobs or prestige.[101]

The issue, however, became quickly academic for a more substantial reason. By 1910, the socialist tide was surging in. In one year, from 1908 to 1909, the party membership had dropped slightly, but in 1910 the membership was up to 58,011 (from 41,479) and by 1912 had made a sensational jump to 125,826.[102] Electoral victories, too, began to multiply. In 1910 socialist mayors were elected in Milwaukee, and Schenectady, New York, and in the fall of that year Victor Berger was elected as the first socialist congressman. By May 1912, the national secretary reported a total of 1,039 socialists elected to office, including 56 mayors, 160 councilmen, and 145 aldermen.[103] The victories were largely in municipalities, and apparently an outcome of exposures of municipal corruption; only 18 state representatives and 2 state senators were in office. Nevertheless, the trend to reform via socialism was seen as a good omen. Also, the socialist press had grown mightily as well: by 1912, there were 8 foreign-language and 5 English dailies, including the New York *Call*, which had been

[99] *International Socialist Review*, Jan. 1910, p. 594; cited in Jessie Wallace Hughan, *American Socialism of the Present Day* (New York, 1911), pp. 233-34.

[100] Fine, *op.cit.*, p. 300.

[101] That the issue was not solely a left-right fight, as indicated by the *International Socialist Review*, is the fact that three right-wingers named to the national executive committee in 1910 (James Carey, George Goebel, and Lena Morrow Lewis) opposed a labor party.

[102] Report of the national secretary, *Proceedings*, 1912, p. 219.

[103] *Ibid.*, p. 220.

started in 1908; in addition there were 262 English and 36 foreign-language weeklies.[104]

In 1910 the whole country was going "progressive," and the "leftist" groups, including the socialist movement, were benefiting from the general trend. If the increasing vote was a product of a national swing to progressivism, equally relevant was the fact that the socialists were also tempering their dogmatism and widening their appeal. The socialist increase in great measure was probably due to the new appeal to the small middle class. The tone was set by Morris Hillquit. In 1910 he drew up a convention report entitled *The Propaganda of Socialism*, which is the first detailed assessment of past socialist propaganda tactics in the United States and an outline of future appeals. In this important document Hillquit said:

"Our principal efforts must be directed towards the propaganda of Socialism among the workers. But they should by no means be limited to that class alone. . . . the ultimate aims of the movement far transcend the interests of any one class in society, and its social ideal is so lofty that it may well attract large numbers of men and women from other classes . . . [the workers] are by no means the only class which has a direct economic motive for favoring a change of the existing order. The vast majority of the farming population of our country . . . is mortgaged to the money-lenders, exploited by the railroads and controlled by the stock jobbers. Vast masses of the small traders and manufacturers are beginning to realize the hopelessness of their struggle against large capital concentrated in the hands of modern industrial monopolies and trusts, and in the ranks of the professionals the struggle for existence is growing ever fiercer. . . . A movement like ours, which has set out to recast the entire modern social structure, cannot afford to banish the 'intellectuals' from its ranks. A Socialist movement consisting exclusively of 'Jimmie Higginses' would be as impotent as such a movement made up entirely or overwhelmingly of 'intellectuals' would be preposterous. . . . *Within very recent years a tendency has manifested itself in some sections of our movement to limit it entirely to wage-workers, and to reject the co-operation of all persons from other classes,* no matter how sincere they may be in their professions of Socialist faith and how valuable their services may be for the cause. This is not a rational application of the Marxian class-struggle doctrine, but an absurd caricature of it."[105]

Such an attitude was viewed by the left wing as a desertion of socialist principles. In the winter of 1911 Debs charged that the party held "not

---

[104] As against 3 English and 6 foreign-language dailies, and 29 English and 22 foreign-language weeklies in 1910.

[105] *Proceedings of the National Congress of the Socialist Party*, 1910, pp. 63-64. Italics added.

a few members who regard vote-getting as of supreme importance, no matter by what method the votes are secured, and this leads them to hold out inducements and make representations which are not at all compatible with the stern and uncompromising spirit of a revolutionary party."[106] But Debs never followed up these salvos. He refused even to be a delegate to the 1912 convention, where the issue would be put to a test.

The 1910 congress of the Socialist Party had in other ways moved slowly to meet contemporary problems. The two chief issues were immigration and the farm resolution. On both, the party had adopted moderate positions. Because the American Federation of Labor favored restriction of immigration, the party moved in a similar direction. A majority resolution, written by Berger, favored the "unconditional exclusion" of the yellow peoples, but the compromise, drafted by Hillquit, denounced exclusion on the basis of race yet favored legislative measures limiting immigration of "strike breakers and contract laborers." The party also reversed its previous demand calling for the socialization of land and adopted a statement which said: "Only to a very small extent is the land now, only to a very small extent is it likely to be for many years to come, a socially operated means of production. Even to declare in any dogmatic manner that all land must eventually become social property is somewhat utopian; to demand that the ownership of all land shall be immediately socialized is to make ourselves ridiculous."[107] The importance of the resolutions lay not only in the moderate and anti-utopian conclusions but in the fact that for the first time they had been based on careful reasearch rather than on a priori dogma.

The emphasis of the Socialist Party administration on being "practical," and the determination of the left wing to halt the drift to "reformism," drew the battle lines sharply for the 1912 convention. The year before, in a distinct gain for the left, Big Bill Haywood had been elected a member of the national executive committee. Other left strivings were visible. The I.W.W., for one, was becoming involved in nationally significant strikes culminating in the giant strike at Lawrence, Massachusetts, which shut down the town's textile industry drum tight. In the midst of this agitation the McNamara case broke. Two brothers, John and James McNamara, officials of the A.F.L. Structural Iron Workers, were arrested in early 1911 and charged with bombing the Los Angeles *Times* building on October 1, 1910, a bombing in which twenty persons were killed. Industrialists cited the case as proof of labor's belief in violence, but the entire labor movement rallied to the McNamaras' defense. Debs toured the country on their behalf. The national executive committee of the Socialist Party wired the Structural Iron Workers the support of "the entire power of its 4000 organizations, and its press consisting of ten

[106] Ginger, *op.cit.*, p. 307.   [107] *Proceedings*, 1910, p. 219.

dailies, over a hundred weeklies and ten monthlies (in all languages) to be used in the defense of the McNamaras. . . ." The American Federation of Labor, too, voted support of the defendants.

For the Socialist Party the Los Angeles mayoralty was directly at stake. Job Harriman, the party's candidate, had been given a 50-50 chance of being elected. Five days before the election the McNamaras suddenly pleaded guilty, and with their confession the socialist chances plummeted. Unionists and socialists hastened to disavow earlier support of the two men. But the damage had been done.

Six months after the McNamara case the Socialist Party nominating convention opened. Tensions between the "reds" and the "yellows" ran high. Some effort would be made, it was felt, to curb the growing power of the left wing. The first incident of the convention was a caricature of a decade of party strife. A day before the convention opened, the Indianapolis socialists, the hosts, appointed one of their number to make an address of welcome clad in a pair of overalls. John Spargo, a leader of the right wing and author of many of the party's expositions of socialist doctrine, protested. He declared that the proposal was undignified and would give the capitalist press an opportunity to mock. The issue swelled in importance and became a major order of business of the socialist national executive committee. The local socialists contended that "the overalls were . . . a symbol of the fact that the Socialist Party represented the workingman. . . ." Spargo proposed that if the Indianapolis socialists persisted in their "insult," the members of the national executive committee show their displeasure by leaving the hall. For a time it looked as if the national executive committee would be rent in twain over the question of a fifty-nine cent pair of overalls. On a vote, the overalls won. The incident was the subject of much heated debate and dismal prophecies were voiced on the opening day that the event foreshadowed a split in the convention, but the welcoming speaker, in mild socialist compromise, appeared in "plain, ordinary bourgeois pants."[108]

The big question at the convention was the trade-union resolution. Everyone expected a heated conflict between a majority report endorsing the American Federation of Labor and the minority urging industrial unionism. To everyone's surprise the resolution which was brought to the floor took neither position. It stated that the party had "neither the right nor the desire" to interfere on questions of "form of organization," but it also called attention to the need for "organizing the unorganized, especially the immigrants and the unskilled laborers."[109] The resolution was a skillful bit of political compromise, for each side felt its own position

[108] "The National Socialist Convention of 1912," *International Socialist Review*, June 1912, p. 808. Berger wished it known that in the pinch he voted for overalls.
[109] *Proceedings*, 1912, p. 195.

carried, while only rhetorical concessions were made to the other side.

A glow of optimism prevailed, and amid the moments of good feeling Big Bill Haywood arose and said: "To my mind this is the greatest step that has ever been taken by the Socialist party. . . . as Tom Hickey has shaken hands with Job Harriman for the first time in twenty years, I feel I can shake hands with every delegate in this convention and say that we are a united working class."[110]

For a day the convention went along in this glow. A platform which ringingly reaffirmed the class struggle ("Society is divided into warring groups and classes, based upon material interests. . . . All political parties are the expression of economic class interests.") was unanimously adopted. The platform also called for a set of "immediate demands," such as unemployment relief, minimum wage scales, graduated income tax, curbing of injunction, etc. But efforts by Victor Berger to force a stand on immediate *issues*, such as a plank calling for tariff reduction, evoked little response. The sentiment of the delegates was that the Socialist Party was not concerned with the tariff one way or the other, and the plank was overwhelmingly tossed out.

The storm which seemingly had passed broke unexpectedly the following day. The committee on the constitution was reporting and came to article II, section 6, which had created a furious debate four years before. At that time, the phrase "political action" had been vaguely defined. Now the section was tightened and its meaning made unmistakably clear. It read: "Any member of the party who opposes political action or advocates crime against the person or other methods of violence as a weapon of the working class to aid in its emancipation shall be expelled from the party. Political action shall be construed to mean participation in elections for public office and practical legislative and administrative work along the lines of the Socialist Party platform." On the motion of a delegate the more fateful word "sabotage" was inserted in the section instead of "crime against the person." The McNamara case had quickened the issue.

In the debate that followed, the right-wing leaders left no doubt that they had made up their minds to drive the "Wobbly" and reckless elements out of the party. National executive committeeman Goebel reported: "I find the movement in locality after locality disorganized, I find them fighting amongst themselves. . . . Because men have come into the Socialist party and . . . advocated . . . sabotage." Victor Berger chimed in: "In the past we often had to fight against Utopianism and fanaticism, now it is anarchism again that is eating away at the vitals of our party." The opposition retorted that the issue was between progressives and "another element that stands conservative, reactionary, monkeying with old out-

[110] *Ibid.*, p. 100.

75

worn machinery."[111] The lines were at last cleanly drawn, and on a standing vote the section on sabotage was adopted by a vote of 191 to 90.

The convention action provoked a long and bitter dispute inside the party. Haywood, not Debs, was the target of the resolution. Haywood was outspoken and direct; Debs, evasive and vacillating. In the February 1912 issue of the *International Socialist Review*, two articles by Haywood and Debs became, in effect, a debate of the issue. Haywood wrote: *". . . no Socialist can be a law-abiding citizen. When we come together and are of a common mind, and the purpose of our minds is to overthrow the capitalist system, we become conspirators then against the United States government. . . . I again want to justify direct action and sabotage. . . .* the trade unionist who becomes a party to a contract takes his organization out of the columns of fighting organizations; he removes it from the class struggle. . . ." (Emphasis added and sentence order changed.)

Emotionally Debs agreed with Haywood. "If I had the force . . . I would use it . . . but I haven't got it, and so I am law-abiding under protest—not from scruple." But politically, Debs saw the futility of such an appeal, and turned against Haywood. The American workers, he said, are law-abiding, and "direct action will never appeal to any considerable number of them while they have the ballot and the right of industrial and political organization. . . . My chief objection to all these measures is that they do violence to the class psychology of the workers. . . ." Then Debs voiced his flat objection: ". . . I am opposed to sabotage and 'direct action.' I have not a bit of use for the 'propaganda of the deed.'[112] These are the tactics of anarchist individualists and not of Socialist collectivists."

Some of the right-wing leaders felt that Debs should not be the presidential nominee. However, they could not agree on a candidate. The New York group named Charles Edward Russell, the muckraker who had joined the party in 1908. However, the Wisconsin crowd, suspicious of "New York," named Emil Seidel, the mayor of Milwaukee. But the personal popularity of Debs was still high and he won the nomination with 165 votes to 56 votes for Seidel and 54 for Russell.

Debs made his usual colorful campaign crisscrossing the country in an emotional outpouring that stirred the hearts of people. Wilson and Teddy Roosevelt were running on "reform" platforms in 1912 and while their campaigns probably drew votes from the socialists, their frenetic activity also stirred greater interest in the campaign. Debs rolled up 897,000 votes in 1912, more than doubling the vote of the last campaign. This

[111] *Ibid.*, pp. 123, 128, 130.

[112] The phrase, *"die Tat,"* "the deed," was common as an anarchist tactic of rallying the working class behind some heroic action. This was the motive, for example, of Alexander Berkman in shooting H. C. Frick during the Homestead strike in 1893. See Emma Goldman, *Living My Life* (New York, 1931), I, p. 96.

vote, almost 6 per cent of the total, was the highest percentage of a presidential vote ever polled by the Socialist Party in the United States.

The anomalous fact was that while the vote increased, the party membership declined during the campaign, and as a drive opened against the direct actionists it continued to fall. In February 1913 William D. Haywood was recalled from the national executive committee of the party on a national referendum vote. Within a year, from June 1912 to June 1913, the *Party Builder* reported a loss of more than 50,000 members.[113] Some writers, for example James Oneal in his *American Communism*, deny that the expulsion of the I.W.W. elements affected the party.[114] Such a view is untenable. There is little question but that the onslaught against the left wing hit the party hard, and the great losses in membership resulted, in large measure, from the defections of the left.

In 1912 Haywood and the I.W.W. were at the height of their popularity. More than twenty-eight I.W.W. strikes took place in which nearly 1,500 persons were arrested for strike activity. In addition, the Wobblies had perfected their mass-action "free speech" technique which had begun so successfully in Spokane in 1909.[115] Most important for Wobbly fame was the strike at Lawrence, Massachusetts, and the free-speech fight in San Diego, both in 1912, which "really introduced the Industrial Workers of the World to the American public. . . . [They] made the name of this little group of intransigeants a household word, hardly less talked about and no whit better understood than the words 'socialist' and 'anarchist.' . . . Lawrence was not an ordinary strike. It was a social revolution *in parvo*. . . . It stirred the country with the alarming slogans of a new kind of revolution. Socialism was respectable—even reactionary—by comparison."[116]

Those years, too, were the years of awakening for the rebel spirits. A new intellectual generation was tearing away the caudal vestiges of puritanism. Van Wyck Brooks' *America's Coming of Age* was a call to arms urging writers to rise above the debilitating materialism that grayed American life. The *Masses*, founded in 1911, became the calliope through

[113] Cited in Perlman and Taft, *op.cit.*, p. 286.

[114] "Following this decision [i.e., the antisabotage clause], a small group left the Socialist Party, but in the following November the party received the largest vote in its history. Its membership also increased. . . . This force tendency in the Socialist Party was checked in the convention of 1912 and it rapidly declined." James Oneal, *American Communism* (New York, 1927), pp. 27-28. Oneal, one of the leading Socialist Party publicists, was employed in the national office for many years and edited the *New Leader* from 1924 to 1940.

[115] When their orators were refused the right to speak from street corners and were arrested, the Wobblies flooded the town—and the jails—with more of their number, mostly lumberjacks, sailors, and other migratory workers, until the groaning city said "uncle": in the years 1911 to 1913 there were some fifteen free-speech fights.

[116] Brissenden, *op.cit.*, pp. 281, 282, 291.

which the young rebels whistled and hooted at the effete culture of the East and the gargoyle mansions of the new crude rich in the West. To these Greenwich Village free spirits, however, the Socialist Party under its right-wing leadership was too stodgy; insurgency could ride the wild wind more easily among the less disciplined doctrines of the left. Other intellectuals found sympathy with Haywood, too. This Polyphemus from the raw mining camps of the West had dedicated himself to the organization of the unskilled, the poverty-stricken and forgotten workers. And so he had become a hero. Haywood was defended by a group of New York intellectuals who now attacked the antisabotage clause. "We know Comrade Haywood to believe in political action," they wrote, "and to have been of great service to our party in helping it to solve the difficult problems that confront the working class upon the industrial field. Instead of exaggerating inevitable differences of opinion, instead of reviving De Leonistic tactics of personal incrimination, heresy-hunting, and disruption, we should make use of the special talents of every member within our ranks, and in this way secure loyal service and cooperation. We believe in a united working class." Among the signers were Walter Lippmann, Max Eastman, Margaret Sanger, Osmund K. Fraenkel, J. G. Phelps Stokes, William English Walling, Louis B. Boudin. Independently of this statement, Helen Keller made a deep emotional plea for unity.[117]

In May 1913 the revolutionary elements made a last effort, at the national committee meeting of the party, to repeal the antisabotage clause. They pointed out that in West Virginia, where fifty-two socialists had been imprisoned in a drive by the state against the Socialist Party, a number of socialists had captured guns and used them against the police. With the clause in the constitution, they said, the party would be unable to support the West Virginia socialists. The move was defeated, however, 43 to 16.[118] In later years Haywood voiced his bitter condemnation of the party's action. "Criminal Syndicalism laws have been upheld by the United States Court. . . . It is under such a law that the Communists were tried in Michigan. . . . The many who have been persecuted can thank the traitors of the Socialist Party who adopted Article 2, Section 6 against the working class."[119]

[117] *International Socialist Review*, Feb. 1913, pp. 606, 623.
[118] *Ibid.*, June 1913, pp. 878, 879.
[119] *Bill Haywood's Book*, p. 259. One caution should be noted: Haywood's autobiography was written in Moscow in 1927 and the charge has been made that the book was doctored. Benjamin Gitlow writes: "After Haywood died the manuscript was turned over to Alexander Trachtenberg, representative of the Comintern Publishing Department in the U.S., for final revision and publication. He changed and revised the book to conform to the Party Line and had the Party okay his revisions, and then had it published by International Publishers." See *The Whole of Their Lives* (New York, 1948), p. 51. Gitlow, an ex-communist, was a high official of the Communist Party at the time of the publication of the Haywood book.

Nineteen hundred and twelve was the high mark of socialist influence in the United States. It was the turning point as well. From that year, socialist strength and influence ebbed. After 1912, the party membership fell off rapidly and regained its earlier peak only in 1919 when membership rose to 108,000 from 81,000 in the previous year. But that new membership rise itself reflected the changed character of the Socialist Party and foreshadowed its role in the next decade. In 1912, when the party reached its zenith, it had an average of 118,000 dues payers of which 16,000, or about 13 per cent, were in the foreign-language federations. In 1918 about 25,000, or 30 per cent, were members of the foreign-language divisions. In 1919, when the membership again jumped, "practically the entire increase was furnished by recent arrivals from Russia and its Border States. The membership in the foreign-language federations rose to 57,000 or 53 per cent of the total, the bulk of it was represented by Russian, Ukrainian, South Slavic, Finnish, Lithuanian and Lettish organizations."[120]

The War and the defections of many party leaders merely completed, but were not themselves the cause of, the isolation of the socialist movement from American politics. The eclipse of American socialism took place in 1912; the rest of the years were a trailing penumbra.

We can adduce five major reasons for the decline of the Socialist Party after 1912.

1. The expulsion of the left wing, accounting for a large share of the 50,000 decline in membership from mid-1912 to mid-1913. This precipitous decline, however, obscures a salient fact: the Socialist Party always had a high turnover in membership; in usual course the falling away of old members was compensated by a new recruitment, resulting in net gains. In this respect, the loss of membership in 1912 had a dual meaning: the loss itself is attributable to the stand on sabotage, an internal party matter, but this time there was no compensating gain. For an explanation of this fact we have to turn to external factors, particularly the influence of Woodrow Wilson.

2. The use of the Socialist Party, in the period from 1910 to 1912, by old-line party politicians for electoral manipulations. This created in many cases a rising illusion of socialist strength. Thus, in the Mississippi election of 1911 the genteel wing of the Democratic Party, in order to defeat Theodore Bilbo, sought to elect a socialist lieutenant-governor and did in fact swing to the Socialist Party candidate a third of the vote. In the South particularly, remnants of the old populist groups sought to use the Socialist Party as a club against the Democrats or as a means of pressuring the Democrats for an acceptable candidate.[121]

---

[120] Morris Hillquit, *Loose Leaves from a Busy Life*, p. 290.
[121] Arthur W. Calhoun, "Can American Politics Be Socialized?" *Politics*, Feb. 1945, pp. 48-50.

3. The rigidity of rules imposed on socialist office-holders, which proved quite irksome for many. Once in power, socialist legislators and administrators faced the problems of compromises, concessions, deals, and other problems of the "practical" side of politics. As a result, many who wanted to "get things done" soon left the party. In Schenectady, for example, Socialist Mayor George R. Lunn, a minister, joined the Democratic Party after being defeated for reelection. In North Dakota, socialists evolved the technique of the Non-Partisan League in order to utilize the primary system and capture control of one of the major parties. Although the Non-Partisan Leaguers won control of the state in a sensationally short time, they were repudiated by the party.

4. The loss of support of the agrarian groups. The greatest degree of socialist strength, paradoxically, was always among the discontented farm elements. After 1912, the farm support of the socialists fell off. One reason was the newly gained protection from government which eased the farmers' plight. The Federal Reserve Act of 1913 expanded credit, permitted national banks to loan money on farm mortgages, and allowed six months for the rediscounting of agricultural paper against three months for commercial paper. More directly, the Federal Farm Loan Bank System, created in 1916, eased the seedtime-to-harvest credit problem. A second factor was the rising farm prosperity as a result of exports to Europe. Thus the value of wheat exports more than tripled from 1914 to 1917, rising from almost 88 to 298 million dollars, while the value of meat exports rose in similar proportion.[122]

5. Finally, of unquestioned but neglected weight was the influence of Woodrow Wilson. The presence in the White House of a man who was an intellectual had great appeal to individuals who had been socialists or were close to the party, men like Walter Lippmann and the group led by Herbert Croly which founded the *New Republic*. But Wilson's appeal was more than to the intellectuals and the echoes which their voices could magnify. The light of "The New Freedom" had an incandescence which seemed to many to shine with a clearer light than that of the socialists. In his speeches, Wilson denounced the growing centralized control of finance, the choking of opportunity by monopoly, "the control over the government exercised by Big Business," and the blight of municipal corruption.[123] Wilson himself pointed out that where many socialists had been elected it was not a socialist but a protest vote that put them in office. It was Wilson's achievement to draw off the protest vote before it jelled into a solid bloc of dissent. The solid body of social legislation which he enacted in his first term drew that reform vote tightly to himself.

[122] H. U. Faulkner, *American Economic History* (New York, 1937), pp. 461, 462, 694.

[123] Woodrow Wilson, *The New Freedom* (New York, 1933), pp. 3-32.

As a result of all this, after 1912 few socialists could believe in the "inevitability" of socialist triumph in the United States. In the years thereafter this failure of belief was to pose new problems for the existence of socialism as a *political* movement in the United States.

VII. *The Inner World of American Socialism*

One other factor in the decline of American socialism should also be discussed—the structural weakness of the Socialist Party itself as an instrument of propaganda, social change, or revolution. An environment provides, in Toynbee's sense, the *challenge* to a social movement; the character of the party and its leadership determine its ability to respond.

Within the American Socialist Party there was rarely any effort made to think through systematically, as Lenin had, the organization of the party and the relationship of the special character of membership to other roles in the labor movement or among the broad masses of society. Actually, the organizational structure of the Socialist Party was primarily a reflex to the type of discipline in the Socialist Labor Party. Like the founding fathers of the Continental Congress, the socialists sought in "states rights" a defense against oppression. The party constitution stated that each state ". . . shall have . . . sole control of all matters pertaining to the propaganda, organization and financial affairs within such state or territory."[124] In fact, this power was so vigorously exercised that in Wisconsin, for example, no lecturer could enter the state without the permission of the state committee, and on occasion Victor Berger, the state boss, went so far as to bar Eugene Debs himself. The party acutely feared centralization and bureaucracy. An early convention was nearly rent apart on a motion to increase the salary of the national secretary from $1,000 to $1,500 a year because one faction argued that to do so would make the post so lucrative, and the salary so out of line with proletarian tastes, that bureaucracy would result. To make sure that the will of the party membership decided all issues, referenda were ordered at the drop of a resolution, and much of the party's time was consumed in holding these town meetings by mail.[125] Local autonomy was so complete, under party structure, that strong cliques could arbitrarily run city branches or state organizations, refusing to admit outsiders or possible challengers. And in such instances the national office had little power of discipline.

Under these conditions it is not hard to understand the turnover of six

[124] Article x, section 4, of the Socialist Party constitution, in Appendix, *Proceedings*, 1912, p. 202.

[125] At one point the referenda were coming so thick and fast that national secretary Mailly reported: "Recently two referendums were taken upon the same subject within thirty days of each other, and as a result there are now two contradictory clauses in the present national constitution." *Proceedings*, 1904, p. 58.

different national secretaries in the eighteen years from 1901 to 1919 and why no official served more than five years. There was no real continuity in the national office. Nor was there any full-time responsible party leadership. Debs, the titular leader, never took administrative responsibility; Hillquit was busy with a law practice in New York; Berger edited several Milwaukee papers. Thus, unlike many European socialist parties and the later Communist Party, the leaders were not functionaries.

A different type of weakness in the party was the cult of proletarian chauvinism, the practice of endowing all virtue in the man with the horny hands merely because he was a worker. "When it comes to a pick between the intellectual, the preacher, the professor, and the working man, that man who is fresh from the ranks of the working class and who in his every day life is in actual contact with the work and the struggle," declared George Goebel, a right-wing spellbinder and longtime member of the national executive committee, "I am with that man that . . . more nearly represents the working class."[126] Thus the words "middle class" and "intellectual" became cuss words, and both sides competed violently in the effort to emphasize their working-class social origins and allegiances.

The problem, like original sin, was present at the very birth of the party. In the first fierce debates between the Hillquit "Kangaroo" group and the Berger faction of Social Democracy, the most heated epithet was the charge of being middle class. Max Hayes, a Hillquit lieutenant (who proclaimed himself a printer and a proletarian), sneered at the Berger group: "The anti-unionists were marshalled by Berger a school teacher and editor, Stedman a lawyer, McCartney a preacher, Edwards another editor, Cox another lawyer, Miller another editor, London, still another lawyer; Margaret Haile, a lachrymose woman, and one or two others—all so-called academic socialists, theorists."

To which A. S. Edwards, the editor of the *Social Democratic Herald*, wryly replied: "Comment is uncalled for, except that we might direct our attention to the fact that Harriman is a lawyer and ex-preacher, Hillquit is a lawyer, Schlueter an editor, Feigenbaum an editor, Morgan a lawyer, Jonas an editor, Stone an editor, Sissman a lawyer, Benham an editor, Taft a lawyer, Lee an editor, and finally, not to continue such trivialities to too great length, Max Hayes himself an editor and a good one."[127]

When Victor Berger attacked Debs for participating in the formation of the I.W.W., Debs's angry retort was: "Berger and Heath probably never worked for wages a day in their lives, have no trade, never had on a pair of overalls and really have no excuse to be in a trade union at all."[128] The charge was untrue. Actually, Berger and Heath had been wage

---

[126] *Proceedings*, 1908, p. 154.
[127] Fine, *op.cit.*, pp. 201-2.
[128] Ginger, *op.cit.*, p. 241.

earners for a longer period than Debs. Debs had worked on a railroad less than five years in his early youth, and when he took the job as secretary of the firemen's union he had left the road several years before. Most of his life, after union office, he worked as a lecturer and editor.[129]

In symbolic terms the motivation for these claims is obvious. Being a worker meant a proletarian (i.e., good) policy; being bourgeois meant a middle-class (or bad) policy. This distinction has been used by the communist historian Philip Foner to explain the decline of the socialist movement, through devitalization by the "bourgeois" elements.

"The Socialist movement," Foner writes, "was running at flood tide but a considerable portion of the new membership came from outside the working-class—lawyers, doctors, dentists, preachers, educators, small manufacturers and business men and an occasional millionaire. Being persuasive speakers and excellent parliamentarians they quickly rose to leadership in the Party and came to control its policies, pushing the working-class members into the background. As one socialist put it they were 'soft and shifty stuff for Socialism to build on.' "[130]

But how does one make these identifications? At times the judgment is made on the basis of *social origin*, so that working-class parentage automatically endows one with virtue; at other times, when convenient, the basis shifts to one of current *occupation*. Actually neither the left nor the right wing could claim a monopoly of working-class adherents. Most of the right-wing leaders came from working-class parents. The leadership of the left wing was largely "bourgeois" both by social origin and occupation: William English Walling was an intellectual, J. G. Phelps Stokes a millionaire, Frank Bohn a writer, Jack London a writer.[131] The

---

[129] The legend of Debs as a proletarian will not down. At the I.W.W. convention, Haywood in attacking De Leon said, "Debs was the workingman who laid down his shovel on the locomotive when he took up the work of organizing the firemen. . . . De Leon's only contact with the workers was through the ideas with which he wished to 'indoctrinate' them. . . ." By that criterion, neither Lenin, nor Trotsky, nor Stalin, not to mention Marx or Engels, would have been allowed leadership of a working-class movement.

[130] Philip S. Foner, ed., *Jack London, American Rebel* (New York, 1947), pp. 64-65.

[131] London, the modern Rover Boy of socialism, was loudest of all in his denunciation of reformism. His letter of resignation in March 1916 attacked the party "because of its lack of fire and fight, and its loss of emphasis upon the class struggle. I was originally a member of the old revolutionary up-on-its-hind legs, a fighting Socialist Labor Party." Yet London, who had gone down to Mexico during the Pancho Villa uprising, advocated the annexation of the land below the Rio Grande by the United States. And when the Socialist Party in 1917 denounced the war, London, whose socialist views were based on the Nietzschean image of a race of supermen, raged at the party. "Civilization," he wrote, "at the present time is going through a Pentecostal cleansing that can only result in good for human kind." See Foner, *op.cit.*, pp. 123, 126. To London's letter, the New York *Call* replied, ". . . the rank and file of the Socialist Party are fighting—not always an exhilarating, romantic, spectacular fight—not always the sort of fight that makes good copy for the magazines or good

International Socialist Review, the monthly voice of revolutionary social-ism, said bitingly of the representation at the 1912 convention, ". . . among other representatives of the proletariat were 21 lawyers, 18 preachers and assorted real estate agents, teachers, doctors and trade unionists."[132] Yet, as Oneal points out, "self-advertised as a proletarian wing, a later survey of its members by W. J. Ghent showed that nearly 75 percent were not proletarian."[133] And as Victor Berger stated: "Our party in Milwaukee is absolutely proletarian. . . . I may say that above ninety per cent—ninety-five per cent probably—of our vote is a working class vote. We have only about two and a half lawyers in our ranks—not enough to fill the offices."[134] In the later years the growing support of socialism in the colleges and among the rebel spirits who settled in Greenwich Village usually went to the left wing of the party. A John Reed out of Harvard, a Max Eastman off the Columbia campus, were restless souls whose spiritual hunger could not be fulfilled by the prosaic right-wing program which emphasized child-labor laws, minimum wages, and other bits and pieces of social legislation, and tended to slight the revolution. Actually, if a sociological distinction regarding the factions could be made, it would be between the rebels, the romantics, the declassed and dispossessed, all leaning to the left,[135] and the reformers, social workers, ministers, professionals, and craft-union members, who supported the right wing.

The net effect, however, of this cult of proletarian chauvinism was a repetitive litany of revolutionary rhetoric and phrase mongering. A person would claim respect solely on the basis of the length of time he had been in the party, or on the basis of his proletarian origin, his devotion to the principles of orthodox Marxism, and a genuflection to the word revolu-tion.[136] The result was a sterile and doctrinaire set of policies. The cult

---

films for the movies—but the steady, unflinching, uncomplaining, unboasting . . . fight. . . ."

[132] *International Socialist Review,* June 1912, p. 810.

[133] *New Leader,* April 28, 1934, p. 4.

[134] *Proceedings,* 1908, p. 28. The same speech was made with little variation in 1910 and 1912.

[135] " 'Meet Comrade Joseph Medill Patterson' (County Secretary Fraenkel beamed). My hackles were up at once. I resented his bourgeois overcoat. It was beautifully tailored and adorned with a luxurious fur collar. . . . I couldn't see a millionaire with Patterson's background fitting into the proletarian revolution," wrote Ralph Chaplin in his autobiography, *Wobbly* (Chicago, 1948), p. 85. It was an attitude shared by many others. Joseph Medill Patterson, later the founder of the New York *Daily News* and a bitter isolationist and Roosevelt hater, was a member of the Socialist Party and its national executive committee in 1908. Another major stockholder in the Chicago *Tribune,* millionaire William Bross Lloyd, grandson of former Illinois Governor William Bross, a founder of the *Tribune,* and son of Henry Demarest Lloyd, was a founder of the American Communist Labor Party.

[136] Perhaps the worst sinner in this respect was Victor Berger. To the extent that he was readier to compromise and adapt to immediate political realities—going even

of proletarian chauvinism reached its most absurd heights in convention debates on such issues as paying the carfare of delegates to conventions. One can in fact almost trace the evolution of socialist reformism on this question. In 1904 the party first voted to reimburse delegates for travel expenses. In 1908 the convention, on Hillquit's motion, voted to pay the sleeping-car fare for delegates, although the minority claimed that "working class money should not be spent for palace car accommodations." Finally in 1912 the convention voted to pay Pullman car allowances; the opposition could only offer the feeble motion to limit travel to second-class or tourist accommodations "because the sleeping is just as good and costs just half as much."[137]

Equally slight amidst the weightier problems of history but equally symbolic of the basic mentalities of the socialist leadership was the Gridley affair, which took up almost two days of convention time in 1904. The credentials of delegate Gridley of Indiana were challenged on the ground that he had been named to the post of civil engineer of

---

further than the official A.F.L. position in favor of Oriental exclusion and limited immigration—he became more bellicose and "left" in his rhetoric. At one point he wrote: "In view of the plutocratic law-making of the present day, it is easy to predict that the safety and hope of this country will finally lie in one direction only—that of a violent and bloody revolution, therefore I say that each of the 500,000 socialist voters and of the 2,000,000 workingmen who instinctively incline our way, should besides doing much reading and still more thinking, also have a good rifle and the necessary rounds of ammunition in his home." Cited in *Proceedings*, 1912, p. 133. Morris Hillquit tells the story of an occasion where he and Berger represented the Socialist Party at a three-day and three-night "talk-fest" organized by Robert Hunter in an effort to convert twenty-five noted reformers to socialism. Berger at one session launched into a vehement denunciation of capitalist law and proclaimed ". . . wait until we have the power. Then we shall make our own laws, and by God, we will make you obey them." As Hillquit reports: "He was red in the face. His eyes flared and he reinforced his conclusions by striking the table with his clenched fist. An embarrassed silence fell on the gathering. The discussion came to an abrupt end." Later one of the conferees anxiously sought out Hillquit, who pointed out that in a democracy a minority obeys a law until it has sufficient strength to change it, and the former majority must now obey the new law. Did not Berger say practically the same thing? "My friend thought awhile," Hillquit concludes, "then laughed, 'C'est le ton qui fait la musique.' " See Hillquit, *Loose Leaves from a Busy Life*, pp. 58-59. It was this mistaking the tone for the music that later brought Berger into conflict with the espionage laws and resulted in his subsequent expulsion from Congress and in government persecution.

[137] John Spargo, the right-wing leader, summed up the case for comfort: "Comrades there is always the proposition of the man who says that as a working class party we should in all externals represent the working class. . . . it is expressed in the notion that we ought to come in day coaches or on the bumpers underneath the cars, if we possibly can do so. . . . that is not the working class . . . view at all. . . . men who come to the convention tired and outworn and weary are not in a position to make the best resistance to the forces of capitalism which can be made. . . . Finally, comrades, this is the twentieth century. And we of the working class demand for ourselves and our class all the advantages of the twentieth century." *Proceedings*, 1912, p. 30.

Aurora, Indiana, by the capitalist parties in the town. Gridley pleaded that he held the job because of a disability incurred in the Civil War and that he had been elected to it nineteen years before the Socialist Party was formed. The duties, he added, were technical, not political. The credentials committee finally voted to seat Gridley as an individual exception, but propounded a general rule that persons elected to office by the capitalist parties be barred from the Socialist Party. A Connecticut delegate mentioned an instance where a member accepted a job as city scavenger, but the socialist local voted charges against him for taking an appointment from the Democratic Party. So intense was this feeling that when Gridley was seated the minority demanded a roll call of states and lost 28 to 58. At the same convention a protest was lodged against the seating of J. Stitt Wilson, a prominent ex-minister and a California leader, on the ground that he had sent a congratulatory telegram to Mayor Samuel Jones of Toledo on the occasion of his election. "This was such a violation of Socialist ethics," said the delegate, "that it should debar him from taking part in the deliberations of this convention."[138]

Back of these at times outlandish feelings was the fear that traffic with the two major parties would dilute or corrupt socialist ardor and thus betray socialism. It also reflected the protective mortgage of men who, having seen the light first, feared that the late-comers would rob them of their birthright. Such fears of corruption underlay, too, the rigid refusal of the socialists to participate with other parties or reform movements, even on local issues. In June 1903 when Henry Demarest Lloyd sought to enlist Debs's support for a municipal ownership campaign in Chicago, the party standard bearer replied that he did not believe that "single taxers, socialists and anti-socialist trade unionists can successfully harmonize on any question whatsoever. . . ."[139] This attitude carried over into the heated denunciation of the labor party proposal in 1909 and ended only in 1922 with the formation of the Conference for Progressive Political Action.

And yet, underneath this proletarian cult lay a queer strain of soaring middle-class, get-rich-quick fantasies. If, as Max Scheler says, moral indignation is a disguised form of envy, underneath the proletarian veneer was a hot desire for riches. One can find regularly in the pages of the *International Socialist Review*—which labeled itself "the fighting magazine of the working-class," and of which William D. Haywood was an editor— a large number of advertisements which promised quick returns through land speculation. In the June 1912 issue, a full-page advertisement proclaimed: "DOUBLING OR TRIPLING YOUR MONEY THROUGH CLEAN HONEST

---

[138] *Proceedings*, 1904, pp. 15, 49.   [139] Ginger, *op.cit.*, p. 258.

INVESTMENT." It stated (shades of Henry George): "Getting in ahead of the railroad and the resulting rise in real estate values is the way thousands of people have made fortunes, especially in Western Canada. The wise real estate buyers of yesterday are wealthy people today." And in the text following: "Lots in Fort Fraser B.C.—destined to be the hub of the Canadian West." Nor were these isolated instances. Similar advertisements kept appearing in the *International Socialist Review* for many years, indicating their "pulling power." (The cover of the January 1916 issue is a painting of a hungry man in the snow, the inside half-page has an ad stating that a salesman could make $300 a month selling a cream separator.)

But this type of get-rich-quick appeal was not limited to the *International Socialist Review*. It was a mania throughout the party. In 1909 the Chicago *Daily Socialist* was carrying page advertisements for gold-mine stocks, whale-oil stocks, Florida lands, and other speculative ventures. John M. Crook, a party official and employee of the Chicago *Daily Socialist*, sold stock in a floor-surfacing-machine company; Bentall, former state secretary of the party in Illinois, promoted a flying-machine company; Kaplan, a national executive committee member from Minnesota, had other stock schemes; these, as well as Dickson's Matterhorn Goldmine and Insurance and Florida land schemes, were actively promoted by the Chicago *Daily Socialist*.

But perhaps the most spectacular promotions were those of Gaylord Wilshire, millionaire socialist and publisher of *Wilshire's Magazine*, a popular muckraking magazine of the period. After selling subscriptions to his magazine, and then common stock in it by flamboyant premiums (gold watches, pianos, etc., as prizes), Wilshire—whose name today adorns resplendent Wilshire Boulevard in Los Angeles—began the active pushing of blue-sky stocks for gold mines in British Guiana and Bishop Creek, Colorado, promising a 30 per cent dividend. The manager of the Colorado mine was Ernest Untermann, the translator of *Das Kapital* and leading socialist theoretician; various leading party officials, including a leading member of the national executive committee and a noted socialist editor, actively engaged in selling *Wilshire's Magazine* and gold-mining stock. After raising several hundred thousand dollars, Wilshire's gold-stock schemes failed in December 1910.

To the degree that any one person can encompass the fantastic contradictions inherent in the history of the socialist movement—its deep emotional visions, its quixotic, self-numbing political behavior, its sulky, pettish outbursts—it is Eugene Debs, so that in summation we must return to him once more. Debs had what the theologians call charism, the inner light of grace, or, as put by a laconic southerner, "kindlin' power." "He was a tall shamblefooted man, had a sort of gusty rhetoric that set on fire the railroad workers in their pine-boarded halls . . . made them want the world he wanted, a world brothers might own where everybody would split even. . . ," wrote Dos Passos.[140] "You felt that he really cared," said Ralph Chaplin.[141] "People loved him because he loved people," wrote Oscar Ameringer.[142] He spoke with Franciscan anguish, and when he said "brother" the recognition of kinship was instant.[143]

Yet while Debs fully *realized* the messianic role of the prophet, he lacked the hard-headedness of the politician, the ability to take the moral absolutes and break them down to the particulars with the fewest necessary compromises. He lacked, too, the awareness that a socialist leader of necessity must play both of these roles, and that in this tension there arise two risks—the corruption of the prophet and the ineffectuality of the politician. But Debs never even had the strength to *act* to the hilt the role of the prophet. A shallow dogmatism gave him the illusion of an inflexible morality. "If his mind failed to grasp a direct connection between a proposed reform and socialism," writes a sympathetic biographer, "he refused to waste time with reform. Then argument became futile; he could not be swayed." This dogmatism had its roots not in an iron revolutionary will, as with Lenin, but in an almost compulsive desire to be "left" of orthodox labor opinion. Nor did this thick streak of perpetual dissidence flow from the spirit of a dispossessed rebel like Haywood. Its wellspring was a sentimental nineteenth-century romanticism. He had been named for Eugene Sue and Victor Hugo, and their concern for the underdog, as well as the naive optimism of a Rousseau, soared in him. Yet in his personal life, manner, and habits (except for a later private addiction to drink), Debs was respectable and almost bourgeois; his

---

[140] John Dos Passos, *The 42nd Parallel* (New York, 1930), p. 26.

[141] Ralph Chaplin, *op.cit.*, p. 84.

[142] Oscar Ameringer, *If You Don't Weaken* (New York, 1940), p. 142.

[143] Debs's home life is of interest for those who, like Harold Lasswell, see in politics a public displacement for private motives. Debs's mother had a strong influence in his life—he left railroading at her urging for the less strenuous life of clerking—but most extraordinary was his deep attachment to his younger brother. "Theodore and Gene were of one flesh," remarked his sister, "they fairly breathed through one another." Debs married late, at the age of twenty-nine, and between his wife Kate and brother Theodore there was such strong antagonism that an open break resulted between the two. Kate Debs seemed to have been so hostile to Debs's socialist activities—it threatened her sense of middle-class respectability—that novelist Irving Stone was led to call her, in the title of his fictional portrayal of the life of Debs, the *Adversary in the House* (New York, 1948). Stone's judgment regarding Kate Debs is vigorously supported by James Oneal, a neighbor of Debs and one of the right-wing leaders of American socialism. See the review of Stone's book by August Claessens, *New Leader*, Jan. 10, 1948, and the reply by James Oneal, Jan. 31, 1948. An attempt to apply Lasswell's psychoanalytic and somatotype classification of political personalities—see his *Psychopathology and Politics* (Chicago, 1930)—to Debs is made by Kathryn Rogers, unpublished M.A. thesis, University of Chicago, 1930.

wife Kate was even more so. His literary tastes were prosaic: his favorite poet was Elbert Hubbard. But in his politics, Debs wore the romanticism like a cloak—and this was his strength as well as his weakness. It caused him to shun the practical and to shirk the obligations of day-to-day political decision. His fiercest shafts were reserved for the bureaucrat and party boss; his warmth and affection for those who led turbulent and dissident careers like his own.

How these sentiments could cruelly mislead him is illustrated in his attitude toward Tom Watson, a magical name among the populists of his day. Tom Watson of Georgia was a flaming agrarian rebel. A forceful speaker and writer, he was nominated with Bryan in 1896; but Watson refused to go along with the Democrats. Watson went to Congress, attacked the monopolists, founded *Tom Watson's Magazine*, among whose contributors were Theodore Dreiser and Edgar Lee Masters, and at the turn of the century was one of the leaders of the radical South. In later years he soured. Pressed by the race issue he became a champion of white supremacy, a vigorous antisocialist, and a defender of the Old South. The logic of crabbed populism led him to a vehement attack on the Negro ("Lynch law is a good sign: it shows that a sense of justice lives among the people"). Following the Leo Frank case in 1913 (in which a northern Jew was accused of murdering a Gentile girl, and lynched after his death sentence had been commuted), Watson became the most outspoken Jew-baiter in the country. As one biographer has written, ". . . if any mortal man may be credited (as no one man may rightly be) with releasing the forces of human malice and ignorance and prejudice, which the Klan merely mobilized, that man was Thomas E. Watson."[144] Yet, when Tom Watson died, Eugene V. Debs, recently released from the penitentiary, wrote in a letter to Mrs. Watson: "He was a great man, a heroic soul who fought the power of evil his whole life long in the interest of the common people, and they loved him and honored him."[145]

Withal, the lonely figure of Debs, his sagging, pleading gauntness, pierced all who beheld him. It was perhaps because in a final sense he was the true protestant. Debs stood at the end of the long road of the reformation. He had an almost mystical—at times omniscient—faith in the dictates of his inner self. Like the Anabaptists of old, all issues were resolved by private conscience. From the priesthood of all believers he had become the solitary individual, carrying on his shoulders the burdens of humanity. That sense of loneliness—and grandeur—touched others who were equally afflicted with the terrible sense of isolation. By his standing alone, he emphasized the individual and his rights, and at best, such an attitude of "autonomy" provides a unique defense of the dignity of the

[144] C. Vann Woodward, *Tom Watson, Agrarian Rebel* (New York, 1938), p. 450.
[145] *Ibid.*, p. 486.

person. But in its extreme antinomianism, in its romantic defiance of rational and traditional norms, it shirks the more difficult problem of living in the world, of seeking, as one must in politics, relative standards of social virtue and political justice instead of abstract absolutes. It is but one pole—a necessary one—in creating standards of action. But as the isolated protestant refuses to join the community of "sinners," so the isolated prophet evades the responsibility of political life. The prophet, once said Max Scheler, stands on the mountain as a signpost; he points the way but cannot go, for if he did, no longer would there be a sign. The politician, one might add, carries the sign into the valley with him.

VIII. The Decline and Fall of American Socialism

The subsequent history of American socialism is the story of breakup and decline. Although 1912 was the high-water mark of the socialist vote, it also brought an uneasy awareness that the party would never be a major force in American politics. After a dozen years the party could only poll about 6 per cent of the total vote and elect one congressman. Many members raised the question: Is American capitalism more resilient than socialists have credited it with being, or are the party's policies wrong? A feeling of tiredness was evident in the party leadership. This was particularly apparent in the case of Debs, who was wearying of the constant round of speaking and writing and felt, along with the gnawing sense of advancing age, that he was increasingly unheard. Various elements felt the party was insufficiently militant. In the far West some syndicalist-minded elements dropped off wholesale; in the Ozarks the dispossessed farmers began forming the secret and military-style Working Class Union. Thus, chunks of the left wing fell away. At the other end of the scale, the New Freedom of Woodrow Wilson, if not bringing the millennium to American labor, was, at least, furnishing tangible evidence that labor could promote gains through legislative activity. Within short order, a Department of Labor of cabinet rank was created, with William Wilson, a former secretary-treasurer of the mine workers, as secretary; the La Follette bill aiding the seamen had been passed after years of pleading by haggard Andrew Furuseth; government employees won the right to join unions and lobby for measures in their behalf; the Clayton Act, although not "Labor's Magna Carta," as Gompers had grandiloquently hailed it, did curb injunctions against labor by federal courts, thus withdrawing the sword which had been held over labor leaders by the Danbury Hatters and Buck's Stove injunction cases. Not only in Washington, but also in the various states, there were being enacted industrial safety laws, workmen's compensation, minimum wage laws, apprenticeship rules, and state anti-injunction laws. In short, the minimum beginnings of social legislation and union protection were under way. Thus the Wilsonian magnet pulled at reform elements in the Socialist Party and drew them out.

Other elements were now restless too. In its heyday, the Socialist Party had attracted a varied crew of drifters, promoters, speculators, and pitchmen who had found no place in capitalist society. Many were sincere socialists, but by temperament they needed a quick ascent if they were to stay hitched to the party. When the shooting star of socialism began to fall, these freebooters soon drifted away. Nevertheless, it was through many of them that socialism continued to exert a subtle yet unmistakable influence in American life. A case in point is the career of A. C. Townley and the meteoric rise of the North Dakota Non-Partisan League, one of the truly original phenomena in American politics.

Arthur C. Townley, like so many other Americans, started in poverty and dreamed of a fortune. In his youth he engaged in various speculative land ventures, and in 1909, a failure at the age of twenty-nine, moved to western North Dakota for his biggest plunge. He leased on credit thousands of uncultivated acres, bought tractors and farm implements, again on credit, and sowed on the wild virgin soil a huge crop of flax. But the long silky plant refused to grow and Townley went bankrupt, owing $80,000. Shortly afterward he turned to socialism and became an itinerant party organizer. But socialism, too, in North Dakota was a feeble stalk. Early in 1915, a small group of socialists decided that a third party had no tangible future in the state. They decided instead to organize the Non-Partisan League, stressing only the immediate needs of the farmers, and seek to capture one of the established parties through the primaries system. "The word socialism frightens the farmer," Townley is reported to have said. "I can take the name non-partisan . . . and use it to sugarcoat the principles of socialism and every farmer in the state will swallow them and call for more. . . . The farmers are ready."[146]

Townley's words were prophetic. The League spread like a dry prairie fire. In one year it elected Lynn Frazier governor of the state.

Hostile critics have dubbed the League a socialist front;[147] but this misreads its curious role. True, most of the backstage operators were or had been well-known socialists.[148] But its appeal and strength were populist; it was literally and figuratively straight corn. Essentially the

---

[146] Rev. S. A. Maxwell, *The Non-Partisan League from the Inside* (St. Paul, 1918), p. 45.

[147] Andrew A. Bruce, *The Non-Partisan League* (New York, 1921), p. 2.

[148] Townley was the League's chief organizer. Its legal adviser was Arthur LeSeur, a former railway attorney turned socialist who was also president of the People's College of Fort Scott, Kansas, a socialist correspondence law school whose letterhead featured Eugene V. Debs as chancellor. Charles Edward Russell, the socialist muckraker, was editor of the League's paper, while Walter Thomas Mills ("the little giant"), former Methodist minister, stock promoter, and peripatetic socialist educator, wrote the League's platform.

League's grapeshot was aimed at the *middleman* and the *speculator*, the two millstones grinding the farmer. The one—the processor in Minneapolis—controlled the price of grain storage; the other, by his speculative activities, forced up the price of land. The League program called for the state ownership of grain elevators, flour mills, etc.; state inspection of grain; hail insurance; rural credit banks; and the exemption of farm improvements from taxes. Its demands were thus simply those of a specific interest-group.

What the socialists contributed to the program was the rhetoric, the strategy, and the organizational technique. Townley's latent flair for promotion found a dazzling outlet. (The basic idea was a simple one and later to be copied by the Klan and many other rural and neighbor-based organizations.) Working farmers in each county were designated as organizers, assigned sales territory, and given a high commission for each man recruited. Paradoxically, it was the model-T Ford which in great measure made this scheme possible. With his little jalopy the farmer, rather than the outside organizer, could easily make the necessary calls to his neighbors, who knew and trusted him, and return in time to do his own chores. In less than a year, the League enrolled 50,000 members. Dues were high, but Townley promised results. The scheme of the direct primary allowed him to make good. By voting as a tight bloc, the League was able to capture the Republican Party and, in a traditionally G.O.P. state, win the election. It was one of the most notable examples of pressure-bloc manipulation in United States politics.

The old-line socialists in North Dakota resented the League: they feared it spelled the end of the party. And they were right. In 1912, the Socialist Party vote for governor was 6,834. Shortly after the formation of the League it sank to 2,615 and finally failed to place on the ballot altogether.

However, the Non-Partisan League soon came to an abrupt end. In 1921, the regular Democrats and Republicans combined their forces and succeeded in recalling Governor Frazier. Shortly thereafter, the Townley movement itself waned. The reason was peculiarly an agrarian one. Because farmers usually are short of cash, they were accustomed to pay dues by postdated checks. The result was that the farm depression in the early twenties drove the Townley movement into bankruptcy.

As a practical experiment in protest politics, the North Dakota Non-Partisan League was a striking innovation. In immediate terms, it reached its goals. It set up a state-owned mill and elevator, instituted crop insurance, etc. Its success in North Dakota stimulated the movement toward farmer-labor political action which began after World War I, and its tactic was copied in the thirties by Upton Sinclair's E.P.I.C. movement, and in some measure by the Political Action Committee in the forties.

In final assessment, however, the Non-Partisan League was less a progressive achievement than a demonstration of the retrogressive, crabbed, narrow, and xenophobic nature of agrarian socialism come to its logical conclusions. In the two decades following, the Non-Partisan League reorganized and sent a number of "progressives" to Congress, including Frazier, Nye, Lemke, and later Langer. What the end of the road turned out to be, however, can be seen in the career of William Lemke, one of the first political bosses of the League. A bull-headed Fargo lawyer, Lemke was born in poverty, and in his youth migrated to Mexico, where he engaged in various unsuccessful land speculations. Returning to North Dakota, he entered League politics. In 1932, after the revival of the League, he was elected to Congress and served until 1940, returning in 1942 and retaining a seat until his death in 1950. With the typical political narrowness of the small-town mind, his enemy was always called by the vague, amorphous name, the "interests." Politics in this view is always a "plot" and the devil, in this instance, the bankers, particularly the "international bankers." It was no accident that in 1936 Lemke, the populist, finally became the presidential candidate of Father Coughlin's Social Justice ticket, and that his appeal was a strange compound of crank money reform, free silver, isolationism, and other appeals to anxious and distressed petty-bourgeois elements. The blackish reactionary dye in populism had suffused through the cloth.[149]

If the populist pressure for immediate reform led some socialists to the tactic of the North Dakota Non-Partisan League, the strain of adventurism and agrarian violence led others to the Green Corn Rebellion and the destruction of the socialist movement in Oklahoma. Because the rebellion illustrates the other side of the populist aspect of American socialism, it is a story worth explaining.

Sparsely settled Oklahoma may not have had a working class, but it did have, in the most literal sense of the word, a proletariat—a dispossessed propertyless group with little visible means of support. These rural "proles" were an "aggregation of moisture, steam, dirt, rags, unshaven men and slatternly women and fretting children,"[150] tenant farmers who were little more than serfs to the cash crop demanded by the landlords. Many had settled as early as 1894 when the Cherokee strip had been thrown open; others had been members of Debs's American Railway Union who after defeat and blacklist had wandered into the area. Like most of the South and West, Oklahoma had been swept by populism. But, recalcitrant to the last, Oklahoma's populists had not softened and gone with Bryan into the Democratic Party. They were ridden by an

---

[149] See Daniel Bell, "The Grass Roots of American Jew Hatred," *Jewish Frontier,* June 1944, pp. 15-22.

[150] Oscar Ameringer, *op.cit.,* p. 229.

all-consuming hatred of their lot—the bare and uncertain living which a thin topsoil could provide.[151] This resentment was fueled by a stomping revivalism whose periodical outbursts provided relief for pent-up feelings and stifled emotions. The volatile mixture that resulted found its outlet in socialism.[152]

It was the adaptation to this religious temper that gave Oklahoma socialism its peculiar flavor. The new gospel was spread through the medium of week-long encampments, similar in form to the old-style evangelist camp meetings. Thousands of families would come from miles around, arriving in old buggies, chuck wagons, and buckboards, pitch their tents, cook, eat, and sleep on the camp grounds. A typical encampment would be opened with a rousing horseback parade, followed by a pickup mixed chorus which sang socialist versions of old populist songs to the tune of well-known religious melodies. Then followed the fire and brimstone oratory, often by noted socialist spellbinders such as Gene Debs, Kate Richards O'Hare, and Walter Thomas Mills. So went the week with a tumultuous round of singing, concerts, speeches, campfires, and memories to last for the next few months of dreary labor.

At its height, the socialist vote in Oklahoma was close to one-third of the total vote. Six socialists sat in the state legislature and the party elected numerous county officers. Proportionately, Oklahoma was the strongest socialist state in the country. But most of these socialists were "reds," and therefore against the reformist "yellows" who led the national party. Tad Cumbie ("the gray horse of the prairies"), the leader of Oklahoma's intransigeants, always flaunted a flaming red shirt at party conventions in order to show his convictions.[153] Because the official Socialist Party was considered too tame, the left-wingers organized two secret societies, the Working Class Union and the Jones Family. The members met at appointed rendezvous, gathered arms and dynamite, and waited for a moment to demonstrate that direct action could gain their

[151] "A poor man ain't got no chance in this country," raved George Hadley, looking over his untidy acres. "I've worked like a nigger all my life and look what I've got. I should 'a been rich by now and by God I will be if ever we get any justice in this country." Such was the mood of one socialist, as reported by Angie Debo in her *Prairie City*, a composite but authentic reconstruction of Oklahoma life. Angie Debo, *Prairie City* (New York, 1944), p. 131.

[152] "Pressure was upon them. . . . They were looking for delivery from the eastern monster whose lair they saw in Wall Street. They took their socialism like a new religion. And they fought and sacrificed for the spreading of the new faith like the martyrs of the old faith." Oscar Ameringer, *op.cit.*, p. 263. Ameringer, famous socialist editor and wit, had been a party organizer in Oklahoma and his salty memoirs are an invaluable sourcebook for the flavor and color of the period.

[153] At the 1912 convention Victor Berger likened the simon-pure leftists to the Hebrews who on journeys carried bundles of hay so as not to sleep on spots contaminated by Gentiles. The next day Cumbie appeared with a tiny bundle of hay pinned to his shirt.

ends. In the spring of 1917, these secret societies, which had spread through Arkansas as well, claimed 34,000 members.[154]

When the United States entered World War I and the draft act was passed, the night riders moved into action. With Tad Cumbie as commander-in-chief, they proposed, like Daniel Shays of old, to secede from the Union. They thought they could halt Oklahoma's participation in the war by seizing the banks and county offices, controlling the money and the press of the state. Several "armies" did take the field and, raiding at night, burned down some railroad bridges, cut telephone lines, and destroyed some pipelines. Because they subsisted on barbecued beeves and Indian green corn, the insurrection was called the Green Corn Rebellion.[155] The rebellion, which involved in all some two thousand farmers, including Negroes and Seminole Indians, collapsed early in August 1917 when 450 of the rebels were rounded up by the militia. Three persons were killed and eighty-six convicted and sent to the penitentiary. Though not a single official of the Socialist Party was connected with the Green Corn Rebellion, thousands of socialists were arrested: other thousands fled to the Winding Stairs mountains of adjacent Colorado, Arkansas, and Texas to escape arrest.[156] Shortly after the trial of the ringleaders, an emergency convention disbanded the Oklahoma Socialist Party. The move was taken to prevent the government from linking the overt acts in Oklahoma to Victor Berger, who was then on trial in Chicago for violating the "Espionage Act."

To this wartime opera bouffe, a tragicomic footnote needs to be appended. The war had discredited the Socialist Party, and its leaders sought a new approach. Spurred by the example of North Dakota, Oscar Ameringer and others in 1921 organized the Farmer-Labor Reconstruction League, and nominated for governor J. C. ("Our Jack") Walton. A flamboyant character, Walton was the mayor of Oklahoma City and a cardholder in the railroad unions. His campaign was typical. He flayed the "interests" and spoke out, although side-tongued, against the Klan. This was the Indian summer of progressivism. In the Senate were Frazier and Nye of North Dakota, Shipstead and Johnson of Minnesota, Norris and Howell of Nebraska, Brookhart of Iowa, and La Follette of Wisconsin. Oklahoma was not one to lag behind. The League captured the Democratic Party, and "Our Jack" was swept into office in 1922 by a 60,000 plurality.

[154] *Oklahoma: a Guide to the Sooner State* (Norman, Okla., 1941), p. 48.

[155] Another version fixes the name as resulting from the coincidence with the annual green-corn dance of the Shawnee Indians, as well as the staple item of Indian green corn or "tomfuller." See the novel by William Cunningham, *The Green Corn Rebellion* (New York, 1935).

[156] Charles D. Bush, *The Green Corn Rebellion* (University of Oklahoma Graduate Thesis); cited by Ameringer, *op.cit.*, pp. 347-49, 353-54.

The farmer-laborites waited for reforms to start. Instead disquieting rumors reached their ears. "Our Jack" was seen playing golf in "tasseled knickers and silver-buckled sport shoes" on a Muskogee links, surrounded by oil derricks; worse still, remarks Ameringer, a caddy was carrying his bag! Appointments promised to farmer-laborites failed to materialize. Soon after, "Our Jack" traipsed off to Cuba with lobbyists for the oil-cement-asphalt-utilities "interests" and on his return began to build an elaborate house. A year later Walton capped this betrayal by openly joining the Klan. It was the end of socialist politics and influence in Oklahoma. Populism, of a sort, finally won out when trumpeting "Alfalfa Bill" Murray was elected governor of the state in 1930 on the Democratic ticket. But Alfalfa Bill was a far cry from old populist idealism. Like Tom Watson of Georgia he had traveled a familiar course. Beginning against the "interests" he ended as a rancorous isolationist and bigoted nativist. It was a shriveled ending for a grass-roots American radicalism.

But above all these—the defection of the left, the slipping away of the reform elements, the loss of populist support—the final gust that shattered the old Socialist Party was the whirling sandstorm of the European war. For years the international socialist congresses had blustered that a European working class would not permit a general world war to erupt. But war had come and the European socialist parties broke on the reefs of national patriotism: the German socialists supported the Kaiser, and the Russian socialists the Tsar; English socialists rallied behind the King, while French socialists, after the tragic assassination of their powerful antiwar leader Jean Jaurès, responded to the Marseillaise. Only the Italian socialists, a tiny handful of English pacifists around Ramsay MacDonald, and small groups of left-wingers, notably the Russian Bolsheviks, maintained the classic socialist position. American socialists, three thousand miles away from the conflict, were confused. Officially, the American party opposed both the war and American preparedness, but influential individuals began doubting the party's stand; others became disillusioned by the unexpected and shattering failure of European socialism.

To shore up the crumbling walls Debs in 1914 appealed for solidarity of all the left-wing forces. Once more he called for the merger of the United Mine Workers and the Western Federation of Miners to form "a revolutionary industrial organization"; and in the political field he urged the reunion of the Socialist and Socialist Labor Parties.[157] The old phrases were there, but by now they were meaningless.

By 1915 the party membership slipped to below 80,000 from the high of 125,000 in 1912. Membership rose after 1915, but it was an alien

[157] E. V. Debs, "A Plea for Solidarity," *International Socialist Review*, Mar. 1914, reprinted in *Writings and Speeches of Eugene V. Debs*, p. 372.

element, the foreign-language federations, which largely accounted for the gain; and these new groups began to dominate the party. The once vigorous socialist press began to disintegrate. By 1916 there were only two socialist dailies alive (as against five in 1912), the ineffectual New York *Call* (with a pale circulation of 15,000) and the Milwaukee *Leader* (circulation 37,000). Significantly the number of foreign-language socialist dailies rose from eight to thirteen. In the weekly field the toll was greatest. Of the 262 periodicals that flourished in 1912, only 42 remained.

It would not be too rash to say that the Socialist Party of 1917 bore little resemblance to the heterogeneous movement which had made so vigorous a dent in American life in the first dozen years of the century. Three major factors account for this difference and are explored below: a radical shift had taken place in the geographical centers of party electoral strength; a decisive transformation had taken place in the composition of the party membership; and almost the entire intellectual leadership of the party had decamped to support America's role in the war.

Before 1912 socialist strength was concentrated largely in the agrarian and mining areas of the West and Southwest. In the next years this support decreased while the strength of the Socialist Party increased proportionately in the Northeast and urban areas, particularly in New York. By 1920, in fact, New York contributed more than one-fifth of Debs's total of more than 900,000 votes, although in previous campaigns New York had never provided more than 10 per cent of the socialist total.[158] The reasons for the decline in the West have been partially enumerated. The rising strength of the Socialist Party in the urban East, and particularly in New York, was due in greatest measure to the high tide of European, and particularly Jewish, immigration. These new immigrants—again particularly the Jewish group—provided the sinews which sustained the American Socialist Party until 1932.

For a variety of historical reasons, the Jewish immigrants from eastern Europe were inclined to support radical movements. Like Carl Schurz and the German Forty-Eighters, they had participated actively in revolutionary movements in their own countries and fled because of oppression. On coming here they retained much of their radical fervor, and, as with Schurz and the German Republicans, it was only after a period of accommodation that the European enthusiasms were tempered. A goodly number of immigrants were younger men and women of education who were of necessity forced to enter the garment shops as workers. But the sweatshop conditions to which older workers had resigned themselves

[158] This was both a relative and an absolute shift, i.e., the Socialist Party vote had decreased in its old strongholds yet the new role of New York as the number one center of socialist strength was not merely a displacement of other centers but a rise in total vote as well.

stirred these young firebrands to action. In 1909, beginning with the waistmakers' strike and with the Triangle Dress Factory fire, which shocked the community into awareness of the miasmic factory conditions, unionism took hold. In less than five years, the International Ladies' Garment Workers, the Amalgamated Clothing Workers, the Furriers, and the Millinery Workers unions had won contracts and a permanent footing. With their rise came a young and new leadership that was almost wholly socialist in inclination; and the new unions became the financial backbone and chief organizational props of the Socialist Party. Besides these unions the new Jewish immigration also created a powerful fraternal and insurance organization known as the Workmen's Circle, and this also became an important source of socialist financial strength. Started in 1905 with less than 7,000 members, it grew within a decade to a membership of 52,000 with assets exceeding $625,000.

A word also needs to be said concerning the distinctive role in the American socialist movement played by the *Jewish Daily Forward* and its controversial editor, Abraham Cahan. At its height the *Forward* had a remarkable circulation of 250,000 and it was undoubtedly the most influential paper in the Jewish community of New York. The *Forward* made its unique mark because it was a Yiddish newspaper among a Yiddish folk. The early Jewish intellectuals had become separated from the Yiddish masses by their disdainful refusal to speak Yiddish. The *Forward* mirrored and articulated the pathos and deep self-pity, the despair and indignation of a bewildered immigrant folk. Characteristically, the *Forward* won its first popular support and ousted its dominant rival, the Socialist Labor Party *Abendblatt*, when it took an undogmatic and even "antisocialist" stand on two crucial issues. The *Abendblatt* attacked the Spanish-American War and, along with other doctrinaire socialist papers, refused to be roused by the Dreyfus case in France. But hatred of Spain was deep in Jewish consciousness, and Dreyfus himself was a Jew. On both issues the Jewish mass feelings were aroused and the *Forward* followed its tribal instincts.

Probably in few other instances has a newspaper had so great a cultural influence on a community. The *Forward* bound together the Jewish community and made it socialist.[159] In doing so, the *Forward* replaced the rabbi, although synagogue modes of discourse were adopted. Propaganda was carried on by *De Proletarischer Magid* (the proletarian preacher) and the lessons were called the *Red Sedre* (the weekly portion of the *Torah*). The first walking delegate, said the *Forward*, was Moses, because he led the strike against the Egyptian overseers. For many years the *Forward* exercised a decisive, and at times arbitrary, voice in the affairs of the Jewish unions, and in the period from 1920 to 1932 was the most powerful influence in the Socialist Party.

[159] Melech Epstein, *Jewish Labor in the U.S.A.* (New York, 1950), pp. 318-34.

With the successful rise of Jewish labor, fostered as this was by the *Forward*, the Socialist Party was able for the first time to elect a congressman from New York in 1914 when Meyer London carried the lower east side. For years New York had been an embarrassingly weak spot in the socialist armor because of the depredations of William Randolph Hearst, quondam reformer. "The ability of Hearst," said the New York *Call* in 1909, "to cut heavily into the Socialist vote every time he chooses to be a candidate for office must be a source of bitter humiliation to every sincere Socialist." However, the new immigration created a solid base of socialist votes which could not be swayed by the reform breezes.

The immigration as a whole was responsible for a remarkable change in the composition of the membership of the Socialist Party. After 1915 the number of party members began to rise steadily until, by 1919, it was back to almost 110,000. This new growth was due almost entirely to the foreign-language groups. Starting in 1908, the Socialist Party had begun the organization of foreign-language federations in order to reach the foreign-speaking voters. In actual practice the federations were really small national socialist parties attached to the American organization but responsive largely to the passions and concerns of the land of their origin. By 1919, at the new peak of the party, over 53 per cent of the members—a majority—were members of foreign-language federations. In 1912, these federations had constituted less than 12 per cent of the total membership. The growth in the federations was less a product of conditions in America than of enthusiasm for events in Europe. For example the Slavic federations in the Socialist Party (Russian, Ukrainian, South Slavic, Lithuanian, Lettish) almost doubled their membership in the four months following December 1918, and by April 1919 constituted a decisive bloc of 20 per cent of the party membership—a fact which was instrumental in the emergence of present-day American communism.

The third factor which transformed the character of the Socialist Party was the loss of almost the entire body of intellectuals, publicists, public figures, union leaders, etc., as a result of World War I. In fact, except for Hillquit, Berger, and Debs, not one major "name" remained in the ranks of American socialism after the war.

These defections had been foreshadowed in 1916 when the Socialist Party vote plummeted. Old and tired, Debs had refused to run. No party convention was held that year, and a national referendum nominated a journalist, Allan Benson, for president. But with the war issue casting so large a shadow, many socialists felt that their trust would reside better in Wilson and that their votes should not be wasted. Consequently, a number of prominent socialists openly supported the Democratic ticket. Among these were William English Walling, the intellectual leader of the left wing who had attacked the German social democrats for voting the Kaiser's war credits; Ernest Poole, whose novel *The Harbor* had been one of the great successes of radical fiction; Ellis O. Jones, a professional humorist;[160] Mother Jones, famed union organizer and heroine of the coal fields; and John Reed and Max Eastman of the *Masses*. This enthusiasm for Wilson was strengthened by Max Eastman's report of an interview at the White House between the President and a group of *Masses'* editors. According to Eastman, Wilson represented "our popular sovereignty with beautiful distinction." And reflecting possibly the solidarity which the intellectuals felt with the professor in the White House, Eastman remarked that Wilson was "a graciously democratic aristocrat." The Woodrow Wilson Independent League, formed by these intellectuals, helped swing away much of the liberal vote from the socialists. Benson's total of about 590,000 votes represented a decline of about a third from the high point of 1912.

When the United States declared war in April 1917, the intellectuals and the union leaders continued to follow Wilson. For them, the greatest danger was German militarism; if the Kaiser won, they saw no hope for world peace. The roll call of bolters is impressive. Among those who left the party were: John Spargo, editor of the *Comrade* and the leading popularizer of socialist ideas in America who was also the theoretician of the right wing; William English Walling, perhaps the most provocative mind in American socialism and the theoretician of the left wing; A. M. Simons, editor of the Chicago *Daily Socialist*, and author of *Social Forces in American History* and *Farmers in American History*, the first attempts to see U.S. history in Marxist terms; Charles Edward Russell, the noted muckraker whom the right wing had nominated against Debs in 1912; William J. Ghent, a perceptive writer whose neglected book, *Our Benevolent Feudalism*, had in 1906 pictured with remarkable accuracy the emergence of fascism as a reaction to the socialist threat; Allan Benson, the party's presidential candidate in 1916; George D. Herron, the leader of the Christian socialist movement in America whose mother-in-law, Carrie Rand, had on his request set up the Rand School in New York; Upton Sinclair and Jack London, the two literary firebrands who had started the Intercollegiate Socialist Society; Carl D. Thompson of Wisconsin, who had sought the Socialist presidential nomination in 1916; State Senator W. R. Gaylord, the party's public spokesman in Wisconsin; Ernest Untermann, who had translated Marx's *Das Kapital* and was one of the theoreticians of the party; Robert Hunter, noted social worker whose exposés of the consequences of poverty had attracted national attention; Henry Slobodkin, one of the founders of the party; J. Stitt

---

[160] Among the numerous paradoxes in socialist history, shortly after Pearl Harbor, Mr. Jones—now pro-Nazi and an anti-Semite—was convicted on July 11, 1942, of sedition and sentenced to five years in prison.

Wilson, mayor of Berkeley, California, and a leading Christian socialist; Chester M. Wright, editor of the *Call*; Lucien Sanial, Gompers' old foe; Arthur Bullard, well-known writer; Frank Bohn, theoretician of syndicalism; J. G. Phelps Stokes, millionaire leftist, and his fiery wife, Rose Pastor. This capitulation of almost the entire Socialist Party intelligentsia was not unique. Almost the entire leadership of American progressivism had followed Wilson too, among them John Dewey, Clarence Darrow, and the prophets of the *New Republic*, Herbert Croly, Walter Weyl, and Walter Lippmann.[160a]

In addition to the intellectuals, the trade unions which formed the progressive and socialist bloc within the American Federation of Labor joined Gompers in support of the war. The coal miners, machinists, even the International Ladies' Garment Workers, all backed the American Alliance for Labor & Democracy. The final blow, perhaps, was the loss of the *Appeal to Reason*. The famous *Appeal*, the most popular success in socialist publishing, the paper to which Debs had contributed for many years as an associate editor, changed its name to *The New Appeal* and endorsed Wilson.

When news of the European war reached the United States, the national executive committee of the Socialist Party issued a statement on August 12, 1914, extending the sympathy of the party "to the workers of Europe in their hour of trial," and stating that "The workers have no quarrel with each other but rather with their ruling class." In December 1914, the party issued an antiwar manifesto putting forth a socialist analysis of the nature of the war. While the immediate causes of the war were stated as "thoughts of revenge . . . imperialism and commercial rivalries . . . secret intrigue . . . lack of democracy . . . vast systems of military and naval equipment . . . jingo press . . . the fundamental cause was the capitalist system." This position was endorsed in a referendum vote by a large majority in September 1915.

For a party leadership that had been attacked as middle-class, soft, and compromising, these were strong words. How are they to be explained? One viewpoint ascribes the antiwar stand of the Socialist Party to the high proportion of German, Jewish, and foreign-language elements in the party.[161] Another points to the party's distance from the scene and

---

[160a] Max Eastman opposed the war, and together with other editors of the *Masses* was indicted under the Espionage Act. During the trial, Eastman was won over to support of the war when, following the Russian Revolution, President Wilson virtually endorsed the Soviet peace program. See Hillquit, *Loose Leaves from a Busy Life*, pp. 222-33.

[161] See, for example, Charles Edward Russell's autobiography, *Bare Hands and Stone Walls* (New York, 1933). Russell reports (p. 288) a conversation related to him about Victor Berger in which Berger stated: "You know, I have always hated the,

consequent lack of involvement. Both of these carry a degree of truth. But equally relevant is the fact (obscured by the taunts of "yellow" and "reformist" made by extremist elements) that the American Socialist Party was heavily a doctrinaire socialist party, more so than most of its European counterparts because of its lack of commitments to the labor movement. With none of the strings of responsibilities which held the European socialists, the party, reacting by formulas, branded the war "imperialist" and then stood apart from it.

War was declared on April 6, and the following day the emergency convention of the party opened in St. Louis to announce its opposition. The antiwar statement that was adopted restated the classic Marxist analysis of war.[162] The manifesto proposed a seven-point program of opposition calling for demonstrations, petitions, opposition to conscription, and ". . . the extension of the campaign of education among the workers to organize them into strong, class-conscious and closely unified political and industrial organizations to enable them by concerted and harmonious mass action to shorten this war and establish lasting peace. . . ."

The St. Louis declaration was written by Morris Hillquit, Algernon Lee, and Charles Ruthenberg—a strange combination of two "right-wingers" and an extreme leftist. Wrote Hillquit later, "We worked on it earnestly and tensely, carefully weighing every phrase and every word, but determined to state our position without circumlocution or equivocation, to leave nothing unsaid."[163]

Although the intellectuals had deserted the party, in the two months following the adoption of the manifesto party membership jumped more than twelve thousand. Because the Socialist Party was the only one that was antiwar, it found new and surprising support for its stand, especially in the northern industrial and foreign-language centers. Thus, in 1917 the Socialist Party vote reached new spectacular heights in the municipal elections of that year. In New York, where Morris Hillquit ran for mayor, newspapers speculated freely on a possible victory, although four years before Charles Edward Russell had received less than 5 per cent of the votes. The threat was real enough for Hillquit's opponents—John F.

Kaiser, but when I see the world taking arms against him I feel that I must seize a rifle and take my place in the ranks and fight for him."

[162] "The capitalist class of each country was forced to look for foreign markets to dispose of the accumulated 'surplus wealth.' . . . The mad orgy of death and destruction which is now convulsing unfortunate Europe was caused by the conflict of capitalist interests in the European countries. . . . Our entrance into the European war was instigated by the predatory capitalists in the U.S. who boast of the enormous profits of seven billion dollars from the manufacture and sale of munitions and war supplies and from the exportation of American food stuffs and other necessities."

[163] Hillquit, *Loose Leaves from a Busy Life*, pp. 165-66.

Hylan, a nonentity picked by William Randolph Hearst; reform Mayor John Purroy Mitchell, who four years earlier had beaten a divided Tammany; and William F. Bennett, a Republican hack—to level their fire chiefly against him rather than at each other. Hillquit openly took an antiwar stand, and declared he would not support the Liberty Loan. Over the city, particularly in working-class districts, the nightly street-corner meetings reached a fever pitch. In a furious speech Theodore Roosevelt denounced Hillquit as cowardly, pacifist, and pro-German and climaxed an impassioned speech with "Yellow calls to Yellow." On election day Hillquit received 145,332 votes (an increase of nearly 500 per cent): 22 per cent of the city's voters (31 per cent in the Bronx) had voted Socialist. In addition, the party sent ten assemblymen to Albany, seven aldermen to City Hall, and also elected a municipal-court judge.

Nor was the New York vote an isolated event. In Chicago the party received nearly 34 per cent of the vote, carrying five wards (as against 3.6 per cent in the previous election). In Buffalo the Socialist vote was over 25 per cent of the total, and throughout Ohio significant totals were registered in every major city—Dayton, 44 per cent; Toledo, 34.8 per cent; Cleveland, 19.3 per cent; Cincinnati, 11.9 per cent. A survey by Paul Douglas of the 1917 vote in fourteen cities showed that the Socialist Party had polled an average of 21.6 per cent of the entire vote, a total which, if projected nationally, would have meant four million votes. The war thus gave the Socialist Party a new tone and purpose; it minimized the differences of left and right, in the first year at least, and the fever glow which resulted gave an illusion of ruddiness and new health.

The 1917 elections were the only means of socialist protest during the war. Soon thereafter, the government moved swiftly to crack down on the party. The chief instrument was the so-called Espionage Act, passed in June 1917, which forbade obstruction to recruitment, insubordination in the armed forces, etc. A year later the act was drastically widened to include such offenses as "profane, scurrilous and abusive language" about the government and constitution, "or saying or doing anything" to obstruct the sale of government bonds or the making of loans by the United States. Moreover, the Post Office Department was given the power to exclude from the mails all matter violating the provisions of the act. The Post Office acted swiftly. In short order the *American Socialist*, the official weekly of the party, the Milwaukee *Leader*, the New York *Call*, the *Jewish Daily Forward*, the *Masses*, Frank O'Hare's *Social Revolution* (formerly the *National Rip-Saw*), the *International Socialist Review*, and several German, Russian, and Hungarian socialist dailies, all had their mailing rights suspended. The only avenue open for expression was the public platform, and this, too, was soon pulled out from under.

103

Antiradical hysteria had begun with the Tom Mooney campaign. At a preparedness-day parade in San Francisco in July 1916 a bomb exploded, killing eight and wounding forty. Shortly afterward, Warren K. Billings and Tom Mooney, a radical labor leader, were arrested. An anarchist paper, the *Blast*, edited by Alexander Berkman (who had shot H. C. Frick at Homestead) was raided. Mooney came to trial in January 1917 and was sentenced to death. World-wide protest, including demonstrations in Moscow, caused Wilson to intervene and the sentence was commuted to life imprisonment. During the Mooney hysteria Wilson ordered the investigation of the I.W.W. On September 5, 1917, simultaneous raids took place in more than a dozen cities, and 166 members of the I.W.W., including Haywood, were indicted for violation of the Espionage Act. All the members of the general executive board, the secretaries of the industrial unions, the party editors, and anyone of slight standing in the organization were picked up. As new leaders replaced those imprisoned, these too were arrested. "If the government had set out not only to render the I.W.W. ineffective during the war but also to prevent its resurgence, it could not have performed its tasks with more thoroughness and completeness."[164]

The government sought to wreck the Socialist Party as well. In September 1917 the national office in Chicago was raided, and in February 1918 the chief officers, including Adolph Germer, the executive secretary, J. Louis Engdahl, editor of the *American Socialist*, the party's national publication, William F. Kruse, of the Young People's Socialist League, Irwin St. John Tucker, former head of the party's literature department, and Victor Berger were indicted. In Ohio, the leaders of the party— Charles Ruthenberg, Alfred Wagenknecht, and Charles Baker—were sentenced to one-year terms for opposing conscription. Across the country hundreds were indicted.

In the period following America's entry into the war, Gene Debs was strangely silent. He had refused to attend the St. Louis convention, although urgently requested to come by Ruthenberg. He discontinued his lecture tours. The conscription act, the Liberty Loan, the subsidies to England and France went by without protest. One biographer has implied that Kate Debs sought to deter him; Debs himself may have thought any gesture hopeless. "He still longed for peace; but he had no program. He was lost."[165] After the Russian Revolution had broken tsarist autocracy (now making plausible the slogan of a war for democracy), and Wilson had declared his war aims, many of the socialists wavered. Max Eastman and Floyd Dell, although on trial as editors of the *Masses* for antiwar propaganda, came out in support of the war. The seven socialist aldermen in New York declared themselves in favor of a Liberty Loan

[164] Perlman and Taft, *op.cit.*, p. 421.
[165] Ginger, *op.cit.*, pp. 345-48.

drive. Meyer London, the only socialist in Congress, left-handedly supported Wilson's war aims by declaring that they were similar to socialist objectives. It was at this point that Debs first began to stir. Happiest when in the opposition, he began to attack this trend in the party. In May 1918 Debs issued a statement on socialist policy, his first word in thirteen months. Stating his unqualified opposition to the war and attacking the majority socialists in Germany, he proposed another convention because the St. Louis manifesto contained "certain propositions . . . which are now impossible." After fifteen months of inactivity Debs began a speaking campaign. But the federal government took no notice and "Debs became increasingly angry. . . . Although he . . . vehemently denounced the President, nothing happened. Half of his beautiful plan [either to free socialist prisoners or get himself jailed] was being spoiled by the callous indifference of the law-enforcement officials. This was the final insult," writes biographer Ray Ginger.[166]

Finally, at Canton, Ohio, the government took notice. Actually, little that Debs said in a two-hour speech was devoted to the issues of the war. He did—for the first time—lash out at those who had deserted the party. "They lack the fiber," he said, "to endure the revolutionary test."[167] In his peroration Debs touched once on the war. On the charge of using "profane, scurrilous and abusive" language, he was arrested for violating the amended Espionage Act. The Cleveland trial was a stage which the Debs of old utilized to the fullest measure. In the hushed, tense courtroom, Debs made his own plea to the jury. His whole life was at stake and in moving sentences he summed up his credo. The ruling class, he said, was helpless against "the rise of the toiling and producing classes. . . . You may hasten the change, you may retard it; you can no more prevent it than you can prevent the coming of the sunrise on the morrow." Before the sentencing Debs made an address which included the oft-quoted ". . . while there is a lower class, I am in it; while there is a criminal element, I am of it; while there is a soul in prison, I am not free."[168] He was sentenced to ten years in prison, and sent to Atlanta.

Except for Hillquit, who had been hospitalized for tuberculosis,[168a] almost every major Socialist Party official was indicted during the war. Berger and the national officers were convicted, but two years later, while still out on bail, their convictions were set aside by the Supreme

---

[166] *Ibid.*, p. 354.

[167] The Canton, Ohio, speech in *Writings and Speeches of Eugene V. Debs*, p. 421.

[168] Statement to the Court, *ibid.*, p. 437.

[168a] Hillquit asserts that his large mayoralty vote in 1917 won him "immunity," for the government feared that an indictment "might antagonize a considerable body of people in New York" (Hillquit, *Loose Leaves from a Busy Life*, p. 234). In the summer of 1918, however, when he was preparing to defend Debs and Berger, Hillquit learned of his ailment. He spent two years in a sanitarium, thus missing the intense fratricide of the 1919 split.

Court. All told, about two thousand persons were tried under the wartime Espionage Act.

The February Revolution that overthrew the Tsar in 1917 was a lightning bolt that cleared the air. The rumbling noise of the following November was the apocalyptic thunderclap. The first *word* signaling the new world revolution had been spoken, incongruously, in the rest room reserved for the Tsar at the Finland station in Petrograd. Returning in April from Switzerland, Lenin said: "I am happy . . . to greet you as the advance guard of the international proletarian army. . . . The war of imperialist brigandage is the beginning of civil war in Europe. . . . The hour is not far when, at the summons of our Comrade Karl Liebknecht, the people will turn their weapons against the capitalist exploiters. . . . In Germany, everything is already in ferment! Not today, but tomorrow, any day, may see the general collapse of European capitalism. The Russian revolution you have accomplished has dealt it the first blow and has opened a new epoch. . . ."[169]

Lenin's remarks had been completely unexpected. His old rivals, the Mensheviks, had come to the Petrograd station to greet him. His party central committee, including Stalin, was in favor of an alliance with the other socialist parties. Lenin rejected this course. His single aim now was power, and the Bolshevik Party, the instrument he had fashioned, had to be ready for its seizure. The same night, in the marble corridors of Kshesinskaya Palace, once the house of the Tsar's ballerina-mistress and now the headquarters of the Bolshevik Party, Lenin spoke for two hours filling his audience with "turmoil and terror." In hoarse accents he denounced any policy of collaboration; he mocked the agrarian reforms of the provisional government; he denounced its war policy. The aim was clear: the peasants must seize the land, the workers the factories, all support to the provisional government must cease. "We don't need any parliamentary republic. We don't need any bourgeois democracy. We don't need any government except the Soviet of Workers', Soldiers', and Peasants' Deputies!"[170]

In November, fired by Lenin's inexorable will, the Bolsheviks seized and held power. Within a year, Europe caught fire. A socialist government was established in Finland. A revolution began in Hungary. The Kaiser abdicated. The Austrian emperor fled. The Romanovs were shot. It was the most dramatic moment in European working-class history since the Paris Commune less than fifty years before. To Europe's socialists it meant still more. Here were not the meek and humble but the revolutionary and disinherited claiming the world. For more than forty years

---

[169] Cited in Edmund Wilson, *To the Finland Station* (New York, 1940), p. 471.
[170] *Ibid.*, p. 475.

European socialism had been lumbering along, growing fat, talking of eventual victories through parliamentary elections; here in one swift surgical stroke, the body of European capitalism was pierced, and was collapsing like a stuffed strawpiece. What equally captured the minds of socialists everywhere was the dazzling spectacle of power seized by men who had been obscure individuals, mocked and derided when they had suggested those "absurd" and "utopian" theories of insurrection. As recently as 1915 Lenin's name had been known to but few European socialists (his reply to an article by Rosa Luxemburg was rejected as unclear by the *Neue Zeit*, the venerable theoretical organ of Marxian socialism). He was almost completely unknown in the United States: when he wrote a letter to the Socialist Propaganda League of Boston, an extreme leftwing antiwar organization composed largely of Slavic members, they ignored it and apparently threw the letter in the wastebasket. The *International Socialist Review* in 1915 reprinted the antiwar manifesto of the Zimmerwald conference, an effort by left socialists to proclaim their opposition to war. But Lenin's name passed unnoticed. Trotsky and Bukharin, however, were both known in New York, where they had come in 1916. Socialists had met with them, argued with them, measured their own ability against theirs; and many felt that if Trotsky, an obscure journalist, could rise to become the Marshal of the Red Army, their own stars were not far off in the heavens.

All American socialists now rushed to acclaim the Bolshevik victory. A few moderate voices, such as that of the veteran Russian socialist editor, Dr. Sergius Ingerman, were howled down. James Oneal, in a speech on November 7, 1919, the second anniversary of the Bolshevik Revolution, mocked the critics: ". . . they say there has been violence in Russia. Some violence in a revolution! Just imagine! Do they think a revolution is a pink tea party . . . every great revolution . . . [has] been accompanied with more or less violence, and it is impossible to dispense with it."

Everyone rushed to become a Bolshevik—the right wing as well as the left! The right wing even announced its readiness to join the new Third International. But a new left wing had arisen in the Socialist Party, and it would have none of the old leaders, no matter how strong the new protestations of revolutionary faith. The taint of reformism, they said, would not wear off these new wearers of Lenin's mantle. They sneered at Hillquit's " 'splendid' Mayoralty campaign for cheap milk." "A Babbitt of Babbitts is Hillquit, the ideal Socialist leader for successful dentists," wrote Trotsky later, recalling his experiences in America during the war.[171]

[171] Leon Trotsky, *My Life* (New York, 1930), p. 274. Trotsky scorned the U.S. socialists: "To this day, I smile as I recall the leaders of American socialism. Immigrants

The left of 1918 was completely unlike the left of 1912.[172] The latter had been a motley collection, loosely organized, of populists, untutored syndicalists, rebels, etc. The new left wing was led by a group of tough-minded young men, many of them fresh out of metropolitan colleges, who found in the Bolshevik Revolution what a left wing had long lacked— a program around which to organize.

The emergence of the left wing in American socialism owes much to the presence here of the Russian émigrés who had been deported from France. One of the earliest meetings leading to the formation of the left-wing caucus was held in Brooklyn in the winter of 1916-1917. About twenty persons were present, including Leon Trotsky, Nikolai Bukharin, and Alexandra Kollontay of the Russians, and Ludwig Lore, Louis C. Fraina, and Louis B. Boudin of the American Socialist Party.[173] Trotsky and Fraina attacked the American Socialist Party for not resisting conscription more strongly and for not resorting to sabotage. "We intended to organize the left-wing under the direction of Comrade Trotsky and Madame Kollontay," wrote Katayama, a leading Japanese communist then in exile here, "but the Russian Revolution called them back." The group which met in Brooklyn later issued an organ called *Class Struggle*, which became the official left-wing voice within the Socialist Party. Meanwhile, an independent left wing had started in Boston, where a group of Slavic socialists formed the Socialist Propaganda League and published the *New International*. When the left wing captured control of the party in Boston, they changed the name of the periodical to *Revolutionary Age*.

---

who had played some rôle in Europe in their youth, they very quickly lost the theoretical premise they had brought with them in the confusion of their struggle for success" (p. 274). And yet, unconscious of the irony, Trotsky tells of his own living here: "We rented an apartment in a workers' district, and furnished it on the instalment plan. That apartment, at eighteen dollars a month, was equipped with all sorts of conveniences that we Europeans were quite unused to: electric lights, gas cooking-range, bath, telephone, automatic service-elevator, and even a chute for the garbage. These things completely won the boys over to New York" (p. 271).

[172] The mood of the young left at the time is caught in an incident related by the former communist writer, Joseph Freeman, in his autobiography. During the 1917 campaign Columbia students found it difficult to get a Columbia professor to sponsor Hillquit because of the expulsions of Dana and Cattell for their antiwar views. Freeman called Hillquit, who said: "Go to my friend Professor Seligman." Freeman was taken aback. Seligman for years had been attacked by socialists as "archreactionary" and as the "chief economic apologist of capitalism." Seligman readily agreed, saying he and Hillquit were friends who for many years had sought inconclusively to convince each other about socialism. "Personal intimacy between the champion of our cause and the apologist for capitalism was beyond our understanding," Freeman wrote. "Was it possible that the leaders of both sides did not take seriously the ideas they professed?" Joseph Freeman, *An American Testament* (New York, 1936), p. 110. Freeman's memoirs is one of the best accounts of the attraction of communism for the young intellectual.

[173] Sen Katayama, "Morris Hillquit and the Left-Wing," *Revolutionary Age*, Vol. 2, No. 4 (July 26, 1919), p. 4.

The Russian Federation of the Socialist Party became the idol of the left wing. Quite naively, its members were looked upon as the only ones who understood bolshevism, apparently through some mysterious osmosis of the language. Actually, the majority of the large membership of the Federation (which now constituted one-fifth of the party) had joined within the past year and knew little of bolshevism or socialism. But the leadership of the Russian Federation, ambitious for power, encouraged this illusion, quoted and misquoted Lenin from the Russian, and acted as the papal delegates of bolshevism. The strength of the left was concentrated in the foreign-language federations, in Michigan and Ohio (whose leaders were Charles Ruthenberg and Alfred Wagenknecht) and in New York, which now contained the bulk of party membership. Except for Ruthenberg, the leadership of the new opposition were almost completely new to the Socialist Party and virtually unknown. In a real sense, the left wing was a Young Turk movement. Programmatically, there was at this time little difference between the wings. But the left was in the position of asserting: "You were wrong before, it is now our turn." If the old guard had been willing to share power, the shape of the split would have been different.

In February 1919 a formal left-wing caucus was started in New York to capture power in the party. The left-wingers held a convention, quite aptly, in the Odd Fellows Hall, on St. Mark's Place in New York's east side, and adopted a document which came to be known as the Left Wing Manifesto. The manifesto, drafted by Louis Fraina, was written with the oracular self-consciousness of taking up where Marx's *Communist Manifesto* had left off. It reviewed the events of the past and condemned the right-wingers for "sausage socialism." The revolutionary sentiment among American workers, it proclaimed, was growing. "The temper of the workers and soldiers, after the sacrifices they have made in the war, is such that they will not endure the reactionary labor conditions so openly advocated by the master class. A series of labor struggles is bound to follow—indeed, is beginning now. Shall the Socialist Party continue to feed the workers with social reform legislation at this critical period? Shall it approach the whole question from the standpoint of votes and the election of representatives to the legislatures? Shall it emphasize the consumers' point of view, when Socialist principles teach that the worker is robbed at the point of production? . . ." The manifesto then turned to the immediate tasks ahead. It called upon the American people to organize Workmen's Councils as the instrument for the seizure of power and the basis for the proletarian dictatorship, which is to replace the overthrown government; workmen's control of industry to be exercised by industrial unions or soviets; repudiation of all national debts, with provision to safeguard small investors; expropriation of banks; expropriation of the railways and the large (trust) organizations of capital; the socialization of foreign trade.[174] In addition, the manifesto called for a disciplined party structure, a press and educational institutions owned by the party, and the centralization of party propaganda to avoid private opinions. It was thus a carbon copy, slightly smudged, of Bolshevik manifestoes during the Russian Revolution.

The left-wing convention set up an executive committee to carry the campaign to other states. "With the exception of Larkin, Lindgren and myself," said Ben Gitlow, "the rest of the members of the executive committee [there were six others] were entirely unknown in the Socialist Party and had never before acted in a leading capacity in the movement."[175]

"An astounding state of affairs resulted," said a report of the old national executive committee. "Veterans and pioneers of the movement, who had served the party in many ways for ten, twenty and thirty years, suddenly found they had no rights within the party but to pay dues. Members of the Left Wing, some of them never having joined the Socialist Party, some of them having only a card of the Left Wing, some of them being members only a few weeks, usurped all rights within the party organization."[176]

Although the left-wing leaders were relatively unknown, they had the new magic of Lenin's name behind them. A powerful factor was Lenin's letter to the American workers which was published in *Class Struggle* in December 1918, and a month later in the *Liberator*, the intellectual magazine which had replaced the *Masses*.[177] No revolution, said Lenin, ever had a smooth and assured course. Those who cried out against the horror of the Russian civil war were "sickly sentimentalists." The class struggle in revolutionary situations always provoked counterreaction and terror, and limitations of democracy were the necessary midwives of the revolution. Lenin appealed to the revolutionary traditions of America including the "war of liberation" against the English and the Civil War. Denying any absolute standards of morality and using a *tu quoque* argument, Lenin argued that the bourgeoisie had used terror in its own struggles against the feudal elements, citing 1649 and 1793. Yes, said Lenin, the revolution made mistakes. It had not suddenly turned men into saints, but the 'dead, rotting, polluted, decayed' corpse of the bourgeoisie

[174] Reprinted in *Revolutionary Radicalism, Report of the Joint Legislative Committee Investigating Seditious Activities Filed April 24, 1920, in the Senate of the State of New York*, i, pp. 706-14. This report, in four volumes, generally known as the Lusk Report (and hereafter so cited) after the committee's chairman, is an invaluable source book of socialist and communist documents during the years of World War I.

[175] Benjamin Gitlow, *I Confess* (New York, 1940), p. 27.

[176] Quoted in Fine, *op.cit.*, p. 345.

[177] Reprinted as a pamphlet by International Publishers, New York, in 1934.

could not be put into a coffin without mistakes. Only through mistakes can one learn. The letter was widely cited and used to good effect.

In March 1919 the Third International was born. Under the slogan of "Back to Marx," it adopted the name Communist, as Marx had, to distinguish itself from the social democracy. Rosa Luxemburg, who headed the German *Spartakusbund*, the left wing of German socialism, felt that the creation of the International was premature. She argued presciently that if an International came into existence when the revolutionary movement in the West was still weak, it would mean that the center of gravity of world communism would be Moscow, not Berlin. Hence, the German delegate, Hugo Eberlein, went to Moscow in March 1919 with instructions to oppose the founding of the International. Thus in the founding document of the Communist International, the signature of Germany, key to the advance of communism in Europe, is missing.[178]

One of the first acts of the new International was to order splits in every Socialist Party in the world. The revolution is sweeping Europe, declared the Comintern, and a resolute left-wing movement is necessary to speed it along. In the United States the left wing grew steadily. It seemed as if it would shortly win control of the party. No convention had been held since April 1917 in order to avoid exposing party members to persecution and imprisonment. As a result, the old Hillquit-Berger leadership was still in control. In the spring of 1919 a national referendum was held to elect new officers. The left wing won twelve of the fifteen seats on the national executive committee. For the now crucial post of international delegate, John Reed defeated Victor Berger, and for the equally important post of international secretary, the correspondent with other socialist parties, Kate Richards O'Hare beat Morris Hillquit. Quite coolly, however, the old administration charged election fraud, set aside the vote, and appointed a committee to investigate the election and bring in a report to the party convention in August. It then proceeded systematically to eliminate the left wing. In May, the old national executive committee suspended the seven left-wing foreign-language federations (Hungarian, Lettish, Lithuanian, Polish, Russian, South Slavic, and Ukrainian) thus sloughing off one-third of the party membership. It expelled outright the Michigan state organization for rejecting parliamentary methods. A month later, it eliminated the Massachusetts state body, and in August expelled the Ohio organization. When the Socialist Party convention opened on August 30, 1919, the right wing had saved its hold on the party name and machinery, but had lost two-thirds of the membership. It found official rationalizations for its actions, but the real reason for this summary procedure was the feeling of the old leaders that

[178] E. H. Carr, *Studies in Revolution* (London, 1950), p. 184.

no group of intruders, merely by virtue of signing a party card, was going to take over a party they had spent their lives in building.

The left wing had acted, meanwhile, to consolidate its forces. A national conference was called in New York on June 21. But immediately the fatal amoebic process took hold, and the conference split. The sessions opened while the Lusk committee raids were going on, and the conference was forced to move from one hall to another and conduct its meetings in semisecrecy, thus adding to the heavy conspiratorial feeling which inspired the delegates. Although the conference had been called to map plans for the capture of the Socialist Party, an impatient and substantial minority led by Harry Waton pressed for the immediate formation of a communist party. The Russian Federation and the other Slavic groups also favored this step. Most of the American-branch delegates opposed the step and won. Waton shouted "Betrayers!" and bolted to set up the first communist splinter group in the United States.[179] The left wing set up a national council (including Charles Ruthenberg, Louis Fraina, James Larkin, Ben Gitlow, and Bertram D. Wolfe), but the Russian Federation refused membership, and in June, together with the Michigan state organization, issued a call for a convention in Chicago on September 1, 1919, for the purpose of organizing a communist party. In August the majority of the national council, including Fraina, Ruthenberg, and Wolfe, decided that capturing the Socialist Party was impossible, and joined the Russian Federation in sponsoring a communist party. Gitlow and Reed, however, headed a faction which held the fort on the old tactic.[180]

The Socialist Party convention opened in Chicago on August 30, 1919. Various delegates from the Gitlow-Reed faction sought entry but were "screened" by convention manager Julius Gerber and bounced with the help of the Chicago police. When the convention opened, the old leadership elected Seymour Stedman as chairman over Joseph Coldwell, 88 to 37. Thereupon the minority bolted, and with the clamoring Gitlow-Reed faction moved downstairs and formed the Communist Labor Party. Two days after the Socialist convention opened, and a day after the Communist Labor Party was formed, the delegates from the Slavic Federation, the Michigan state organization, and the Fraina-Ruthenberg group met and organized the Communist Party of America, the subsequent history of which will be traced later in this chapter.

However, the Socialist Party was still not out of the factional woods.

---

[179] In later years, Waton renounced Marxism and organized the Spinoza Institute of America, which during the thirties and forties met regularly in the Labor Temple on New York's Fourteenth Street, where Waton conducted classes and regularly debated with members of various left-wing splinter groups.

[180] See *The American Labor Year Book*, 1919-1920, Pt. 6, pp. 414-17.

The major problem at the 1919 convention was the relationship of the Socialist Party to the international socialist movement. Some efforts had started at Berne to revive the war-torn Second International. In the spring the party had sent James Oneal abroad to observe, and his recommendations of May 7, 1919, rejected affiliation with the Berne conference because it admitted the German "social patriots."[181] At the convention, after the left wing was completely ousted, the majority resolution opposed immediate endorsement of the Third International and called for a new, all-inclusive world body. A minority resolution called for immediate adherence to the Comintern. Both sides agreed, however, that "no party which participates in a government coalition with parties of the bourgeoisie shall be invited." Such was the temper of the "reformist" Socialist Party in 1919! Both resolutions were submitted to referendum, but the *minority* resolution carried by a vote of 3,457 to 1,444—a striking indication of the calamitous decline in party membership and the revolutionary mood of the socialist remnant. Shortly afterward the Socialist Party's application for affiliation was forwarded to Moscow. In other actions as well, the party showed that it was moving left. For the first time the Socialist Party took a stand that it had never dared to take before and unqualifiedly endorsed industrial unionism. Hillquit, who was unable to attend, went even further and in tones reminiscent of the early Debs called for amalgamation of the industrial bodies into one working-class union.

By 1920, the new found revolutionary temper of the party was cooling somewhat. In the spring of 1920 the five socialist assemblymen had been expelled from the state legislature because their pledges of party membership were deemed incompatible with their oaths of office. Hillquit moved, therefore, to rewrite the party bylaws and program.[182] As a result, a new minority led by Alexander Trachtenberg and Benjamin Glassberg, both Rand School teachers, left the party, charging that Hillquit was kowtowing to "Albany" and was seeking to "paint the Socialist Party as a nice, respectable, goody-goody affair. . . ."[183]

On the issue of affiliation with the Comintern, the majority weaseled. It voted to affiliate with the Third International provided "no formula such as 'The Dictatorship of the Proletariat in the form of Soviets' or any other special formula for the attainment of the Socialist commonwealth be imposed . . . as condition of affiliation. . . ." A revolutionary minority,

[181] Lusk Report, *op.cit.*, i, pp. 531-36.
[182] A section calling for the expulsion of a party member in public office who voted for war appropriations was dropped. A proviso requiring members of party committees to be citizens was passed. Two provisions of the St. Louis war program, one calling for resistance to conscription and the other calling for repudiation of the war debts, were also dropped.
[183] Lusk Report, *op.cit.*, ii, p. 1778.

led by J. Louis Engdahl, which had not bolted, again called for immediate adherence to the Third International. A third resolution, by Berger, opposed any international organization for the time being. Both the majority (Hillquit) and the minority resolutions were again submitted to a referendum; this time the majority carried by the slim vote of 1,339 to 1,301. The Socialist Party also retreated from the fiery statements of 1919. It redefined its aims as seeking ". . . to secure a majority in Congress . . . to attain its end and by orderly constitutional methods, so long as the ballot box . . . [is] maintained." Debs was once more nominated for the presidency even though—in jail and far removed from the scene—he was unable to campaign. He had always maintained his affiliation with the party.

In August of 1920, the Comintern once and for all settled the issue of Socialist Party affiliation. It issued twenty-one points which it demanded that each party obey as a condition of affiliation. The effect of these conditions was to tie securely each national party to Moscow's orders. The Communist International, said Zinoviev, was not a hotel where each member party could pick and choose its course.[184]

In November 1920 the Socialist Party application was rejected. The minority Engdahl-Kruse group then bolted. A month later the Finnish Federation withdrew.

By the quixotic whim of political fate, at a time when the flame of American socialism was guttering, Debs polled 919,799 votes, the highest total of votes in the two decades of American socialism. There was no money and there was little campaigning. But it was a personal vote, a gesture of homage to a gallant individual, a protest against the inept Democratic and Republican choices, and a protest against the government's brutal repressions of 1919. Although Debs did not follow the party quarrels closely, he reacted sharply to the twenty-one points. "The Mos-

[184] Among the twenty-one conditions were these: (1) all propaganda to be of Communist character, and the party press to be centralized under the control of the Central Committee; (2) removal of all "reformist" and "centrist" elements; (3) creation of a parallel underground apparatus and preparation for immediate revolution—"In nearly every country in Europe and America the class struggle is entering upon the phase of civil war. In such circumstances the Communists have no confidence in bourgeois legality"; (7) the repudiation of [and here the Comintern was specific] Turati, Kautsky, Hilferding, Hillquit, Longuet, MacDonald, Modigliani [It is interesting to note that except for the Italians, these men were not reformists, but the representatives of orthodox Marxism and its recognized interpreters. These men, not the reformists, were the ones Moscow feared.]; (12) acceptance of the principle of democratic centralism; (16) all resolutions of the Comintern to be binding on the constituent parties; (17) adoption of the name Communist.

When Zinoviev was asked what he would do if one of the center socialist parties (particularly the Hilferding group in Germany, which was wavering) accepted the twenty-one conditions, he replied, "We would find a twenty-second." See Ruth Fischer, *Stalin and German Communism* (Cambridge, Mass., 1948), pp. 141-43.

cow program wants to commit us," he said, "to a policy of armed insurrection. . . . [It is] ridiculous, arbitrary and autocratic."[185] In other ways, too, Debs reacted against the Bolsheviks. Emotionally sympathetic to their revolution, he was critical of its methods and recoiled from its ruthlessness. Although the communists today seek to canonize Debs, he expressed himself from the beginning against the continued use of terror by the Bolsheviks. He was angered at what he thought was the unnecessary murder of the Tsar, and when in June 1922 the socialist revolutionaries were put on trial, he cabled to Moscow a strong protest against their possible execution or "the unjust denial of their liberty."[186]

By 1921, the Socialist Party had almost turned its back on communism. The Jewish and Bohemian federations had left. The last adherents of the committee for the Third International had also gone. At the June convention, for the first time in its history, the party lifted its ban on cooperation with other radical and liberal groups. It now talked of a labor party in which it would find a place, and voted to join the Conference for Progressive Political Action. There was, however, little left. On paper the Socialist Party claimed 10,000 members; it was a paper membership.

There is a simple human tendency to try to read the present backwards into the past. For that reason, and because the communists shrilly cried reformism, there is a tendency among historians to obscure the fact that the Socialist Party in the period from 1919 to 1921, purged as it was of the communists, had in fact succumbed to the Bolshevik aberration, and that Hillquit, the arch-symbol of the "right," had come out vigorously as favoring revolutionary action. Nor was this wholly rhetorical. Hillquit prided himself on being an orthodox Marxist, in this respect following Kautsky, and was in those years a believer in the possible necessity of force in defending a socialist revolution against the capitalist class. Following the 1919 split, Hillquit wrote in the *Call* on September 22, 1919: "The division was not brought about by differences on vital questions of principles. It arose over disputes on methods and policy, and even within that limited sphere it was largely one of emphasis rather than fundamentals."[187] Hillquit's differences with the left lay primarily in his estimate of American conditions and his objection to the mechanical and slavish copying of bolshevism's illegal work, which he felt unnecessary in the United States. In his analysis of the failure of the Second International he applied an economic determinist analysis and concluded: "It was the economic organization of the European workers, and the pressure of their

[185] James Oneal, *American Communism* (New York, 1927), p. 104.
[186] David Karsner, *Talks with Debs in Terre Haute* (New York, 1922), pp. 171-73.
[187] Lusk Report, *op.cit.*, I, p. 557.

immediate economic interests (as understood by them) that broke the solidarity of the Socialist International . . . not parliamentarism. . . ." And, in an analysis which reflects both Lenin and De Leon, he continued: "The fundamental weakness of the organized labor movement has been that it was a movement of a class within a class, a movement for the benefit of the better-situated strata of labor—the skilled workers. . . . They had certain 'vested interests' in the capitalist regimes of their respective countries." Such a condition creates, he said, craft rather than class solidarity and deflects the worker from the ultimate goal to concern with immediate benefits. "In such conditions, the parliamentary activities of labor's political representatives cannot but reflect the narrow economic policies of their constituents." Turning to the present, he said, "In countries like Germany, in which the struggle for mastery lies between two divisions of the Socialist movement, one [the independent socialists, led by Haase, Dittmann, and Hilferding] class-conscious and the other opportunist [led by Ebert and Scheidemann], one radical and the other temporizing, the support of the Socialist International must . . . go to the former."[188]

Hillquit later gave these ideas theoretical expression in a remarkable little book called *From Marx to Lenin*, published in New York in 1921. Although criticizing the Communist International because "it is essentially Russian in structure, concept and program," Hillquit defended the idea of the dictatorship of the proletariat and of soviets, which he regarded merely as "occupational representation." "The Dictatorship of the Proletariat contrary to widespread popular assumption is not the antithesis of Democracy. In the Marxian view the two institutions are by no means incompatible. . . . it is frankly a limited form of democracy but it is a higher form than the democracy of the bourgeoisie because it means the actual rule of the majority over the minority while the latter represents the rule of a minority over the majority."[189] Thus, the socialist picture from 1917 to 1921 is not a simple one of "left" vs. "right" but a complete shift of the *entire* socialist movement to a frame of reference completely outside the structure of American life. By opposing World War I (I am not passing judgment but analyzing consequences) the Socialist Party cut itself off from the labor movement and created a widespread distrust of itself among the American people. In its rush to embrace a policy which bordered on adventurism, the party isolated itself completely from the main streams of American political life. When, in 1921, it had come back to even keel, it was by then a broken shell.

[188] The New York *Call*, May 21, 1919; quoted in Lusk Report, *op.cit.*, I, pp. 524-30.
[189] Morris Hillquit, *From Marx to Lenin* (New York, 1921), pp. 57, 59.

IX. *The Melancholy Intermezzo*

Nineteen-nineteen—for one brief moment the revolution flared, like a pillar of fire, and then guttered, leaving the American radical movement sitting among the gray, dry ashes. Nineteen-nineteen—almost every issue of the *Nation*, the *New Republic*, and the *Dial* carried articles with "revolution" in their titles. The specter that haunted Europe for sixty years was no longer distant but immediately overhead. It seemed, too, that America might have to face the same ghost. The war had produced a set of social tensions that could not be released gently. The uprooting of hundreds of thousands of persons, the patriotic sentiments that had been whipped to a high frenzy, all churned American society into an emotional jag which sought relief in violence or vicarious outlets.

The measure of recognition that labor achieved during the war evaporated quickly. The cost of living was soaring and wages lagging. Unemployment was rising and employers becoming more demanding. The result was an eruption of mass strikes on a scale never before seen in American society. Four days after the armistice, the Amalgamated Clothing Workers called a general strike which sent 50,000 tailors into the streets of New York. In January 1919 the city's longshoremen and harbor workers called a general strike that stopped all harbor traffic. The next month the entire labor movement of Seattle walked out in a general strike shutting the city down tight for five days: street cars stopped running; theaters and barber shops closed; labor guards patroled the streets; garbage wagons and funeral cars could proceed only with permits from the strike committee—it was a vignette of the Paris Commune. Over the border in Winnipeg a general strike was smashed by government forces with the deportation of the strike leaders. And across the United States there spread a demand for an eight-hour day which brought a general strike to strife-torn Lawrence, Massachusetts. The fever spread rapidly: New England telephone workers, New York actors, printing pressmen, longshoremen, railway shopmen and switchmen, in Boston even the policemen, the "armed minions" of the capitalist state, walked out, frightening the town and bringing Governor Calvin Coolidge in quickly with the state troops to break the strike. Some 367,000 workers challenged United States Steel, the great behemoth of American industry, in a strike which ran four months before being crushed by the iron hand of Judge Elbert Gary. A threat by John L. Lewis to call a national coal strike was halted only when a federal court injunction tied up strike benefit payments, and when Woodrow Wilson had denounced the proposal. More than 4,160,000 workers were out on strike that year. It seemed as if the revolution were coming.[190]

[190] J. B. S. Hardman, "Postscript to Ten Years of Labor Movement," *American Labor Dynamics* (New York, 1928), pp. 9-14.

Nineteen-nineteen was also a year of reaction. Woodrow Wilson's attorney general, A. Mitchell Palmer, led the pack in a series of "Red Raids" to exorcise the revolutionary threat. Palmer warned that 60,000 subversive radicals were loose in the country, and obtained 6,000 warrants for the arrest of dangerous aliens. On January 2, 1920, Palmer's men swooped down and in simultaneous raids in thirty-three cities netted 2,500 suspected radicals. In many cases, individuals were held incommunicado, persons were picked up without warrants, agents-provocateurs infiltrated radical sects and prodded the groups to violence. In New York, the five socialist assemblymen were ousted from Albany. In all, four thousand persons were arrested, one thousand ordered deported. Throughout the land, roving bands of vigilantes and ex-servicemen added to the hysteria by raiding I.W.W. headquarters, foreign-language clubs, etc., and beating up anyone found there. Xenophobia was rampant and found endorsement in a magazine article by the new vice-president, Calvin Coolidge. The hysteria against foreigners boiled up so that no one considered it odd that two Italian anarchists, Nicola Sacco and Bartolomeo Vanzetti, were arrested in May 1920 and charged with murder during an ordinary payroll robbery.

The outrages mounted so high that in the same month a group of lawyers headed by Charles Evans Hughes issued a report on the illegal practices of the U.S. Department of Justice stating: "We cannot afford to ignore the indications that, perhaps to an extent unparalleled in our history, the essentials of liberty are being disregarded. . . . [We know of] . . . violations of personal rights which savor of the worst practices of tyranny."[191]

In this atmosphere American industry launched its union-busting campaign under the slogan of the American Plan. By the autumn of 1920 the country was covered with a network of open-shop organizations. Fifty open-shop associations were active in New York State alone. In every industry the drive was carried on. By 1923 unionism had less than 3,620,000 members, as compared to more than 5,000,000 in 1920.[192]

Nineteen-nineteen was also the year that labor took a plunge into national independent political action. The impulses behind this move were varied. Many socialist trade unionists, forced out of the Socialist Party by the left wing, were looking for new paths; the railroad brotherhoods, who had fared well when the government took over the roads during the war, endorsed the Plumb Plan for government ownership, and sought to implement this move through political action; other unions, in reaction

[191] Chief Justice Charles Evans Hughes, *Two Addresses Delivered before the Alumni of the Harvard Law School*, Cambridge, June 21, 1920; cited in G. Louis Joughin and Edmund M. Morgan, *The Legacy of Sacco and Vanzetti* (New York, 1948), p. 211.
[192] Leo Wolman, *Ebb and Flow in Trade Unionism* (New York, 1936), p. 26.

to the events of 1919, endorsed public ownership of basic industries as a desirable goal. And, as if in prevision of what an alert labor movement could do, the solid success of the farmers' movements raised hopes that a *native* political appeal would enlist the voters where the socialists had failed. In Chicago, long the home of independent parties (one had been formed in 1851), the American Federation of Labor took the lead and organized the Labor Party of Cook County. In April 1919 it polled a sizable 50,000 votes for John Fitzpatrick, local A.F.L. head, for mayor. Satisfied with this showing, Fitzpatrick continued to take the initiative and in November 1919 called a national conference in Chicago out of which emerged the American Labor Party. Though new born, the party felt ready to enter the 1920 presidential campaign and named a ticket headed by Max Hayes, the veteran socialist leader who had left the Socialist Party after Ruthenberg had captured the Ohio movement, and Duncan MacDonald, head of the Illinois Federation of Labor, a miner and also a former Socialist Party member. In July 1920 the new Labor Party merged with the Committee of Forty-Eight, a group of liberals and ex-Bull Moosers headed by Amos Pinchot, and created instead the Farmer-Labor Party. This new coalition nominated for president a lawyer of Utah, Parley Christensen (one of the forty-eighters), and Max Hayes for vice-president. The Socialist Party refused to consider a joint slate and nominated Debs. Although the Farmer-Labor Party started from scratch and with a set of political unknowns, it managed to roll up a creditable 300,000 votes. The following year it won the official endorsement of the United Mine Workers. In 1922, seeking to broaden its base, the Farmer-Labor Party sent out an appeal to labor unions and leftist political parties to join. The socialists refused, but the communists, reversing their sectarian tactics, set out to capture the new party. When the convention opened on July 3, 1923, the genuine farmer-labor delegates found themselves outnumbered by a flood of disguised communist delegates. It was the first demonstration of the successful use of the front technique. A motley array of organizations claiming to represent workers sought credentials: sports clubs, workers' choral societies, vegetarian outfits, etc. (Sample: The Lithuanian Workers Vegetarian and Chorale Singing Society.) Fitzpatrick repudiated the conference, but the communists took over and built the first of its many "Potemkin Village" fronts, naming this one the Federated Farmer-Labor Party. The net effect of this Pyrrhic victory, however, was to send a chastened and bitter Fitzpatrick back to the Gompers fold and to destroy the tolerance of the Chicago Federation of Labor for the communists.

Meanwhile, the Minnesota Farmer-Labor Party, proceeding on its own, sought to push national independent political action. In June 1924 it called a national conference to launch a national Farmer-Labor Party. Again the communist cohorts arrived in depth and captured the party; the genuine farmer-laborites withdrew in dismay.

The large national unions, meanwhile, had kept aloof from the political efforts centering in Chicago and Minnesota. A number of them, however, favored coordinated political action on a national scale, and in February 1922, on the initiative of the railway brotherhoods, set up the Conference for Progressive Political Action (C.P.P.A.). The garment workers joined, and other unions endorsed the conference. The socialists, who had remained aloof from previous attempts, now expressed their interest. The basic idea of the C.P.P.A., however, was to follow the tactics of the North Dakota Non-Partisan League and nominate reliable candidates on old-party tickets. It would name labor candidates only when circumstances made it impossible to capture an old-party nomination. From the start the socialists sought to turn the movement into a full-fledged labor party. A motion to that end was defeated in December 1922 by the close vote of 64 to 52. Clashes between the socialists and the laborites continued, and an especially sharp conflict on the issue arose in New York in 1923. In the normal course of such events the friction among the incompatible groups would have been sufficient to disrupt the conference. But two incidents after 1922 served to hold the movement together. One was the spectacular postwar success of the British Labour Party in its replacement of Lloyd George's rapidly fading Liberal Party, a success giving rise to the hope that a repetition was possible here. The second was the Harding Ohio-gang scandals, in which William G. McAdoo, "labor's friend," was "smeared with oil." It is likely that if the Democrats had nominated McAdoo, there would have been no third-party campaign in 1924. But when the G.O.P. named Calvin Coolidge and the Democrats nominated a safe and respectable Wall Street lawyer, John W. Davis, the unions felt no alternative was possible. La Follette, aging and eager to run, clinched the decision.

If the socialists had hoped that the La Follette campaign would open the way to a firmly based Labor Party, the election events showed, as Hillquit put it, that the campaign was only an "intermezzo." The socialists and the farmer-labor groups came to the 1924 convention fully prepared to organize a permanent new party. But La Follette was against one; so were the large unions. La Follette was nominated beforehand in order to avoid the formal issue from the floor and the embarrassing attempt to organize a third party. Hillquit challenged the procedure, but the free railroad passes of the members of the Brotherhood accounted for the good attendance and the socialists were beaten.[193] Hillquit then pleaded that the progressives nominate supporting tickets in various states, pointing out that only on that basis could an effective campaign be carried on.

[193] David McKay, *The Progressive Movement of 1924* (New York, 1947), p. 119.

But even this motion was defeated. The unions endorsed La Follette but remained nonpartisan in the congressional and local campaigns. In New York the Socialist Party put La Follette at the head of its ticket and ran Norman Thomas for governor. But Thomas got only traditional socialist union support because Al Smith was running against Theodore Roosevelt, Jr., and the unions feared to jeopardize his chances. Hillquit's prediction that the lack of supporting tickets would immobilize the La Follette campaign in many states proved true. But the unions were caught in the "practical" dilemma and could find no way out. Gompers and the American Federation of Labor endorsed La Follette, the first such act in their history, even though they warned that they were not supporting any third party, only the man. Although officially supported by the American Federation of Labor, the moral and financial support from the organization was small, and it dwindled to nothing by election day. Some unions bolted. The pressmen, led by George Berry, supported Davis. Hutcheson of the carpenters and Lewis of the miners supported Coolidge.

The communist-dominated Farmer-Labor Party nominated Duncan MacDonald and William Bouck, and then sought to make a deal with the C.P.P.A. for a common ticket. However, neither La Follette nor any of the unions would have anything to do with the farmer-laborites. Suddenly, on Moscow's order, the communists reversed their position, dumped the bewildered MacDonald and Bouck, abandoned their dummy organization, and nominated William Z. Foster and Benjamin Gitlow on the Workers Party ticket.

In the election La Follette polled a disappointing 4,826,471 votes, or approximately 17 per cent of the total. In the apathetic nation only half the eligible voters had turned out to vote. La Follette had carried Wisconsin, run well in North Dakota, and had carried the city of Cleveland, but little else. His strength, as one historian of the campaign analyzes it, was drawn largely from the farmers (to the tune of 2,530,000 votes). Of the remainder, a million votes had been contributed by the socialists and a million came from labor.[194] Officially, La Follette was credited with 3,797,974 votes from the Progressive Party, 858,264 from the socialists, and 170,233 from farmer-laborites.

When the C.P.P.A. met in February 1925 it was a defeated and dispirited organization. The socialists pressed for the continuance of the movement, but the unions opposed any new third-party venture and the conference was liquidated. "Time and common cause," writes McKay, "would never quite overcome this basic weakness in the progressive movement. The labor men always suspected the Socialists; the latter, in turn, reciprocated the distrust."[195]

An era was drawing to a close. One year after the campaign, La Follette

[194] *Ibid.*, p. 221.   [195] *Ibid.*, p. 73.

was dead. A year later Debs passed away. The critics were writing off the Socialist Party as well. In *Current History* for June 1924 David Karsner wrote of "The Passing of the Socialist Party," while two years later in the same magazine William J. Ghent wrote the party's epitaph.[196] The Socialist Party, he argued, was the victim of the nationalism of the war and the lessened interest in social progress that came in the twenties. In 1928 the vote of 267,835 for Norman Thomas seemed to confirm the gloomy predictions; it was the lowest vote the party had received since 1900. Socialism was at ebb tide.

X. *The Caligari World of Underground Communism*

If in 1919 the United States had a whiff of class warfare, to the communists this whiff was a heady potion. To them it was the wind that heralded the apocalypse. "Workers, the United States seems to be on the verge of a revolutionary crisis. The workers, through their mass strikes, are challenging the State. . . . Out of these mass industrial struggles must issue the means and the inspiration for the conquest of power by the workers. BOYCOTT THE ELECTIONS," declared the *Communist World*, the organ of the new Communist Party, in its first issue on November 1, 1919.[197]

With "victory" so near on the horizon, it was almost inevitable that the communist movement would split into innumerable sects, each claiming to possess the political formula for victory and denouncing others as an enemy greater than the capitalist class—for the competitor could only "mislead" the ready-to-be converted and so take them down the political primrose path.[198]

In September of 1919 two communist parties opened their conventions in Chicago. The one, calling itself the Communist Party, opened its sessions at the "Smolny."[199] No sooner was Louis Fraina elected chairman

---

[196] W. J. Ghent, "The Collapse of Socialism in the United States," *Current History*, May 1926, pp. 242-46.

[197] Lusk Report, *op.cit.*, p. 758.

[198] The sociology of sects has rarely been explored. We know that sects arise most frequently in periods of disorganization when the crust of convention has cracked, and cosmic and apocalyptic answers find more ready acceptance. In such periods, also, there is a tendency for the sects to divide and become two, typically more bitter toward each other than toward the "world" which they formerly united in opposing. The religious experiences also suggest the analogy that in the moments before salvation, or ecstasy, one must achieve *purity*, hence such rituals as absolution, purification baths, etc. The literature on the Hellenistic, Oriental, and Christian mystery sects is vast, beginning with the fount, Sir James Frazer's *Golden Bough*. For a formal sociological analysis see Georg Simmel, "The Secret and the Secret Societies," in *The Sociology of Georg Simmel* (tr. and ed. by Kurt H. Wolff; Glencoe, Ill., 1950), and Ellsworth Faris, "The Sect and the Sectarian," *Papers and Proceedings . . . American Sociological Society*, XXII (1927), pp. 144-58.

[199] The headquarters of the Russian Federation of the party, so named in imitation of the Bolshevik Party headquarters in Petrograd where the revolution had started.

than the convention broke into three factions. One was the Slavic bloc, another the Michigan state delegation (with which the Slavic bloc had united in June), and the third the Fraina-Ruthenberg group from the left-wing national conference. Formally the disagreements arose over phraseology and tactics. The Michigan delegates were suspicious of the Slavic bloc's phrase "mass action" in the party's declaration—fearing it meant approval of insurrection—and sought a commitment to "political action." The Ruthenberg wing wanted unity with the Gitlow-Reed communist group, but the Russians of the Slavic bloc feared they would be outvoted in a larger party. Finally Ruthenberg and the Russians reconciled their differences, and the Michigan delegates bolted to form a third communist party. The Communist Party platform called for "mass action" to destroy the bourgeois state[200] and to ensure its replacement by the dictatorship of the proletariat. The platform affirmed its purity by declaring that the party would not collaborate with the Socialist Party, Labor Party, Non-Partisan League, People's Council, Municipal Ownership League, etc., and would name candidates only for the legislature, shunning all nomination for executive offices.

The rival Communist Labor Party had its troubles, too: it had to face the damning charge of containing "centrists," i.e., unreliable petty-bourgeois elements. A small group of delegates, including Louis B. Boudin and Ludwig Lore, had refused to accept the extreme positions of bolshevism. Boudin, with a reputation as a foremost Marxian scholar, worried the Communist Labor Party leaders with his pronouncement that their program was un-Marxian and in violation of the *Communist Manifesto.* The issue was dissipated, however, when Gitlow informed Reed, who was to answer Boudin: "Don't worry, I have the Communist Manifesto with me and I have just the quotation you need to show up Boudin."[201] "Exposed" thus as "diluting" the revolutionary content of the program, Boudin fled the convention, and Bolshevik purity was maintained.

The Michigan delegates who bolted formed the Proletarian Party in June 1920 with branches in Detroit, Rochester, and Buffalo—the first communist "splinter" party in the United States. The Proletarian Party, under the leadership of John Keracher, survived down through the depression, and spurted briefly in the 1930's, principally in Detroit. It was effaced, however, when a number of its active members rose in the United Auto Workers' hierarchy and found themselves, of necessity, going along in support of the Political Action Committee and the Democratic Party.

In the winter following the conventions each of the parties exhausted its energies in attacks on the other. The Communist Party, composed in

---

[200] Interestingly enough, in revolutionary rhetoric at this time the phrase "the state" replaced the older "ruling class."

[201] Gitlow, *op.cit.*, p. 52.

the main of foreign-language groups, derided the Communist Labor Party as "desiring to be a revolutionary proletarian party without the proletariat," since nearly 60 per cent of the wage workers were of foreign birth. The Communist Labor Party declared that its opponent held a philosophy of revolutionary splitting—that is, "the more you split, the 'clearer' and stronger you become." It recalled that Nick Hourwich, the leader of the Russian Federation, had explained that "in order to have a group of uncompromising leaders competent to lead the working class when the final crisis comes, you must constantly 'split and split and split.' You must keep the organization small and constantly bring about situations within the party that will result in splits." In this way the membership would be refined so that a small group would be "clear" and thus determine who was "not clear."[202] The position, while a caricature, was a logical extension of the tactic of Zinoviev, the head of the Third International, in splitting every European socialist party and creating new "purified" parties to carry through the revolution. This logic was matched by the German communists (Spartacists), under the leadership of August Thalheimer, who refused in 1920 to support the general strike called by the German trade unions against the rightist Kapp *Putsch*, on the ground that these were both "counter-revolutionary wings."[203]

However "logical" the tactic may have been, it did have the mathematical consequence of reducing the membership of the communist parties, and scaring away thousands of others. Before the September 1 cleavage in the Socialist Party, the left wing had approximately 60,000 members (about a tenth of whom belonged to the nonforeign-language sections). After the splits, and the Department of Justice raids of November 1919, the two communist parties had less than 13,000 members.

In May 1920, following a letter from Zinoviev, the two parties met in secret convention and fused into the United Communist Party. Retreating from the flamboyant proclamations of the previous six months, the new party abandoned the idea of mass action as the means of freeing wartime political prisoners still in jail, although it declared that "the working class must be prepared for armed insurrection as the final form of mass action by which the workers shall conquer the state," and declared that the

[202] For those who worried about splits, a communist magazine was reassuring. It justified the numerous splits on the basis of a biological analogy. "The law of life in biology is division of cells and so it is the law of social science," the editor observed. "The more active divisions, the larger the great body of trained men and women at the crisis." There are those who lament that "the past year has witnessed more division than at any time in the history of the movement," he continued, but this should really not be a matter of discouragement. "Don't worry about division; rather fear the opposite," was his conclusion. See the *Western Worker*, Oakland, Calif., May 20, 1921; cited in Oneal, *op.cit.*, p. 77.

[203] Ruth Fischer, *op.cit.*, p. 126.

state was the coercive organ of the ruling class and that democracy was the empty privilege of periodically voting to confirm this rule.[204]

This "retreat" was not to the liking, however, of a substantial faction at the unity convention, which forthwith bolted and called itself the Communist Party. This faction attacked the new party as insufficiently revolutionary, as led by "adventurers and charlatans," and denounced the platform which "reeked with '*the bourgeois capitalist horror of the destruction of property and lives.*'" It denounced the United Communist Party also for considering force "*as a purely defensive measure—not as an offensive measure* for which the Communists must consciously prepare." It further mocked the new party for its lack of theoretical clarity in "the use of the term 'soviet rule under a working-class dictatorship' [which] shows a fundamental lack of understanding, [for, as everyone knows,] the Soviet Government is a form of proletarian dictatorship."[205] The bolters claimed 8,000 members, almost all of whom were of the Slavic federations, while the new United Communists had less than 3,500 members.[206] Despite the low estate of the membership of the United Communist Party, and perhaps because of its high élan, Zinoviev regarded it as the destined instrument of the revolution. He ordered the new party "immediately to establish an underground organisation even though it is possible for the Party to function legally . . . [in order to] direct revolutionary propaganda . . . and, in case of violent suppression of the legal Party organisation, [to permit] of carrying on the work."[207]

Moscow could not allow the two warring sects to continue their feud, and in 1921, under the watchful eye of a Communist International representative, a partial working unity was restored. But by 1921 the tide of world revolution had receded, and it left stranded in its backwash a number of minor sects each of which desperately sought the northwest passage—or portage—to the revolutionary seas. One of the first was the Industrial Communists, who organized in November 1919 in Terre Haute, Indiana. Their program (a garish blend of De Leon's industrial-union republic and Lenin's soviets) declared that modern society revolved around six basic industries and that the revolutionary party, in its organization, had to be a microcosmic reflection of this fact; thus the assumption of power would automatically produce industrial communism.[208]

[204] Lusk Report, *op.cit.*, II, p. 1882.
[205] Oneal, *op.cit.*, p. 91.
[206] Picayune as these doctrinal formulations may seem, they were, to the parties concerned, as serious and meaningful as that, say, of the Dunkers whose religious sect split on the issue of multiple foot-washing, one party insisting that each person should wash the feet of only one other, while their opponents contended that each should wash the feet of several, as a condition of salvation.
[207] Lusk Report, *op.cit.*, II, p. 1907.
[208] De Leon's Socialist Labor Party went through this period with its doctrinal

A year later they changed their name to the Proletarian Socialist Party, and in two years' time faded into the Rummagers' League. This group, disillusioned by party organization, became an educational society with its announced purpose to "rummage the field of history and science so as to develop the keenest intellects possible."[209] After issuing one number of its magazine, the *Rummager*, the group, to paraphrase Trotsky, was swept into the dustbin of sectarian history. By 1921 other spores emerged. These included, among others, the Committee for a Third International, headed by J. Louis Engdahl, which had left the Socialist Party in 1920; and the Workers Council, which was sympathetic to the Committee for a Third International but refused to accept the Comintern declaration that "the class struggle in almost every country in Europe and Asia is entering the phase of civil war." "By the end of 1921," summarizes Oneal, "no less than twelve communist organizations had been formed, of which eight were of a political character and intended to function as political organizations. Of these . . . seven had either died or merged."

By the end of 1921 a number of the underground communist parties had begun chafing at their burrowed existence. The United Communist Party sent up a periscope in the form of the American Labor Alliance. Shortly thereafter, the New York communists tentatively moved toward legality by forming the Workers League, which nominated Ben Gitlow for mayor, and even formulated a set of immediate demands, a step that had been repudiated two years before. Other straws were in the wind. In October, Max Eastman, the strongest intellectual supporter of the communists, attacked the underground parties for ignoring reality.

By the end of the year a number of open groups converged and in December 1921 formed the Workers Party, headed by James P. Cannon. This new party seemingly united all of the aboveground communists except the Proletarian Party. However, in February 1922 a new group, called the Workers Defense Conference of New England, emerged with a new party called the United Toilers of America. The constituent organizations (the Ukrainian, Lettish, and Polish Publishing Associations, and the Women's Progressive Alliance) made it clear that it was the creation of those underground groups of communists who believed that the organization of the Workers Party was a "betrayal" of the masses. The situation is best explained by an account of the bizarre underground maneuverings written by one of the former participants, Ben Gitlow.

"The underground Communist Party was affiliated with the Third or Communist International, but the Workers Party was not. Among the

---

purity untouched. A fastidious party by now, it scorned the Marxian illiteracy of the communists who would not learn De Leon's formulas intact and accept the Socialist Labor Party as their teacher and leader.

[209] Oneal, *op.cit.*, p. 109.

members in the movement, the underground Communist Party was known as the 'Number One' organization, while the Workers Party was the 'Number Two' organization. A large section of the underground Communist Party split away from the underground movement, feeling that the Workers Party was given too much autonomy and that its program was no more than a remote approach to the Communist program. Regarding the Workers Party as a dilution of Communist principle and a step leading toward the dissolution of the Communist movement, this group which called itself the United Toilers and was nicknamed by Lovestone the 'United Toilets,' published in its official paper, *The Workers Challenge*, edited by Harry M. Wicks, the most violent and vituperative polemics in America.[210] I should say that ninety-nine percent of the United Toilers membership came from the foreign-language federations; they were chiefly Russians, Letts, Ukrainians and Lithuanians with a handful and a sprinkling of English-speaking members.

"It soon became very clear to me that the deciding factor in the situation was Number One, the underground Communist Party, where the internal struggle was over the question of its relations with the Workers Party, or in the broader sense, its attitude toward legal public activity. On this issue Number One was divided into three main caucuses. The largest of these was the so-called Goose Caucus. . . .[211] The name 'Goose Caucus' originated in the course of a stormy debate, when William F. Dunne, exasperated by Jakira's unceasing and persistent stuttering interjected, 'Jakira, you make me sick; you cackle like a Goose,' and Amter, springing to the defense of his fellow factionalist, retorted, 'But the geese saved Rome and we shall yet save the Party,' while Lovestone, counter-attacking with ridicule, shouted back, 'All right then, from now on you're the Goose Caucus.' The name stuck.

"The Goose Caucus looked with suspicion and contempt on those members of Number Two who were not at the same time members of Number One, fought against the immediate liquidation of the underground movement, hoping in time, as soon as the changed situation in the country warranted it, to transform Number One into a legal party espousing the Communist cause.

"The chief opponents of the Geese were the Liquidators (a name bor-

[210] [Special mention should be made of the vituperative rhetoric employed by extreme revolutionary sectarians in their debate. One example from the above-named publication: "That asinine assumption of humanity and pusillanimous purveyor of putrid punk that calls himself managing editor of the official organ of the Workers Party. . . ." At one point, V. I. Lenin, no mean polemicist himself, called this left-wing communism "an infantile disorder." It was a shrewd thrust, with a psychoanalytic overtone beyond the intent of the author. D.B.]

[211] [Its leaders were L. E. Katterfeld, secretary of the party, Abraham Jakira, leader of the Russian Federation, Alfred Wagenknecht, Israel Amter, and Edward Lindgren.]

rowed from the situation in Russian Social Democracy after the revolution of 1905) who allied themselves with the non-members in Number Two, using them as political leverage for wresting control of Number One from the Geese. The Liquidators were led by Jay Lovestone, Charles E. Ruthenberg, James P. Cannon, William Z. Foster and Earl Browder.[212]

"Between these two chief contending forces were the Conciliators, who hoped to gain control by pleading unity and by holding the balance of power between the two extreme factions. While the Liquidators sought to have the Workers Party supersede the Communist Party in effect, the Conciliators recognized it as merely the legal front of Number One."[213]

The underground comedy ended finally in uproarious burlesque. In August 1922 the secret Communist Party held a convention in the woods near Bridgman, Michigan, to settle the question of legality. Three nuncios had been sent by the Comintern to guide the decisions toward open activity. Stealthily the communists converged on the wooded lakelands. Elaborate precautions against detection had been taken. The delegates traveled in small squads of two to five members, each with a captain; the routes were so laid out that the delegates would not converge in large numbers and thus arouse suspicion. Better known communists changed trains a half dozen times to throw possible shadowers off the track. Finally the squads gathered at Bridgman, a small ramshackle town of a few houses, where each stranger stuck out like a drugstore neon sign on Saturday night. The convention opened, the delegates gamboled and frolicked gaily on the lake front. And dancing with them was a Department of Justice agent with the Hollywood monicker of "K-97." When the rites had gone far enough, other agents, who had hidden in the trees, crashed the festivities and rounded up the cultists. Since it was almost as difficult to camouflage the Department of Justice watchers as it was the communists, the underground leaders heard the noise and fled. Before the hurried escape, however, all the party records, including membership lists, were buried conveniently in the presence of K-97, and later deposited in government archives.

[212] [Foster, at that time, was a member of the Workers Party, and only secretly of the underground Communist Party.]

[213] Gitlow, op.cit., pp. 132-34. From the depths of his later disillusion, Gitlow comments: "But it is really a waste of time to discuss principles in reference to this controversy, for principles played a subsidiary role; they were merely verbose rationalizations to cover up the main consideration—to gain control of the Party apparatus." The currently fashionable reduction of all political motives to a power drive does violence both to the complexities of human delusions and the peculiar hold of doctrinal pieties among men whose lives are caught up in compulsive *missions*. Such individuals may be driven to desire power, but such urges can be seen without contradiction and more meaningfully as a desire to make incarnate their own visions as well as to obtain the satisfactions of deference and respect from others. Ideological fanaticism, i.e., the conviction that only the knowing believer has the absolute key to the truth, is a more complex phenomenon than the hedonistic impulse to power.

Before its abrupt end the convention had voted by a narrow margin to continue the Goose Caucus line for an underground existence. But the government raid had made such cloak-and-dagger masquerades a joke, and early in 1923 the communists came up for air.

The Workers Party that emerged from the bramble patch was an emaciated, hollow-chested, feral case. It claimed 20,000 members; other estimates put the figure closer to 13,000.[214] Ninety per cent of the membership, however, was in the foreign-language federations, which led a life of their own separate from the American scene. "If we were to read the nine dailies and twenty-one weeklies of the Workers' Party carefully, one would get the complete picture of all European countries, but a very incomplete picture of political life in America," wrote John Pepper, the Comintern "Rep" (i.e., representative) in 1923.[215] The caption of the article was "Be American," and in that direction the Communist Party now sought to turn. The factionalism, however, remained. It was to continue for six years.

Two major groups had coalesced in the communist movement by 1923. One was headed by William Z. Foster and his two lieutenants, Earl Browder and James P. Cannon. The other was led by Charles Ruthenberg and the Hungarian communist John Pepper; their chief aid was Jay Lovestone.

William Z. Foster, born in 1881, had achieved a reputation as a skillful trade-union organizer. At an early age he had gone to work, and by twenty, diagnosed as consumptive, he headed West. There he was drawn into socialist work, and through his activity in logging camps passed into the I.W.W. He disagreed, however, with the Wobblies' dual unionism; and a trip to Europe brought an acquaintance with the theories of the French syndicalists and the promulgation of his famous tactic of "boring from within."

Foster argued that withdrawal of the radicals from existing unions merely isolated them and that the workers would not turn from unions which ministered to their needs, even ineffectively. Hence the necessity of an organized core for joining and capturing the American Federation of Labor.[216] Foster sought to swing the Wobbly convention of 1911 to his new tactic, but failed. He then formed the Syndicalist League of North America, and later the International Trade Union Educational League, in order to train "cadres" for work in unions. Foster, however, exercised only a small though potent influence in the Chicago labor movement. During the war the militant Foster was quiet. He sold Liberty

---

[214] See Oneal, op.cit., p. 145; Gitlow, op.cit., p. 158.

[215] Oneal, op.cit., p. 145.

[216] David Saposs, Left Wing Unionism (New York, 1926), pp. 48-49; William Z. Foster, American Trade Unionism (New York, 1947), pp. 14-15.

Bonds and some left-winger accused him as well of "having sold out to the officialdom because he abstained from propagating revolutionary doctrines and even conveyed the impression of having forsaken them."[217] In 1918, however, Foster, then a general organizer for the Brotherhood of Railway Carmen, launched a skillful organizing drive among packinghouse workers, and a year later was put in charge of the great steel organizing drive and strike. The two campaigns gave him his reputation in the labor movement. In 1920, inspired by the mass strikes, Foster revived the Trade Union Educational League and dreamed of ousting the aging Gompers.

Formally, Foster never joined the communist underground; at least he always denied his membership. Actually, he was a highly-placed party member who had reported to the Bridgman convention in Michigan but had left before the raid. The Trade Union Educational League was financed by the Profintern, the Red trade-union international. Foster was one of those who vigorously fought the continuance of an underground communist movement. He felt that a legal, disciplined party concentrating on trade-union work would, within a short period of time, be able to bore from within the American Federation of Labor and win control. This was Foster's chief and unyielding goal. It was to this task that he sought to commit the communists.

Foster's chief factional opponent, the real founder of modern communism in the United States and the man who eagerly sought the laurel of "America's Lenin," was a cold, power-minded man named Charles Emil Ruthenberg. Born in Cleveland in 1882, of German-Lutheran stock, Ruthenberg had held various white-collar jobs until he joined the Socialist Party. In 1909 at the age of twenty-seven he became a socialist organizer in Cleveland, and continued as a functionary in the radical movement until his death. Conservative in dress and bearing, calm and deliberate in manner, aloof and restrained socially, he was a puzzle to the more volatile, quarrelsome, frenetic individuals that the left wing attracted. But behind this tightly controlled and faceless exterior was a romantic and conspiratorial nature and a recklessness both personal and political. During World War I, Ruthenberg stacked guns in the Socialist Party cellar and sketched plans for a socialist seizure of the city hall that never materialized. A few years later, while a communist prisoner in Sing Sing, he conceived a plan for a mass escape by having an armed band arrive during visiting hours, surround him, shoot its way out, and escape to Russia to await the outbreak of revolution here. Such was the enigma of Ruthenberg.

The issue between the two factions was the communist attitude toward the labor-party movements burgeoning in the early twenties. No clear-cut

[217] Saposs, *op.cit.*, p. 49.

lines were ever really established, for at one time or another both the factions, while warily circling around each other, momentarily adopted the other's position. But consistency is of little virtue in radical politics, not for Emerson's reason of the open mind but because in most instances the decisive element in winning power is less the nature of the political position than its timing. One step backward to gain two steps forward was Lenin's formulation.

In 1921, with the defeat of the world revolution and the economic crisis in war communism, Lenin proclaimed a one-step retreat. This was signaled in a pamphlet *Left-Wing Communism; an Infantile Disorder,* a tract aimed both at the egalitarians and syndicalists (the "workers opposition" group) in Russia who called for worker control of industry, and at the extreme elements in world communism who opposed parliamentary action. In England, Moscow directed the Communist Party to enter the British Labour Party. In the United States, John Pepper directed the infiltration into the Farmer-Labor Party movements. Thus began, in 1923, the famous tactic of the "united front," the disciplined attempt to capture and control mass groups which held progressive aims.

Foster, at first, was cautious on the Labor Party question but soon made a *volte-face* and became its most ardent advocate. He went so far, in fact, as to call for the endorsement of La Follette. Ruthenberg was quiet on this point. But the entire policy was vigorously opposed by Ludwig Lore, who headed an independent current of thought and was the leader of the German communist sections.

Into this scrabble, Moscow dropped a brick. Foster's policy was declared wrong. Lore's *position* was declared right, but Lore himself was declared an opportunist. Such decisions may make no logical sense, but are extremely intelligible in the dialectic of power struggle. The Ruthenberg-Pepper bloc had been close to the Zinoviev-Stalin faction in the Russian Communist Party (largely through Pepper's connection with Zinoviev, the chairman of the Communist International). Lore, however, judging issues on their abstract and ideological merit, had voiced some support for Trotsky's ideas. Hence he had to be punished. Foster immediately declared his allegiance to Stalin, whom he perceived as the rising force. He reversed his position, denied responsibility for the formation of the Federated Farmer-Labor Party, denounced a labor party, and sought to throw the blame on Pepper for the debacle of the 1924 campaign. Hastily, Foster also dissociated himself from Lore, who had been a member of his caucus.

Since 1923, the Foster faction had held a majority in the Communist Party. Now it set out to consolidate its power. But it did so not by appealing to the membership but by sending emissaries to Moscow. "From Moscow, the contending caucus headquarters received cables, letters, documents, instructions, advice on policy. As soon as cables, or letters, were received by the contending caucuses, the caucus machinery went into immediate operation. Secret caucus meetings were called. The mimeograph machines were flooded with ink, and caucus bulletins went out to every nook and corner of the party. Besides, the caucus spies were kept very busy during those exciting days. They shadowed their factional opponents, penetrated their caucus meetings, rifled letter boxes to get their hands on caucus documents, and at the same time, while covering their tracks as best they could, collected evidence for a case on the 'illegal' factional activities of their opponents."[218]

The only point both factions could agree upon was the witch hunt against Lore. The issue came to a head at the 1925 convention. The Foster caucus was in the majority, but fearing a *Putsch* by their opponents they barricaded the national headquarters in Chicago and guarded the presses of the *Daily Worker*. However, the issue was not to be settled in that fashion. Moscow had created a "parity" commission, with a Russian general, Gusev (or Green as he was called), as chairman. In the midst of the convention, Moscow spoke. A telegram arrived stating curtly:

"Under no circumstances must majority suppress Ruthenberg group, because it has finally become clear that the Ruthenberg group is more loyal to the Communist International and stands closer to its views. . . . Ultimatum to majority that Ruthenberg must remain as secretary and Lovestone a member of the Central Executive Committee. Ultimatum to majority, to refrain making removals, replacements and dispersions against minority. Ruthenberg group must retain co-editorship Daily Worker. . . ."[219]

Ultimatum to majority, and Foster capitulated. From that date on, though factional fights continued, they no longer had meaning in terms of the American Communist Party. The members were simply Janissaries carrying out, at the outposts, the orders from the center at Moscow. Thus, in 1925, the Russian yoke on the American Communist Party was securely fastened. Lore, of course, was expelled. In a tearful speech, he pledged his allegiance to communism and concluded, "Nothing you will do will make a reformer of me, less of a revolutionist than I am today."

In 1927, Ruthenberg died and was succeeded by Lovestone. Factional activity had become more intense, yet no longer represented any real fight for the allegiance of the party membership but only a series of heresy hunts. In 1928 James P. Cannon and Max Shachtman were expelled for supporting Trotsky's position at the sixth world congress of the Comintern. The issue was "left sectarianism," or Trotsky's position of intensifying industrialization, collectivizing the peasantry, and spurring the revolutionary currents in China and Germany. The lead against Trotsky

[218] Gitlow, *op.cit.*, p. 236. [219] *Ibid.*, p. 276.

was taken by Nikolai Bukharin, the president of the Comintern. The following year, Bukharin bit the dust. This time the crime was "right-wing deviationism," or being soft on the peasant question, opposing rapid industrialization, etc. In short, Stalin, sitting in the center of the seesaw, had cleverly shifted his weight until both his major opponents rolled off. Unfortunately for Jay Lovestone, he had sided with Bukharin *too* enthusiastically in the 1928 proceedings. Foster, seeking his opportunity, secretly wooed Stalin and got a pledge of support. It made little difference that Foster had almost no following in the American Communist Party. In the elections to the 1929 convention of the American party he had carried less than 20 per cent of the membership. On Stalin's orders, however, the rival factions were called before a commission of the Comintern, and Lovestone and Gitlow were removed from the party leadership. Fearing such a move, the two "right-wingers" had left orders with their lieutenants, Jack Stachel and Robert Minor, to seize the party property in case of an adverse decision. Secretly, however, both Stachel and Minor had sold out to Stalin, and these instructions were ignored. Gitlow and Lovestone were held in custody in Moscow while the Foster group sped back to reorganize the party. Many of the leading Lovestone followers, such as Mother Bloor and Max Bedacht, capitulated. Lovestone and Gitlow both were expelled and began the melancholy careers of heading a splinter party, calling themselves the C.P.O., Communist Party Opposition. Because Foster, however, had been *unduly* active in promoting factionalism, the wily Stalin "broke" him, too, by naming his subordinate, Earl Browder, the new general secretary of the party. After 1929 the American Communist Party was the pliant tool of Stalin. And it was in this role that it entered the fateful period of the depression.[220]

[220] In view of their subsequent history, it may be of interest to name briefly the leaders of the original factional lines in American communism and note their future careers. In 1924 the leaders of the *Foster* caucus were William Z. Foster, Earl Browder, James P. Cannon, Alexander Bittelman, William F. Dunne, Ludwig Lore, and Juliet Stuart Poyntz. Aligned against them were Charles Ruthenberg, John Pepper, Jay Lovestone, Benjamin Gitlow, Jack Stachel, and Max Bedacht.

Of the latter, Ruthenberg died a natural death. John Pepper was recalled to Moscow and disappeared in the later purges. Jay Lovestone continued as a Communist Party oppositionist until December 1940, when his group voted to dissolve and he took a prowar stand. In 1947 he became secretary of the American Federation of Labor's Free Trade Union Committee, where he directs strategy against the world-wide communist trade-union movement. Ben Gitlow, isolated and ignored for many years, turned up in the late forties as a professional anticommunist, working for various exposure groups such as the Broyles Committee of the Illinois Legislature, the American Legion, etc. Jack Stachel rose as the silent power figure in the Communist Party and was indicted in 1950 by the U.S. government as one of the eleven-man executive committee of the Communist Party. Max Bedacht was for many years executive secretary of the International Workers Order, the communist fraternal organization, and was expelled in 1946, in the post-Browder upheavals, for factionalism.

Of the Foster group, Earl Browder was from 1929 to 1945 the general secretary of

XI. *The Playboys of the Western World*

In early 1920 Warren G. Harding had called for "normalcy, not nostrums." Perhaps it was politically timely, but as a tag of the gargoylish decade to come the phrase was singularly inept. The twenties were, if anything, a period of smugness (on the part of the business community) and self-hate (on the part of the intellectuals). This was the great age of "nothing sacred" selling, and the age of derisive disdain for a mass-consumption culture.

These were the ballyhoo years. Business proclaimed the "new capitalism," and sought to prove it by selling shares of stock to its employees. The Harvard Business School established an annual advertising award, thus "conferring academic *éclat*" on the well-turned sales phrase. The Scriptures became the great source of sales aphorisms. *Moses, Persuader of Men* was the title of an inspirational pamphlet (issued by an insurance

---

the Communist Party until he was abruptly dumped when an article written by the French communist leader, Jacques Duclos, branded Browder as having swung *too* far to the "right" in his optimism regarding postwar Russian-American cooperation. Since then he has published various pamphlets attacking the Communist Party leadership and has vainly sought vindication in Moscow. With Browder's expulsion, William Z. Foster realized his long-cherished ambition of leading the American communist movement. Although named national chairman in 1945, Foster at this point was a figurehead, the real power in the party residing in the hands of Jack Stachel and various secret Comintern "Reps." James P. Cannon, expelled for Trotskyism, has remained faithful to those beliefs and today heads the Socialist Workers Party. Alexander Bittelman was for many years the commissar of the Jewish section of the Communist Party. In 1951 he was indicted under the Smith Act, and an order for deportation to Russia was pending. William F. Dunne was expelled in 1946 for arguing that the Communist Party had not gone left far enough after removing Browder. Together with Harrison George, another former editor of the *Daily Worker*, Dunne sought to form his own splinter communist group. The fate of Ludwig Lore was the most tragic of all. For many years an "independent" communist, Lore gradually became anti-Stalinist and in the late 1930's wrote a daily column for the *New York Post* which was highly critical of the Russian regime. Yet (according to the evidence of Hede Massing, the former wife of Gerhart Eisler, the Comintern "Rep" in the U.S., and herself a courier for the G.P.U.) Lore, all that time, was secretly employed as a G.P.U. agent, reporting to the Russian secret service! Lore, a romanticist, had unwillingly been expelled from the Communist Party. It has been a common tactic of the Comintern to demand of those expelled from the Communist Party that they undertake secret tasks for the G.P.U. as proof of their continued devotion. Others besides Lore have been so accused. Complete mystery still surrounds the fate of Juliet Stuart Poyntz, an associate of Lore. After her disgrace, Miss Poyntz broke all her old friendships and went underground. A few years later she completely disappeared. Carlo Tresca, the anarchist editor who himself was assassinated in 1943, made highly vocal accusations that his friend Juliet Poyntz had entered G.P.U. service and upon her attempt to break away had been spirited away to Russia and executed.

Louis Fraina, the first chairman of the Communist Party, dropped out of sight in 1920 after journeying to Moscow to take a Comintern assignment. He left the communist movement and reappeared in the United States in 1925 under the name of Lewis Corey. Today a professor of political economy at Antioch College, Corey is the author of several notable economic studies and a valiant anticommunist.

134

company, with a foreword by Dr. S. Parkes Cadman, the eminent Brooklyn minister): ". . . one of the greatest salesmen and real-estate promoters that ever lived . . . a Dominant, Fearless and Successful Personality in one of the most magnificent selling campaigns that history ever placed upon its pages." And under the sure touch of Bruce Barton (in the best-selling nonfiction title for 1925 and 1926, *The Man Nobody Knows*), Jesus was no longer a humble carpenter, but "an outdoor man and a great executive. . . . He picked up twelve men from the bottom ranks of business and forged them into an organization that conquered the world. . . . [His parables were] the most powerful advertisements of all time. . . . He would be a national advertiser today."[221] Verily, as *Fortune* said, advertising was the handwriting on the wall, the sign in the sky, and the bush that burnt regularly every night.

Standing outside the gates, the intelligentsia mocked all this in full-throated voice. Babbitt and booboisie passed into word currency. The expatriates flocked to Paris in droves: a civilized life is impossible to live in America, Harold Stearns proclaimed, and the dung and roses school flowered in Branch Cabell; the "lost generation" found a symbol in Scott Fitzgerald and its historian in John Dos Passos; Nineveh had its counterpart in Babylon (Long Island), and the lust of Caligula in the ruthless drive of the "Big Money."[222] It was a mad, careening society. It shot up to the edge of the precipice at a dizzying pace, teetered for an instant, and toppled over with a splintering crash.

By 1932 gluttony had been replaced by hunger:

Item: "CHICAGO, April 1, 1932. Five hundred school children, most with haggard faces and in tattered clothes, paraded through Chicago's down town section to the Board of Education offices to demand that the school system provide them with food."

Item: "BOSTON, June 3, 1932. Twenty-five hungry children raided a buffet lunch set up for Spanish War veterans during a Boston parade. Two automobile loads of police were called to drive them away."

Item: "NEW YORK, January 21, 1933. Several hundred jobless surrounded a restaurant just off Union Square today demanding they be fed without charge. . . . Police riot squads arrived to find the manager stabbed. . . ."[223]

By 1932 the barricades were going up all over America—if not in fact, at least in metaphor. A free-floating anxiety was diffused across America. And in the van was the free-floating intellectual. For him, there was only one perspective ahead—revolution. "I went to New York to hear the semi-scientific captains of industry say in words and facial expressions

[221] Cited by Frederick Lewis Allen, *Only Yesterday* (New York, Bantam ed.), p. 205.
[222] See Alfred Kazin, *On Native Grounds* (New York, 1942), pp. 189-363, for an account of the period.
[223] From contemporary press accounts cited in Mauritz Hallgren, *Seeds of Revolt* (New York, 1933), pp. 167, 169.

that they did not know what had happened or what was to be done about it," said Lincoln Steffens. "Nobody in the world proposes anything basic and real except the Communists."[224] And ". . . now we are all rummaging in our trunks wondering where in hell we left the liberty cap—'I know I *had* it'—and the moujik blouse, . . ." muttered F. Scott Fitzgerald.[225]

There were salient reasons for the intellectual—accepting Schumpeter's rough definition, as those "who wield the power of the spoken and written word"—to veer so quickly to the left. In America the intellectual had matured in a hothouse of moral disapproval of capitalism: America was "mechanistic"; capitalism was characterized by the "cash nexus" rather than an aristocracy of talent; capitalism was anti-heroic—"the stock exchange," writes Schumpeter, "is a poor substitute for the Holy Grail." Bourgeois norms of conduct, rationalistic, prudent, impersonal, and anti-quixotic, oppose the genteel tradition of the Western world, i.e., the code of the gentleman, the ideal of bravery, the myth of the hero, the emphasis on uniqueness. While the intellectual, seeking to transmit that tradition, takes over the aristocratic bias and contempt for the prosaic bourgeois world.[226]

Aristocratic attitudes provided humanistic goals, but no program of action. Marxism did. It had an intellectual system to order the flux of events (i.e., the "laws of history," the material roots of culture, class analysis of society, etc.), a set of powerful predictions (stunningly confirmed in the collapse of world capitalism), and a set of utopian goals. It also had, in the accents of Leninism, the heady language of power, the myth of the invincible Bolshevik hero, the apocalyptic "Kairos" of history, as well as some tangible evidence, in the walled-in enclave of Russian society, that communist planning was maintaining full employment and optimism at the moment of joblessness and fear in the West.

Yet it was not only the intellectual but the Christian moralist and declassed professional as well who found this wave of the future appealing. Teachers without students, lawyers without clients, doctors without patients, above all a student generation that feared its education would be wasted, all sought hope in going left. But in going left, they went, as Koestler later put it, east to Moscow. The world, as they saw it, was anything but gentle, and harsh measures were necessary. "Becoming a socialist right now," wrote Dos Passos in 1932, "would have just about the same effect on anybody as drinking a bottle of near-beer."[227] "I, too,

[224] Quoted in "Communism and the American Intellectuals," by Granville Hicks in *Whose Revolution?* (ed. by I. D. Talmadge; New York, 1941), pp. 81-82.
[225] "Echoes of the Jazz Age," Nov. 1931, in *The Crack-up* (New York, 1945), p. 14.
[226] See "Manners, Morals and the Novel," by Lionel Trilling in *The Liberal Imagination* (New York, 1950). Also see "The Sociology of the Intellectual," by Joseph Schumpeter, in *Capitalism, Socialism and Democracy* (New York, 1942).
[227] Quoted in Granville Hicks, *Small Town* (New York, 1946), pp. 221-22.

admire the Russian Communist leaders," wrote Edmund Wilson in 1932, "because they are men of superior brains who have triumphed over the ignorance, the stupidity and the short-sighted selfishness of the mass, who have imposed upon them better methods and ideas than they could ever have arrived at by themselves. As a writer I have a special interest in the success of the 'intellectual' kind of brains as opposed to the acquisitive kind."[228]

There was, in the excitement of the early thirties, a frosty, tingling sense, almost with cobblestone in hand and Phrygian cap on head, of history being "made." It was a bravura and romanticism that sought to gird itself in the hard angular armor of realism. Yet this mood of steely resolve was also masochistic and immolating—for the intellectual gained a deep satisfaction from vicarious identification with the bull-figures of power. The mood is most sharply reflected in a letter received by Granville Hicks in the summer of 1932. His friend wrote: "It is a bad world in which we live, and so even the revolutionary movement is anything but what (poetically and philosophically speaking) it 'ought' to be . . . from one angle, it seems nothing but grime and stink and sweat and obscene noises and the language of beasts. But surely this is what *history* is. It just is not made by gentlemen and scholars . . . by the Norman Thomases and the Devere Allens and the John Deweys. Lenin must have been (from a conceivable point of view) a dreadful man; so must John Brown, and Cromwell, and Marat, and Stenka Razin, and Mahomet, and all the others who have destroyed and built up. So will our contemporaries in the American movement be. I believe we can spare ourselves a great deal of pain and disenchantment and even worse (treachery to ourselves) if we discipline ourselves to accept proletarian and revolutionary leaders and even theorists for what they are and must be: grim fighters in about the most dreadful and desperate struggle in all history—*not* reasonable and 'critically-minded' and forbearing and infinitely far-seeing men. . . . at this stage . . . everything gives way before the terrible social conflict itself: that the power of imperialism must be fought at every turn at every moment with any weapon and without quarter; that the consciousness of the proletariat—its sense of power and its anger—must be built up by every possible device; and that, meanwhile, the kinds of things we are interested in must take their place, where they belong, out of the thickest dust and along the rim of the arena."[229]

It was a mood which lent itself easily to the justifications of deception, ruthlessness, and terror. It was an attitude toward revolution that Earl

---

[228] "The Case of the Author," in Edmund Wilson, *The American Jitters* (New York, 1932), pp. 310-11.
[229] "Communism and the American Intellectuals," by Granville Hicks, in *Whose Revolution?* p. 84.

Browder once expressed as the "omelet theory"—just as one had to break eggs to make an omelet, one had to break heads to make a revolution. So deep was this genuflection before the altar of revolution, so complete this dedication to the "historical mission of the proletariat," that in the course of the next decade a whole generation of intellectuals found themselves castrated—and gladly accepted their eunuch roles.

Between the romantic image of the communist conjured by the intellectuals and the grubby reality of the sectarian party lay a vast gulf. It is, perhaps, a striking illustration of how compelling a myth can be that the intellectuals ignored the disparity between illusion and actuality. "We did not understand the fine points of Marxist doctrine over which the party fought with the Trotskyites and other factions," recalled Granville Hicks, "and we were not interested in them. It was enough for us to believe that Marxism was in general right and that the Communist Party was in general Marxist."[230]

In 1932 the Communist Party was in the vortex of the "third period" or ultrarevolutionary phase of the party line.[231] The seven years of the "third period" are perhaps the most significant in the history of communism. These were the years of Stalin's consolidation of power and the years of the rise of Hitlerism—to which the "third period" tactics contributed in so large a measure.

The "third period" coincided with the emergence of the first Five Year Plan in Russia. Trotskyism had been defeated, and in wily fashion, Stalin now moved to adopt the "left" posture both to undercut Trotsky's support and to eliminate his erstwhile "right-wing" allies.[232] Abroad, the

[230] Ibid., p. 86.

[231] Roughly speaking, seven twists or "periods" can be distinguished in communist tactics since the formation of the Comintern in 1919. Except for the first, the motives for these changes in the party line stem from the needs of the Russian Communist Party and reflect Russian political conditions. The first period, from 1919 to 1921, was the episode of world revolution. Zinoviev boasted in the first issue of the magazine Communist International of May 1919 that "within a year . . . the whole of Europe will be Communist. And the struggle for Communism will be transferred to America, perhaps to Asia, and to other parts of the world." This was the period of insurrections in Hungary and Bavaria, of Lenin's military adventurism in the Red Army invasion of Poland, of attempted Putsche in Germany, of underground organization in the U.S.A., etc. The second period, opening in 1921 and characterized by the N.E.P. (New Economic Policy) in Russia, was a retreat from the excesses of Russian "war communism"; it accepted the stabilization of world capitalism, evinced friendliness to the British Labour Party, and flirted with farmer-labor movements in the U.S. Except for a brief "left" turn, this tactic continued until 1928, when the "third period" began. In 1935 the "Popular Front" opened, and shut with a bang in the Nazi-Soviet pact of 1939. In June 1941, following Hitler's invasion of Russia, the communists again became cooperative with the democracies, a phase that lasted until 1945 when new aggressive tactics were followed.

[232] Although the "third period" fitted exactly the mood of the depression period, it had been formulated, actually, in February 1928 at the plenary sessions of the

distinguishing feature of the "third period" was the designation as the main enemy not capitalism, or even fascism, but the socialist parties everywhere. Since fascism was the last stage of capitalist decay, it was a transient society, communist theorists declared. Thus it could be disregarded as a serious factor in the onward march of communism. The socialists, however, their rivals in the working class, had to be "exposed." Here is what the communist spokesmen said: "The Social-democrats, in order to deceive the masses, deliberately proclaim that the chief enemy of the working class is Fascism," declared D. Z. Manuilsky in 1932.[233] On the eve of Hitler's victory, the Comintern leader, S. Gusev, once the communist "Rep" in the United States, declared in the official Comintern publication: "It may seem that in Germany, at the present time, for example, the chief social bulwark of the bourgeoisie is Fascism, and that therefore we should deal the chief blows against Fascism. *This is not correct.*"[234]

This was the fatal theory of "social fascism." With the rationale, as declared by O. Piatnitsky, that *"nach Hitler kommt uns,"* the communists joined with the Nazis to destroy the German Republic. In July 1932 they helped the Nazis to paralyze Berlin in transport strikes; in the Prussian *Landtag*, the communists supported a Hitlerite motion to oust the socialist administration of Otto Braun.[235]

Although the victory of nazism shook the American intellectuals, only a few had the political sophistication to understand the enormously tragic consequence of communist policy.[236]

Communist International and formally adopted at the sixth world congress of the Communist International in the summer of 1928. "This third period," stated the resolution of the congress, "renders inevitable a new phase of imperialist wars between the imperialist nations, of wars waged by them against the U.S.S.R., or wars of national liberation against imperialism and imperialist intervention, of gigantic class struggles. Accentuating all international contradictions, accentuating the internal contradictions in the capitalist countries, unleashing colonial movements, this period inevitably leads, through the further development of the contradictions of capitalist stabilization, to the further shattering of capitalist stabilization." The communists, thus, were to adopt the revolutionary crouch and prepare to spring.

[233] D. Z. Manuilsky, *The Communist Parties and the Crisis of Capitalism*, p. 112, a pamphlet cited in George Marlen, *Stalin, Trotsky or Lenin* (New York, 1937), p. 119.

[234] S. Gusev in the *Communist International*, No. 19 (Oct. 15, 1932), p. 674; reprinted in *The Next Step, Report of Twelfth Plenum E.C.C.I.*, p. 9, a pamphlet issued by the Workers Library Publishers, New York. Emphasis added.

[235] "On the basis of our class policy we must in the new situation apply the strategy of the 'main fire' against Social Democracy *more than ever before.* . . . Nothing has changed as far as this principal orientation of ours is concerned," declared Ernst Thälmann, leader of the German Communist Party in the (British) *Labour Monthly*, Sept. 1932, pp. 586-90. For the communist theoretical exposition that fascism is the last stage of capitalism, see R. Palme Dutt, *Fascism and Social Revolution* (New York, 1934). For a detailed analysis of this period see S. William Halperin, *Germany Tried Democracy* (New York, 1946), pp. 444, 459, 508.

[236] A notable exception was Sidney Hook, who in an article, "The Theory of Social

The "third period" of American communism—the early depression years —was characterized by aggressive policies of organizing unemployment demonstrations, exacerbating strikes, promoting ex-servicemen's leagues, and even creating, in imitation of the German communists, a military arm, replete with uniforms, called "Red Front." The A.F.L. unions were labeled "social fascists" and the communists busily proceeded to organize rival or "dual" unions.[237] The new line on unionism was laid down by Stalin himself in an address before the American Commission of the Communist International.[238] In September 1929 the Trade Union Unity League was organized and proclaimed its central slogan as "class against class." One of its chief objectives was the "mass violation of all injunctions against labor."[239] In the next few years dual unions were set up in the clothing, textile, coal, restaurant, shoe, and marine industries. Except for a small but widely publicized coal strike in "Bloody Harlan," Kentucky, some small textile strikes, a number of skirmishes with police, and an unholy alliance with gangsters in the food industry,[240] the net result of five years of communist dual unionism was control of the fur industry in New York and a towering anticommunist bitterness throughout the labor movement of the country.

In the political field, "third period" communism lashed out bitterly at Roosevelt. The New Deal was a capitalist ruse to snare the workers.

Fascism," *Modern Monthly*, July 1934, pp. 342-52, spoke out against this policy. Thereafter, Hook was labeled a "Trotskyite."

[237] In the twenties, the communist policy of "boring from within" had led, particularly in the needle trades and in the mine workers, to bitter clashes with the established leadership. In 1926 the communists gained control of the New York cloakmakers' union, one of the two large divisions of the International Ladies' Garment Workers' Union, and upon the orders of the party called a strike that ran a disastrous six months before being settled on unfavorable terms. The International Union intervened, charged that $3,500,000 had been squandered, and in a bitter fight ousted the communist leadership from the union. For an account of this episode see Joel Seidman, *The Needle Trades* (New York, 1942), pp. 153-86; also David Schneider, *The Workers Party and the Trade Unions* (Baltimore, 1928), chap. 5.

In the coal-miners' union during the twenties the communists supported the efforts of John Brophy and Powers Hapgood against the high-handed and arbitrary rule of John L. Lewis. However, when the two were most sorely in need of aid, the communists, following the new dual union line, pulled out of the United Mine Workers and organized the rival National Miners Union. Foster reluctantly went along with the new policy. Saul Alinsky, an "unauthorized" biographer of Lewis, quotes Powers Hapgood as the source for saying that Foster was unhappy about the new dual union line: see Saul Alinsky, *John L. Lewis* (New York, 1949), p. 58. For a communist version of the story of the National Miners Union see Anna Rochester, *Labor and Coal* (New York, 1931). For a history of the interunion struggle see McAlister Coleman, *Men and Coal* (New York, 1946).

[238] House Committee on Un-American Activities, *Un-American Propaganda Activities* (1940), Address by Stalin, May 14, 1929, in Appendix I, p. 877.

[239] *Labor Fact Book I* (New York, 1931), pp. 136-37.

[240] For an account of these machinations see Sidney Lens, *Left, Right and Center* (Hinsdale, Ill., 1949), pp. 239-46.

Roosevelt was merely the Bruening[241] of American capitalism. The party went so far as to castigate Roosevelt as a Fascist. The chief resolution of the party's 1934 convention declared: "The 'New Deal' of Roosevelt is the aggressive effort of the bankers and trusts to find a way out of the crisis at the expense of the millions of toilers. Under cover of the most shameless demagogy, Roosevelt and the capitalists carry through drastic attacks upon the living standards of the masses, increased terrorism against the Negro masses, increased political oppression and systematic denial of existing civil rights. . . . The 'New Deal' is a program of fascization and the most intense preparations for imperialist war . . . the Roosevelt regime is not, as the liberals and the Socialist Party leaders claim, a progressive regime, but is a government serving the interests of finance capital and moving toward the fascist suppression of the workers' movement."[242] As late as February 1935, the Communist Party manifesto was headed: AGAINST THE "NEW DEAL" OF HUNGER, FASCISM AND WAR![243]

Except for its success in attracting an important section of the intellectual fringe and the student youth, the Communist Party never achieved a wide mass following in America during the depression years. Its influence in the labor movement was nil, its political strength feeble; Foster's vote for president in 1932 was only 103,151, and the party hailed as a great victory the election of a mayor in a tiny hamlet of Minnesota, the only communist mayor in American history. In 1930, at the beginning of the depression, the party claimed 8,000 members. Two years later, after bitter winters of unemployment, "Hoovervilles," hunger riots, etc., the membership reached only 12,000. Actually considerably more had enrolled, but the new recruits, particularly proletarians, found the involved dialectics, the mysterious jargon, the heavy-handed discipline, and the highly verbal disputatious atmosphere of the party such tough sledding that they bolted almost as fast as they were recruited. The *Party Organizer,* the trade journal for party functionaries, complained in 1932 that membership turnover or "fluctuation" was "as high as 75 percent. . . . In the last registration we found that only 3,000 members had been in the party as much as two years." By 1934, the Communist Party had recruited 47,000 new members; but only 12,000 stuck, bringing the membership to a total of 24,000.[244]

[241] Heinrich Bruening, the last democratic chancellor of Germany and the leader of the Centrist party.

[242] "Draft Resolution, Eighth Convention Communist Party U.S.A.," pp. 21-22, in the pamphlet *13th Plenum* which also contains "Theses and Decisions of the Thirteenth Plenum of the E.C.C.I." The pamphlet was issued by the Workers Library Publishers, New York, in March 1934.

[243] In the magazine *Communist International,* Feb. 1935.

[244] Figures cited in Eugene Lyons, *The Red Decade* (New York, 1941), p. 74.

Although communism *never* won a mass following in the United States, it did have for many years a disproportionate influence in the cultural field. At one time, from 1936 to 1939, through the fellow travelers in the publishing houses, radio, Hollywood, the magazines, and other mass media, it exercised influence on public opinion far beyond the mere number of party members.

In 1932 a sizable group of prominent literary figures publicly endorsed William Z. Foster for president. Among them were Sherwood Anderson, John Dos Passos, Edmund Wilson, Matthew Josephson, James Rorty, Sidney Howard, Sidney Hook, Newton Arvin, Granville Hicks, Erskine Caldwell, Malcolm Cowley, Langston Hughes, Robert Cantwell, and Waldo Frank[245] (none of whom are communist sympathizers today; almost all had renounced communism by 1939). It was the first time that such a respectable group of American writers espoused a communist cause. These writers were the spring tide of the flood that followed. A literary generation, depression-barred from Paris, where their expatriate elders had gone, now turned to the revolution. Out of their cavortings emerged "proletcult" and "agitprop"—two words, yet to find their way into Mencken, which signified the first "made-to-order" art in American creative life. "Proletcult," short in communist parlance for proletarian culture, and "agitprop," a similar truncation for agitation propaganda, represented a synthetic effort of middle-class intellectuals to *create* "the" worker, and to use art as a "class weapon." Within a short space of three years a new literature, theater, and dance exploded on the American scene. Jack Conroy, William Rollins, Myra Page, Clara Weatherwax, Robert Cantwell, Albert Halper, Edwin Seaver, Edward Newhouse, Grace Lumpkin, Fielding Burke, all wrote novels which ended on the triumphal note of the downtrodden exploited worker striking off his chains and joining the Communist Party. The Theatre Union produced "Sailors of Cattaro," "Stevedore," and "Black Pit," which struck the same note. The Group Theatre put on "Waiting for Lefty" and discovered Odets. Other groups sprang up—the Workers Laboratory Theatre, Theatre of Action, the Theatre Collective. The small magazines flourished—the *Anvil, Partisan Review, Left, Left Front, Dynamo, Left Review, Blast, New Theatre, New Dance.*

And yet, it all sank, almost without a trace. While literary commissar Mike Gold proclaimed "socialist realism," these cardboard cutouts moldered in the first rains.[246] The "Popular Front," which replaced the revolu-

---

[245] *Investigation of Un-American Propaganda Activities in the United States: Hearings before a Special Committee on Un-American Activities of House of Representatives on H.R. 282,* Vol. 1, Aug. 12-22, and 23, 1938, pp. 379-80.

[246] Writers like Richard Wright, James T. Farrell, John Dos Passos, and Edmund Wilson, who rebelled at using political yardsticks to measure literary values, were driven out of the communist literary world.

tionary line, threw "agitprop" into the discard; the folk song and folk art replaced "proletcult."[247] If little of substance remained from this cultural spasm, the party did learn a tangible political technique: how to *organize* members of the intelligentsia and manipulate their prestige through "front organizations." And the penetration of the cultural field and the myth of Russia as a progressive state bore fruit in the Popular Front, the flowering of communism in American life.

The serious miscalculation regarding the strength of German fascism, Hitler's popular support as demonstrated in the free Saar plebiscite, and the rise of Austrian fascism in 1934 were the hammer blows that shattered the hard "third-period" policy. In its stead came the Popular Front, a soft policy that aimed at coalitions with "bourgeois" governments, at communist support of militarization in their homelands, and at a program of "collective security" among the democratic nations against fascism.[248] The first step was Russia's entry into the League of Nations, which only a few years before a resolution of the sixth congress of the Communist International had branded as "an imperialist alliance in defense of the 'robber peace' of Versailles. . . ." The 180 degree turn was completed at the seventh world congress of the Communist International, held in

---

[247] The depression and its effect of thwarting professional and artistic ambitions does not alone explain the peculiar attraction of communism for the American intellectuals. The other major fact was the lure of the Russian utopia. Russia offered not only "planning," full employment, but most important, the myth of the "new man," purposeful, idealistic, socially rather than profit motivated, engaged in communal creative enterprise rather than in competitive conspicuous-consumption endeavors. In 1933 E. C. Lindemann, a noted social philosopher, argued that human nature is changing in Russia. "There is solidarity. . . . There are other goals which have thus far served to release energies and to promote faith." See E. C. Lindemann, "Is Human Nature Changing in Russia," *New Republic,* Mar. 8, 1933; cited in Eugene Lyons, *op.cit.,* pp. 105-6.

During these years, American intellectuals flocked to Moscow, spent a month or two on guided tours, and returned to report their "first-hand observations." Efforts of more experienced observers to point to the growing conformity in all phases of Soviet life were met either with incredulity or condescending remarks about tender-mindedness. American cultural circles almost completely ignored Max Eastman's book, *Artists in Uniform,* published in 1934, detailing the history of R.A.P.P., the Russian Association of Proletarian Writers, which dictated the propagandistic content of literary production. Eastman's book for the first time told of the suicides of the famous poets Esenin and Mayakovsky, as well as the silences of Isaac Babel and Boris Pilnyak, the most original writers in Russia. Eulogists of the Soviet state, however, such as Walter Duranty, Maurice Hindus, Anna Louise Strong, Harry F. Ward, received wide hearings.

[248] Quite coolly, the rear door to a German agreement was always left open by Soviet Russia. In May 1933, six months after Hitler had come to power, when the German communist movement had been smashed, and when a world-wide anti-Nazi boycott had been started, Russia signed a commercial agreement with the Hitler government. For a general account of Soviet-Nazi trade relations in 1933-1934 see Konrad Heiden, *Der Fuehrer* (New York, 1944), pp. 700-1.

Moscow July 25 to August 20, 1935 (the last public congress, incidentally, of the world communist movement).[249]

The opening address by Wilhelm Pieck struck the keynote. ". . . we communists will fight wholeheartedly to retain every ounce of democratic freedom in company with those who have held in some degree to the principles of bourgeois democracy . . . we are ready to defend the remnants of parliamentarianism. . . . If German fascism attacks the national independence and unity of small independent states in Europe, a war waged by the national bourgeoisie of these states will be a just war in which proletarians and communists cannot avoid taking part."

The report by Dimitrov, the hero of the Reichstag-fire trial[250] and the new secretary of the Comintern, outlined the Popular Front policy. It called for united fronts with the Social Democratic parties and the reformist trade unions, and insisted that in elections these should "participate on a common platform and with a common ticket of the anti-fascist front." In the United States, the communists dissolved the "dual unions" and began wooing the Socialist Party. For a time they energetically pushed the organization of a farmer-labor party; when this effort threatened to interfere with support for Roosevelt, however, the communists discouraged the move. In 1936, although formally nominating Earl Browder for president, the Communist Party actually supported and worked for the election of Franklin D. Roosevelt.[251]

[249] The major speeches and resolutions of this congress were published in November 1935 by Workers Library Publishers in a series of pamphlets. The major ones are: *Resolutions; Freedom, Peace and Bread*, by Wilhelm Pieck, which reviews the intervening years; *The United Front against Fascism and War*, by Georgi Dimitrov, which outlines the Popular Front tactic; *The Fight against War*, by M. Ercoli (Togliatti), which indicates the collective security tactic.

[250] Was Dimitrov actually a hero? Ruth Fischer, former general secretary of the German Communist Party, claims that Wilhelm Pieck, Communist Party chairman, and Maria Reese, a communist Reichstag deputy and intimate friend of Ernst Torgler, chief of the communist Reichstag deputation and a codefendant with Dimitrov, "independently, both told me, the same story: that before Dimitrov stood up in the courtroom to make his courageous peroration, he knew of the secret arrangement between the G.P.U. and the Gestapo that he would leave it a free man." These stories were told her, Miss Fischer says, "while the trial was running its course." See Ruth Fischer, *Stalin and German Communism* (Cambridge, Mass., 1948), pp. 308-9.

[251] "Early in 1936, the Communist Party officially participated in a national conference of Farmer-Labor Party forces, called in Chicago by the Farmer-Labor Party of Minnesota, under the leadership of the late Floyd B. Olson, governor of the state, who had played the dominant role in the rise of his party to power. That conference decided, with the concurrence of the Communists, that the situation was not ripe for the launching of a national Farmer-Labor Party, because the progressive and labor movements were inevitably going to support President Roosevelt for reelection in their overwhelming majority. The Communist Party, while retaining grave reservations toward Roosevelt, whose previous course had been at least ambiguous, agreed that the main task in 1936 was to defeat reaction at all costs, as represented by the Liberty League and the Republican Party, and that its own course should

The turn in line was quite opportune. In November 1935 the heads of eight unions in the A.F.L. formed a Committee for Industrial Organization in order to organize the country's great mass-production industries. A year or so later, when a number of these unions were suspended from the A.F.L., the C.I.O. began its vast organization drives. From 1936 to 1939, "industrial valley"—the long Ohio River and Great Lakes manufacturing areas including Pittsburgh, Buffalo, Cleveland, Toledo, Detroit, and Chicago—was a smoking swath, with the flash fires of unionization spreading in steel, auto, rubber, glass, packing, and other major industries. The C.I.O. needed experienced organizers by the hundreds, and the communist and socialist movements were the most likely sources. In addition, the communists and socialists assigned men by the score to go into factories, establish a political base, and organize caucuses within the growing unions in order to gain control.

Within two years the communists were able to control more than a dozen C.I.O. unions. Additionally, in the national office, Lee Pressman exercised enormous influence as general counsel. Len De Caux, another fellow traveler, edited the *C.I.O. News* and controlled C.I.O. publications. At their height, the communists controlled the United Electrical, Radio and Machine Workers Union, the West Coast longshoremen, maritime union, transport union, fur workers, the Mine, Mill and Smelter Union, and a host of smaller unions including cannery, state, and municipal workers, and communications, etc. In addition, the communists had sizable beachheads in the strategic auto union as well as in the packing and newspaper unions. Among union leaders who were communists or followed the line at this time were Harry Bridges, Joe Curran, Mike Quill, Reid Robinson, James Matles.

Nor were the communists in the political dilemma of the socialists in regard to support of Roosevelt and the Democratic Party candidates. In accordance with the new line, communist unionists went along easily with the C.I.O. policy of support of the New Deal, and in New York State the communists entered the American Labor Party, which had been organized in 1936.[252]

Some of the communist success in the labor field was due in no small measure to communist infiltration of New Deal administrative agencies,

---

be directed toward cementing progressive unity while maintaining its own complete independence. The Communist Party conducted its 1936 election campaign, organized at its Ninth Convention, under this general orientation, with considerable success, which won it a host of friends and sympathizers, and opened many doors to future collaboration with sections of broadest labor and progressive movements." So reported Earl Browder, "Remarks on the 20th Anniversary of C.P.U.S.A.," in the *Communist*, Sept. 1939, p. 801.

[252] For a biting but accurate account of these communist influences, see Ben Stolberg, *The Story of the CIO* (New York, 1938), pp. 145-56.

the scope of which was revealed only a dozen years later. At one time, for example, the communists exercised an influential voice in the National Labor Relations Board, where Nathan Witt was general counsel and Edwin S. Smith was one of the three-man board.[253] The decisions of the N.L.R.B.—and particularly its bias against the craft unions in the definition of a legal bargaining unit—helped the nascent C.I.O. considerably and established precedents which carry down to this day. The *extent* of communist influence, as revealed in the Mundt-Nixon-Wood-McCarthy exposures in 1950 is, I believe, somewhat exaggerated. Such influence was, however, *intensive* in the several agencies where communist cells were able to gain a strategic position and to seed the agencies with their followers. This was particularly true of the Department of Agriculture and the N.L.R.B. in the late thirties, and the Treasury Department and the Board of Economic Warfare during World War II.[254]

During the Popular Front, Browder put forth the slogan "Communism is Twentieth Century Americanism." It was a bold move to gain respectability. "Third period" symbols such as the regular "Lenin-Liebknecht-Luxemburg" memorial meetings were discarded; strict class interpretations of United States history, such as Jack Hardy's *The American Revolution* and Anthony Bimba's *History of the American Working-Class*—first-rate curios of Marxist historiography—were stored in the closet. In fact even Marx and Engels were stashed away. The new heroes were Tom Paine, Thomas Jefferson, and Abraham Lincoln. Party his-

---

[253] Witt was named by Whittaker Chambers, and later by Lee Pressman, as a secret Communist Party cardholder in testimony before the House Committee on Un-American Activities. Edwin S. Smith, after leaving the N.L.R.B., worked for various communist-front outfits and in 1948 became the director of the National Council for American-Soviet Friendship.

[254] The fullest account of the communist elite underground in Washington is contained in the testimony of Whittaker Chambers before the House Committee on Un-American Activities, August 3, 1949, and contained in a forthcoming volume, *Witness* (New York, 1951). Chambers, a former editor of the *Daily Worker*, went "underground" in 1932 and was liaison between the communist Washington apparatus and Soviet espionage. Other disclosures were made by Elizabeth Bentley, a minor courier in the Soviet espionage service, and Louis Budenz, the former managing editor of the *Daily Worker*. Of the dozen or so named by Chambers, two—Alger Hiss, former secretary-general of the San Francisco Conference which founded the United Nations, and Harry D. White, former under-secretary of the Treasury—vehemently denied the accusations. Two others, Julian Wadleigh, an economist in the Department of State, and Lee Pressman, a lawyer in the Department of Agriculture before joining the C.I.O., admitted membership in the Communist Party; Wadleigh further admitted stealing government documents for Russian espionage. The others refused to answer before congressional committees on the ground of self-incrimination. Hiss was convicted of perjury; Harry White died shortly after his appearance before a House investigating committee. Two accounts of the Hiss case are Alistair Cooke, *A Generation on Trial* (New York, 1950), and Ralph de Toledano and Victor Lasky, *Seeds of Treason* (New York, 1950); the former limits itself to the transcripts of the trials alone, the latter includes extracts of the House Committee testimony of Chambers.

torians ransacked their writings and triumphantly emerged with quotations which proved the eternal struggle of the "people" versus the "reactionaries."

The greatest triumph of communist propaganda in the U.S. was the creation of the papier-mâché front organizations. These fronts sought to hook famous names and exploit them for communist causes by means of manifestoes, open letters, petitions, declarations, statements, pronouncements, protests, and other illusions of opinion ground-swells in the land. The viciousness of the front technique was that it encouraged a herd spirit whereby only "collective opinion" carried weight; and if a critic dared challenge a tenet of Soviet faith, he was drowned out by the mass chorus of several score voices. As Eugene Lyons put it: "Did rumor-mongers charge that a horrifying famine had been enforced by the Kremlin to 'punish' forty million Soviet citizens in an area as large as the United States? Half a hundred experts on nutrition and agronomy, all the way from Beverly Hills to Park Avenue penthouses, thereupon condemned the capitalists and Trotskyites responsible for the libel, and the famine was liquidated."[255]

The corruption of the front technique was that many poor dupes, imagining that they were the leaders of the great causes, found themselves enslaved by the opium of publicity and became pliable tools of the communist manipulators behind the scenes. In other instances upper-class matrons and aspiring actresses found in the communist "causes" a cozy nonconformism to replace their passé conventions. The ultimate betrayal was of the masses of front members who gained a sense of participation which they sadly discovered to be spurious when the party line changed and they found that they themselves were victims of party manipulations.

The master of the front technique was Willi Münzenberg, a flamboyant German entrepreneur who had set up many such enterprises in Germany. His greatest success was the organization of an antiwar movement starting in 1932 (a movement whose blueprint was followed almost to the letter eighteen years later in the communist "Stockholm" peace petitions). In the spring of 1932 the French writers Henri Barbusse and Romain Rolland "sent out" a call for a world congress against war, which met in August that year. Subsequently, miniature congresses were held in each country and leagues against war and fascism organized throughout the world. The first national chairman of the American league was a former minister and school teacher in Java, a communist sympathizer within the Socialist Party, Dr. J. B. Matthews.[256] But shortly thereafter,

[255] "When Liberalism Went Totalitarian," by Eugene Lyons, in *Whose Revolution?* p. 122.
[256] Dr. Matthews grew bitter at the left-wing movement when in 1935 employees at Consumer Research, of which Matthews was an officer, called a strike and then

Dr. Matthews, an erratic individual who flirted with many revolutionary groups, was dumped, and in his place Dr. Harry F. Ward, a professor of Christian ethics at the Union Theological Seminary, was made national chairman. In 1937, during the collective security line, when the communists turned prowar, the name of the organization was changed by a semantic sleight of hand to the American League for Peace and Democracy (being "against" war is pacifist, while being "for" peace allows one to decry aggression and call for security measures which might lead to war). At its height, the new league claimed the affiliation of 1,023 separate organizations—women's clubs, religious societies, youth groups, sports associations, etc.—with a total membership of seven and a half million. Allowing for duplications and double counting, the number was still sizable. The league published millions of pieces of propaganda, sent speakers into hundreds of other groups, lobbied in Washington, and carried on many other activities.

Two other springboards for communist influence were the American Student Union and the American Youth Congress. The "youth movement," particularly in Europe, was peculiarly a product of the postwar disillusionment. With the crumbling of older mores and with the economic disintegration of the middle class, a bitter cry arose against the "tired elders." These young "armed Bohemians," as Konrad Heiden called them, the footloose, cynical-romantic, disoriented, déclassé elements from the trenches, flocked in the postwar years to the tough-minded, antihumanitarian, nihilistic, and revolutionary movements of fascism and communism.

In the United States, the traumatic shock of the depression aroused the youth, and youth organizations proliferated. Although the American Student Union at its height never had a membership higher than 20,000 (of the million or so college youth), it claimed the intellectual core of the student body.[257] Members of the A.S.U. went into the professions, government, and trade-union bodies. Because it was the seed bed for the future intellectual elite of the country, the communists worked hard to capture it.[258]

---

organized a rival, Consumers Union. In 1939 Matthews became research director, under Martin Dies, of the House Committee on Un-American Activities, and was largely responsible for its successes. After leaving the Committee, he became a consultant for the Hearst press on communism. See J. B. Matthews, *Odyssey of a Fellow-Traveler* (New York, 1938).

[257] James Wechsler, *Revolt on the Campus* (New York, 1935).

[258] The American Student Union was born in December 1935, fusing the socialist Student League for Industrial Democracy and the communist National Students League. In the original merger agreement, the posts in the new organization were divided evenly between the socialists and communists. The first national chairman and national secretary, George S. Edwards and Joseph P. Lash, were socialists. As the communists moved toward a prowar policy, a rift between the two political groups developed. The pacifist "Oxford Pledge," the feature of the springtime college "peace

Simultaneously with the formation of the A.S.U., the communists and socialists were able to capture the fledgling American Youth Congress, which had been organized by some well-meaning liberals. Hundreds of youth organizations, particularly those of religious denominations, flocked to affiliate, especially when the Youth Congress gained the patronage of Mrs. Eleanor Roosevelt and was instrumental in setting up the National Youth Administration, a junior W.P.A. for student and unemployed youth. At its height, in 1939, the American Youth Congress claimed to represent 513 organizations with a total of 4,700,000 members. Allowing for the inevitable duplications and double counting, the residue was still high.

In the League of American Writers[259] communism gained a medium for enlisting the culture makers of American society. What gave communism its gilded appeal was Spain. The gallant cry of *No Pasaran*, coming soon after the labor movements of central Europe had been shattered so easily, gave a strong emotional lift to anti-Fascist sentiment in the United States. (Although the communists in Spain were only a tiny party and the brunt of the fighting was carried on by the socialists, anarchists, and P.O.U.M., a left-socialist party concentrated mainly in Catalonia, the Loyalist cause in the United States was virtually appropriated by the communists. And it was utilized to the full to enlarge their scope of influence.) The gritty sectarianism of proletcult gave way to the Popular Front in literature. The change was symbolized by the second congress of the League of American Writers, held in June 1937. Among those participating were Ernest Hemingway, Archibald MacLeish, Carl Van Doren, Vincent Sheean, Upton Sinclair, and others of equal repute. Although Waldo Frank, the league's first president, had signed the call to the second congress, he was strangely absent from its proceedings. In the interim he had suggested that some impartial investigation of the Moscow trials was in order, and he was unceremoniously dropped. In his place appeared, without public election, Donald Ogden Stewart, a Hollywood film writer noted for his slick and polished treatments of urbane comedy. The symbolism of the changeover was striking.

But Spain—and the Moscow trials—also drove a strong wedge in the communist influence among the intellectuals. In the unhappy Iberian country, the communists demanded control of press and propaganda, command over several armies, and the right to maintain their own secret police as a price for Russian arms and support. Finally, the intransigeant

strikes" (on the anniversary, April 7, of America's entry into World War I), was dropped. The majority bloc, composed of the communists and Lash's followers—who favored the collective-security program—finally reduced the socialists to an impotent minority.

[259] The League of American Writers grew out of the John Reed clubs in 1935. At the start, the league was affiliated with the International Union of Revolutionary Writers.

socialist premier, Largo Caballero, was pushed out and replaced by Juan Negrín and Alvarez Del Vayo, who were ready to accede to communist demands. As communists moved into strategic position, a reign of terror against political opponents broke out in the Loyalist camp. A P.O.U.M. "uprising" was provoked in Barcelona, and the leader of the movement, Andrés Nin, was shot; Mark Rein, the son of the Menshevik leader Raphael Abramovitch, was kidnapped and disappeared. Camillo Bernieri, an anarchist leader, was murdered. The international brigades, under the command of the French communist leader André Marty, eliminated all noncommunists from command. John Dos Passos returned in July 1937 and told part of the story in the magazine *Common Sense*. The radical *Modern Quarterly* and the socialist *New Leader* carried other bits and pieces. Only after the Loyalist cause was irretrievably lost were other parts of the story fitted together.[260]

The Moscow trials shook the sanity of the political intellectuals of the world. In the years 1936 to 1938 almost the entire palace guard of Old Bolsheviks were ruthlessly shot. Names that for years the world had known as the makers of the revolution were now branded as secret Fascist agents, even at the beginning of the revolution. Most puzzling of all were the "confessions." Kamenev and Zinoviev, Lenin's coworkers in exile, who, with Stalin, had formed the *troika*, the ruling triumvirate of Russia in 1925; Bukharin, leading party theoretician and Stalin's ally in 1927-1928; Rykov, the former premier; Radek, brilliant publicist—all stood up and repeated the same weird tale.[261] Besides these, almost the

---

[260] The most complete account of the Barcelona uprising is contained in "Class War in Republican Spain," by Anita Brenner, *Modern Monthly*, Sept. 1937. Luis Araquistain, former Spanish ambassador to France and a socialist leader, has told the full story of Stalin's role in Spain in a series of articles for the *New York Times*, May 19, 21, and June 4, 1939. A sketch of the events of the civil war is in Gerald Brenan, *The Spanish Labyrinth* (New York, 1943), pp. 316-32. A fictional but accurate account is in Ernest Hemingway's *For Whom the Bell Tolls*, with its savage and thinly-veiled portrait of Marty as the commissar.

[261] Many explanations of the confessions have been advanced, ranging from torture to drugs. Two brilliant fictional accounts of the trials, Arthur Koestler's *Darkness at Noon* and Victor Serge's *The Case of Comrade Tulayev*, interpret the Moscow confessions as the readiness of the Old Bolsheviks to accept "the logic" of opposition—having "thought" of opposition, the consequences were inexorable even if the action never developed. As "Bolsheviks" they should have and might have acted if the opportunity so presented itself. And, having been proved wrong "objectively" by history, they confessed. A devastating story of one person's experience is the Shipkov confessions (*New York Times*, Mar. 5, 1950). Michael Shipkov, a clerk in the U.S. embassy in Bulgaria, was arrested and was told to confess. After a week of torture, Shipkov decided to confess, feeling that the torment would stop. But it didn't. Confession is not the end. Such is the subtle nature of modern terror that the subject cannot be allowed to signal the end of his own torture. To do so would give him some control, some partial dominance of the situation. One must rob the individual of all choice, even the right to choose death on one's terms. The function of terror is to instill a sense of helplessness, to destroy the self and atomize the individual. To

entire general staff of the army, headed by the famed Marshal Tukhachev-sky, were secretly shot after being accused of conspiring with the Nazis although two of the eight generals executed were Jews. It was as Trotsky graphically put it: "Of Christ's twelve apostles, Judas alone proved to be a traitor. But if he had acquired power, he would have represented the other eleven apostles as traitors and also all the lesser apostles, whom Luke numbers at seventy."[262]

The trials provided the first occasion for a counteroffensive by the growing number of anticommunist intellectuals. John Dewey headed a commission of inquiry, which journeyed to Mexico to hear testimony from Trotsky and compile an independent record of the trials. The suggestion, even a mild one, by fellow travelers that some independent investigation ought to be pursued was met by immediate hostility, and the questioner, as in the case of Waldo Frank, was immediately cast out.[263] The two volumes issued by the Dewey commission, the second of which carried as its title *Not Guilty*, precipitated wild melees.[264] The fellow travelers circulated a round-robin letter of protest, initiated by Malcolm Cowley, Robert Coates, Stuart Davis, Marc Blitzstein, and Paul Strand. This letter was signed by "nearly 150 prominent American artists, writers, composers, editors, movie actors, college professors, and Broadway figures," according to the *Daily Worker*, and stated that the trials "have by their

---

be able to choose is the measure of some degree of freedom; therefore the pain stops not on the command of the victim but of the executioner. A comprehensive summary of the various theories on the reasons for the purge cycle in Russia is contained in the excellent *Russian Purge and the Extraction of Confession*, by F. Beck and W. Godin (New York, 1951).

[262] Leon Trotsky, *Stalin* (New York, 1941), p. 416. For a series of exciting vignettes of many of the executed Old Bolsheviks, see Alexander Barmine's *One Who Survived* (New York, 1945), a neglected but brilliant personal history of the postrevolutionary period by a former Red Army general and diplomat.

[263] Frank records his disillusionment over the trials in an extraordinary bit of self-revelation: ". . . could the vision within Marxism not be deepened? Not be made *true*? This was my hope, and my strategy. In my journal of those days i wrote: 'I collaborate with the revolutionists not expecting them to understand me: the bad logic of their dogmatic empiricism prevents that. But I must serve and understand *them*: and part of my service is to let them exploit me.' . . . The Moscow Trials were convincing that this hope had failed. . . . They called the old comrades and cowar-riors *vermin*: and insisted that all their friends throughout the world must do likewise. . . . They destroyed, not only the lives of these men, but their pasts. . . . They defiled their own world. They defiled man. And every inquirer at home they jailed or shot, and every questioner abroad they befouled with cesspool language." Waldo Frank, *Chart for Rough Water* (New York, 1940), pp. 43-45.

[264] The two volumes are *The Case of Leon Trotsky* (New York, 1937), a transcript of the proceedings in Mexico, and *Not Guilty, Report of the Commission of Inquiry* (New York, 1938). The latter was signed by John Dewey, chairman, John Chamber-lain, Edward Alsworth Ross, Benjamin Stolberg, Carlo Tresca, for the American committee.

sheer weight of evidence considered a clear presumption of guilt of the defendants."[265]

By 1939 the warfare among the intellectuals flared into open, deadly battle. The widespread communist influence in publishing houses, book clubs, magazine reviewing, meant that many an anticommunist author was either ignored or ganged up on, while procommunists were petted and built up. Opposed to the communists was the new Committee for Cultural Freedom, initiated by Sidney Hook and headed by John Dewey.[266] The committee issued a statement, signed by 140 Americans, which excoriated those who denounced suppressions of intellectual freedom under fascism but failed to note and speak out against similar denials in Russia. To blast the Committee for Cultural Freedom, the communists began gathering signatures for the biggest rainbow of names yet unfolded in this surrealist universe. They rounded up 400 individuals, writers, college professors, social workers, artists, and issued an open letter which denied "the fantastic falsehood" that Russia could have anything in common with Germany and called the purveyors of such lies "fascists and their allies" who were seeking "to prevent a united anti-aggression front." The letter was released August 14, 1939. Little more than a week later Ribbentrop and Molotov signed the Soviet-Nazi nonaggression pact.[267]

How could the Communist Party, a garish political group with no real roots in American life, exercise such a wide influence in the intellectual and professional strata of American life? An intellectual is one who, almost by definition, seeks to understand and express the *Zeitgeist*. Unlike the scholar, who starts from a given set of objective problems and seeks to fill in the gaps, he begins with his personal concerns, and in the groping for self-consciousness creates intuitive knowledge about the world. The depression and the threat of fascism were the great personal concerns which forced the intellectuals to reconsider their place in the world. At no time in American life, except for a brief period in 1912, had the intelligentsia been recognized as a cohesive social group and given a platform for political articulation: this the communists provided. They

[265] Cited in Eugene Lyons, *The Red Decade*, pp. 246-48.

[266] Among other noted members: Herbert Agar, Sherwood Anderson, Carl Becker, Thomas H. Benton, Percy Bridgman, John Chamberlain, George S. Counts, Elmer Davis, Max Eastman, Irwin Edman, Morris L. Ernst, Dorothy Canfield Fisher, Harry D. Gideonse, Sidney Howard, William H. Kilpatrick, Sinclair Lewis, Eugene Lyons, Wesley Clair Mitchell, Harry A. Overstreet, John Dos Passos, Ralph Barton Perry, James Rorty, George N. Shuster, Norman Thomas, Dorothy Thompson, Ferdinand Lundberg. A goodly number of these anticommunists, it might be noted, had been members of the League of Professional Groups for Foster and Ford seven years before (see note 245).

[267] For full lists of the individuals signing the Committee for Cultural Freedom statements and the opposing open letter, see Eugene Lyons, *The Red Decade*, pp. 345, 349.

gave the intellectuals a status and recognition which they had previously been denied; and to this the intellectuals responded.

In the development of communist intellectual influence in the thirties, and carried over into the next two decades, a strange cycle is apparent. The earliest converts were the literary individuals concerned with the problem of self-expression and integrity—Dos Passos, James Farrell, Richard Wright, Sherwood Anderson, Edmund Wilson. As these became aware of the dishonesty of the communist tactic, a new group appeared, the slick writers, the actors, stage people—in short, "Hollywood"—for whom "causes" brought excitement, purpose, and, equally important, "answers" to the world's problems. The wheel turned and picked up the college professors, the ministers, and lastly the scientists. In the later years the proportion of ministers among the sucker lists of communist fronts was probably higher than any other group. Bewitched by the communist myth, unable to believe evil, attracted by the opportunity to do good, the ministers moved blissfully about, unaware of the shadowy figures behind them. In the latter half of the forties, scientists for the first time began appearing in greater number on communist "innocent" or fellow-traveling fronts, attracted, apparently, not by the utopian and Christian elements in the communist appeal, but by its tough-mindedness and power role.

A number of intellectuals and innocents were also attracted by one or other of the various splinter groups. And certainly no account of the revolutionary Marxist movements in the thirties would be complete without some attempted description of the numerous sects which proliferated during this time. From the vantage point of more than a decade later some of their antics seem exceedingly comic; given their premises, the problem of the "correct" strategy to be pursued in time of revolutionary flux was exceedingly serious. The churchmen who gathered at Nicaea in A.D. 325 to formulate what later became the Nicene Creed had their textual differences regarding the road to salvation. Similarly, the weightiness of "the word" had an equal relevance in revolutionary movements, and the texts of Lenin were scrutinized with all the hermeneutical care that the epigoni gave to the gospels in the first centuries after Christ.

The period of the thirties offered, in the minds of the Marxists, numerous revolutionary situations. It was the task of the "vanguard party" to make the correct assessments and through the correct tactics and slogans give fire at the right moment to the revolutionary moods of the masses. (Revolutions are like births, Trotsky once said. The forceps cannot be applied prematurely.)

There was in the evolutionary history of sects a distinct *rite de passage* (more scientifically formulated as the Law of Faction Formation and Fission). The original splinter groups emerged in the late twenties from the Communist Party. The main factional progeny of the thirties came from the Trotskyites—they who claimed the seal of purity and had the effulgent brilliance of the creator of the Red Army to sustain them. But even Trotsky alive could not guarantee unity; in fact, Trotsky alive was more likely to be the source of splits since it was a great lift to the revolutionary ego of the new sectarian leaders to have jousted with one of the original creators of the Russian Revolution.

The Trotskyites, a band of a hundred or so, were expelled from the Communist Party in 1928. Since they will be discussed at greater length later in this essay, suffice it to say here that for the first few years they remained a "faction" within communism, rather than a general party participating in political life. Because he disapproved of this policy, Albert Weisbord, a leader of the Passaic textile strike of 1926, headed one of the first splinter groups. After flirting with the Trotskyites for several years, Weisbord conclusively broke all relations and on March 15, 1931, formed the Communist League of Struggle.[268] In the heraldic announcement of its birth, he wrote: "Not an isolated sect, but a two-fisted hard group of communists is what we are forming." Its seven years of existence were lean; each one ended with the loss of another member, with Weisbord the lonely survivor at the end.[269]

A second splinter party was formed by B. J. Field, who achieved a limited prominence in the New York hotel strike of 1934. Disagreeing sharply with the Trotskyite trade-union tactics (he thought he was bigger than the party, Cannon declared), Field led out a group of eight and united with two Lovestoneite dissidents, Ben Gitlow and Lazar Becker (who in May 1933 had formed the Workers Communist League), to create the Organization Committee for a Revolutionary Workers Party.[269a] The two ex-Lovestoneites did not tarry long in the O.C.F.A.R.W.P., however, but joined the Socialist Party, and Field settled down with the

---

[268] For much of the ephemeral information of the obscure sects, historians of the socialist movement must be grateful to Max Shachtman, who, anticipating their needs, gathered most of the fugitive data and published it in an article "Footnote for Historians," *New International*, IV (Dec. 1938), pp. 377-79.

[269] In 1937 Weisbord retired from revolutionary activism to revolutionary contemplation and published a huge two-volume work, *The Conquest of Power* (New York, 1937). In the late 1940's Weisbord, his views tempered, became an A.F.L. organizer in New England and Chicago.

[269a] When charged with having ignored the Trotskyites during the strike, Field replied: "I could not get in contact with you even if I wanted to; you haven't even got a telephone in your office." Cannon, the leader of the party, said, "That was true . . . we had no telephone. That deficiency was a relic of our isolation . . . when we had no need of a telephone because nobody wanted to call us up, and we couldn't call anyone. Besides, up till then, we couldn't afford a telephone." James P. Cannon, *The History of American Trotskyism* (New York, 1944), p. 132.

League for a Revolutionary Workers Party. As with similar paramecium organisms, however, such splits are impossible without attempts at fusion, and Field continued in his efforts. He proceeded to negotiations with Weisbord, but these broke down, Field concluding indignantly that "it is impossible to see how such a group with such policies and leadership can contribute anything toward building a genuine revolutionary International." Field tried his luck with the "Italian Left Fraction of Communism" (a three-man group who subscribed to the theories of Amadeo Bordiga, a flaming Italian ex-Trotskyite), the members of which had just previously worn themselves out in fruitless negotiations with Weisbord. In January 1936 Field announced that "eight fundamental questions of the revolutionary movement were discussed and complete political agreement has been arrived at." Mysteriously, however, despite complete political agreement, unity was not forthcoming. Nevertheless, Field still kept trying and two months later sought unity with the Oehler group (see below), but the seed bore no fruit. In May 1936 his membership became restive and Field lost the "Fieldites"; the majority outvoted Field and voted to rejoin the Trotskyites.

The largest of the splinter groups was the Revolutionary Workers League, led by Hugo Oehler, Tom Stamm, and Rosario Negrete, whose differences with the Trotskyite Workers Party arose out of the "French Turn." This was a maneuver, ordered by Trotsky in late 1934, to enter the Socialist parties throughout the world and steer them in a leftward direction. The Oehlerites feared the dilution of their revolutionary purity and bolted.[270] The Revolutionary Workers League was formed in November 1935, but immediately defections, expulsions, and splitlets took place. In November 1937, at the historic third plenum of the R.W.L., Oehler and Stamm had a great falling out. The latter insisted that Trotskyism had degenerated in 1928; the former placed 1934 as the year of the original sin. In addition, differences had cropped up on the trade-union question, on Spain, democratic centralism, and sundry other issues. Stamm upped and left, but claimed the same name for his group of the Revolutionary Workers League. Both organizations elected their comrade Negrete, who at the moment was languishing in a G.P.U. jail in Spain, as a member of their respective executive committees; when he returned to the United States he was greeted at the docks by two delegations, each with banners proclaiming the name of the organization and the an-

---

[270] The chief publications of the Revolutionary Workers League were the *Fighting Worker*, an agitational newspaper; the *Marxist*, formerly the *Fourth International*, which was the theoretical organ; and *International News*, an organ of the provisional International Contact Commission for the New Communist (4th) International. *International News* was issued jointly with the Leninist League of Scotland and the Red Front of Germany.

nouncement that he had been elected to both. (Negrete chose the Oehlerites.)

The idea of schism proved contagious and there soon began a new split in the Revolutionary Workers League led by Karl Mienov, who formed the Marxist Workers League.[271] The initial issue of the inevitable theoretical organ, *Spark* (named in honor of Lenin's prerevolutionary magazine *Iskra*, the title of which meant "spark" in Russian), proclaimed that "to be wrong on the Spanish war means to open the door wide open to social-patriotism in the coming world imperialist war. . . . We are proud that we split from such a centrist group."[272] However, Mienov's group was not immune to the law of faction formation and fission. Mienov himself held that Trotskyism could not be reformed but must be smashed; the minority dissented. A third "faction," a single individual named Stanford, held a unique political position. "I don't like Mienov," he wrote in *Spark*. Appalled by this caprice, Mienov retorted: "What sort of principled position is this . . . we can gauge Comrade Stanford's sincerity, however, by the fact that rather than give out leaflets for the revolution, he prefers to study for exams at Brooklyn College." Mienov, Apocrypha relate, now alone, soon developed schizophrenia and split with himself.

One other Oehlerite split-off deserves mention, the Leninist League, formed at the beginning of 1938. "While definitely anti-gynaicocratic," observes historian Shachtman, "and taking no formal position on exogamy or endogamy, it is based fundamentally on the primitive gens in so far as one must be a blood relation of the immediate family, or at least related to it by marriage, in order to qualify for membership. This has the unfortunate effect of somewhat reducing the arena of recruitment, but it does guarantee against contamination."[273]

This by no means exhausts the number of the Trotskyite splinter groups of the period, or the growth of anarchist sects, deviants from the Socialist

---

[271] Not to be confused with the Marxist Workers League, a previous splinter from the R.W.L. which lasted three weeks before its two members rejoined the Trotskyites. Nor is there much space here for Trotskyites and ex-Trotskyites who renounced Marxism altogether and went syndicalist, as did Joseph Zack (Kornfeder), who started the One Big Union Club and the Equalitarian Society.

[272] Mienov favored a "defeatist" versus a "defensist" position, two terms that were central to Lenin's strategy. The latter meant critical support of a regime, such as Lenin gave to Kerensky in the July days when the Kornilov armies threatened to overthrow the February Revolution; the former meant sabotaging the home government (turning the "imperialist war into a civil war") in order to precipitate a revolution. Oehler advocated that workers in Spain be defensists; Mienov was a defeatist.

[273] Shachtman, *op.cit.*, pp. 378-79. George Marlen, the totem of the Leninist League, was perhaps the most indefatigable collector of the sins of other parties. He published a book, *Earl Browder, Tool of Wall Street*, with a subtitle, *Stalin, Trotsky or Lenin*, which is a vast compendium of quotes by all the fathers of the revolution on the problems of strategy and tactics.

Labor Party, and other political spores that so profusely filled the air in this period.[274] With the coming of World War II, the sects began to decline. An effort to unite the League for a Revolutionary Workers Party, the Revolutionary Labor Group, and the Marxist Workers League failed.[275] Gradually, all these groups faded into oblivion. During the same period the Socialist Party, too, was fading, and its decline will be traced in the pages that follow.

XII. In Dubious Battles

In 1932 the Socialist Party polled 903,000 votes for Norman Thomas. It was by previous standards a respectable total and many felt that socialism was again on the march. But factional discord, like the curse on the House of Atreus, was an ineradicable heritage, and in the next eight years the savage fratricide ripped the party to shreds.

This new conflict was, in one sense, a repetition of the old immigrant-nativist division. The Socialist Party in 1928 had a paper membership of 7,000 concentrated largely in New York. What influence it had depended upon the good will of a few trade-union leaders who, from conviction or nostalgia, still held party cards. But the party had no mass following in these unions nor was it consulted about union policy; it had become a "poor relation" and was so treated. The burdens of the presidential campaign were borne almost completely by a small devoted group of old-timers in New York and the money came largely from the *Jewish Daily Forward* and the small needle-trades unions. This aging group of leaders, clustered about Hillquit, dominated the party.

There was in loose opposition another group, centered around Norman Thomas, which sought to broaden the party's appeal by concentrating on the middle-class and educated groups. In December 1928 Thomas and his lieutenant, Paul Blanshard, along with such nonsocialists as John Dewey, Oswald Garrison Villard, and Paul Douglas, launched the League for Independent Political Action, which they hoped would provide a common platform for progressive and reform elements. The "old-guard" socialist leadership felt this was a move to "liquidate" the party or change its name. When, in 1931, John Dewey invited Senator George W. Norris to "help give birth to a new party, based upon the principles of planning," the old guard, like hard-shell Baptists, reasserted their fundamentalist beliefs. "The Socialist Party is a party of the working-class," a resolution of the New York City convention declared. "[Leaders like Norris] . . .

---

[274] A sober and detailed examination of some of these movements is contained in William Isaacs, *Contemporary Marxian Political Movements in the U.S.* (MS Ph.D. thesis, New York University, 1939).

[275] "Report of Negotiations—RLG, LRWP, and MWL," p. 15 in *Power*, theoretical organ of Marxist Workers League (mimeographed, New York), Vol. 2, No. 1, May-June 1940.

would shift the leadership" from workers "into the hands of political leaders who have minor differences with the parties of capitalism, a policy which Socialists cannot approve."[276] This division was reflected in the social composition of the two groups. The old-guard leadership was largely European-born and/or self-educated, and—although its main leaders were lawyers—it defensively emphasized the "working-class" character of its origin and thinking. The opposition was of professional or middle-class parentage, college educated, ministerial, pacifist. Its main strength was drawn from such institutions as the League for Industrial Democracy (the successor to the Intercollegiate Socialist Society) and the magazine *The World Tomorrow*, a religious periodical whose editors were Norman Thomas, Devere Allen, and Kirby Page. There was, in addition, a personal factor. Norman Thomas, having been the party's standard-bearer in 1928, sought to become, in fact as well as in name, the spokesman of the party. With the sorry lesson of Debs in mind, he was resentful and suspicious of Morris Hillquit, who, he felt, merely wanted him as a figurehead.

Another conflict was one between generations. The old guard were party members of twenty to twenty-five years' standing. Even though many were now furiously pursuing their own professional careers and the years of high prosperity had dampened their ardor and expectations, they were still self-conscious and articulate about their many years of sacrifice for the cause. The youths who began flooding the party in the depression years—membership rose to 15,000 by 1932[277]—resented the "mortgage" on party leadership held by the old guard. They resented more the slack and tired attitude of the local leaders. Although a solid core of experienced and thoughtful men like Morris Hillquit, Algernon Lee, and Louis Waldman steered party policy at the top,[278] most of the local chairmen and organizers had acquired their posts by the mechanical process of attrition and seniority. Many of these second-string leaders looked with fear on the rising tide of new membership with its restless demand for activity. There was, unfortunately, no "middle generation" to bridge the gap.

The younger generation called themselves the "Militants." They issued a strident manifesto attacking "the apologists of gradualness," and demanded that the party "press for a relentless drive for political power instead of reform."[279] The coolness of the old guard toward the Soviets

[276] Quoted in James Oneal, *Some Pages from Party History* (a pamphlet printed by the author, New York, 1935), p. 10.
[277] Report of Clarence Senior, national secretary, to the 1932 national convention in Milwaukee, mimeographed.
[278] Victor Berger and Meyer London, the party's two ex-Congressmen, had both died in tragic street accidents in 1929.
[279] *A Militant Program for the Socialist Party of America*, No. 1, Dec. 1931 (a pamphlet issued by the Program Committee: Theodore Shapiro, Robert Delson,

was further proof to them of the lack of revolutionary temper and tough-mindedness of the party leadership. "The Russian dictatorship," the Militants declared, "was a necessary instrument for the industrialization of Russia. . . ."[280]

To the old guard this talk echoed the manifestoes of 1919. They feared these young tyros would capture the party, and sneered at their parlor radicalism. The younger Militant, wrote James Oneal bitterly, "is all too common. He . . . comes from the middle-class and professional families. Six months or a year in the party and he becomes a 'theoretician' swaggering with erudition. One immediately understands that the Socialist movement began when he joined it. He discusses problems with the gusto of one who has digested everything written since the days of Marx. He is an expert on 'tactics.' In fact this is his speciality. He solves problems of the class war here and abroad with the ease that he flicks his ashes from his cigarette."[281]

The fight came to the surface in May 1932 when the Militants joined the Thomas liberals and the "sewer socialists" of Milwaukee[282] in an incongruous alliance to depose Morris Hillquit as national chairman of the party and to name instead Milwaukee's mayor, Dan Hoan. In the heated debate some ugly charges boiled up. Hillquit's adherents charged "the Thomas alliance with bringing the issue of race and sectionalism into the party under the guise of 'Americanism.'" They stated that "a 'whispering campaign,' emphasizing the fact that Mr. Hillquit was a Jew and that the party should be rid of foreign elements, had been carried on . . . in an attempt to unhorse Mr. Hillquit as leader of the party."[283] Thomas and his chief lieutenants, Paul Blanshard and Heywood Broun, denied the charge. So too did B. Charney Vladeck, an executive of the *Jewish Daily Forward*, a Thomas supporter.

McAlister Coleman), p. 8. When one of the Militant leaders presented the group's viewpoint in the *American Socialist Quarterly*, the editors, dyed-in-the-wool Marxists, commented: "It is difficult to learn from Comrade Shapiro's article just what the militants demand. Suppose they were to get control of the party. What changes would they bring about? They are against reformism. Very well, what does reformism mean to Comrade Shapiro?" See "The 'Militant' Point of View," by Theodore Shapiro, and editor's comment, "Is This Militancy?" *American Socialist Quarterly*, Vol. 1, No. 2 (Apr. 1932), pp. 29-44.

[280] *A Militant Program*, p. 12. Among the endorsers were Devere Allen, Jack Altman, Murray Baron, Andrew J. Biemiller, Paul Blanshard, Franz Daniel, Arnold Freese, Maynard Kreuger, J. B. Matthews, and Upton Sinclair. Subsequently, this view of Russia changed radically and these socialists were among the first to appreciate and point out the danger of Russian imperialism to the world. By 1940 all these men, with the exception of Kreuger and Freese, had left the Socialist Party. Freese, who was elected mayor of Norwalk, Conn., in 1948, resigned in 1950.

[281] Oneal, *op.cit.*, p. 19.

[282] So dubbed by Hillquit to indicate their provincial concern with municipal problems to the exclusion of others.

[283] Dispatch to the *New York Times*, May 24, 1932, p. 1.

On such taut issues, truth bounces quite erratically and is difficult to pin down. This much is true: behind some of the attacks on Hillquit was an attitude characteristic of typical Mid-western provincialisms that "New York is not America." Some others felt, for opportunistic reasons, that the shaggy, shambling Dan Hoan would be a more presentable party symbol than the precise, intellectual Hillquit. In effect, Thomas' bumbling effort to create an "American" party, by which he meant an orientation to the American temperament, was given the worse possible interpretation by the touchy old guard. This saw-toothed issue left crosscuts that never healed.[284] In the final vote Hillquit retained office, 105 to 80; in terms of party membership, however, the division was a closer 7,526 to 6,894, a margin which the old guard knew was too slim to maintain.

Little of this internal feuding was reflected in Thomas' 1932 presidential race. His campaign pledges, after the usual obeisances to social ownership of major industries, spelled out a hard-headed series of meliorative demands, including five billions for immediate relief, five billions for roads, reforestation and slum clearance, unemployment insurance, old-age pensions, government aid to small homeowners, the five-day week, government employment agencies, minimum wage laws, and similar measures that were to become incorporated within the next few years in the New Deal program.

The advent of the New Deal and the events in Europe from 1932 to 1934 accentuated the divergent trends in the Socialist Party. Seeking to capitalize on the impact of the campaign and the restless discontent of the country, the socialists organized in May 1933 a Continental Congress of Workers and Farmers. They hoped it would lead to a new radical party. Despite an impressive list of labor sponsors—including Sidney Hillman, David Dubinsky, and Emil Rieve (who served as chairman)— the venture petered out. For the dulcet voice of Roosevelt was being heard in the land. Norman Thomas could mock: "After all *any* President would have to do *something* in 1933. What Roosevelt did was temporarily to stabilize capitalism with a few concessions to workers that are poor copies of Socialist immediate demands." And the Socialist Party could snap: T.V.A.—"state capitalism"; N.I.R.A.—"state paternalism"; C.C.C.— "looks like forced labor"[285]—but the labor leaders were falling under Roose-

[284] Hillquit himself felt it to be an anti-Semitic bias. In accepting the nomination he declared: "I am here to charge that efforts have been made to introduce the [racial] issue and not on this floor alone. I know the issue of Americanism. I have known it for many years." "Mr. Hillquit," continued the *Times* dispatch, "said he 'apologized' for having been born abroad, being a Jew and living in New York, 'a very unpopular place.'" See *ibid*.

[285] Norman Thomas, *The New Deal: a Socialist Analysis*, pamphlet published by the Socialist Party, Chicago, Dec. 1933, p. 3, emphasis in original; editorials in the *New Leader*, April 22, May 6, June 17, 1933.

velt's spell. The major fact was that the unions were quick to take advantage of the N.R.A. to organize. The almost bankrupt International Ladies' Garment Workers' Union shut down the dress industry in a shrewdly timed general strike and in one week quintupled its membership of forty thousand. Generalissimo John L. Lewis in a series of lightning moves captured the coal fields. In less than six months, the A.F.L. had gained 1,300,000 new members. The socialists were predicting a dire future, but the union leaders were too busy with their immediate problems to listen.

Other defections were taking place. Paul Blanshard, Thomas' floor whip at the 1932 convention, joined the La Guardia campaign in New York less than a year later. In his letter of resignation, he charged the Socialist Party with failure to elect a single alderman in "the natural stronghold of American Socialism," and declared that Roosevelt's program of "managed capitalism" had taken from the socialists the initiative in economic change.[286] The La Guardia administration also claimed three of the bright research men of the Socialist City Affairs Committee, which had uncovered the municipal corruption that had led to the Seabury exposés. Although they sought to remain in the party, the unhappy Thomas asked "almost as a personal favor" that the three, because of the political implications of their public move, resign.[287] The growing public bureaucracy took increasing drain of the Socialist Party. In some cases, socialists who took jobs in Washington resigned from the party in order not to jeopardize their new careers, in other instances the individuals kept silent. Whatever the case, the effect was to immobilize these people politically and weaken the party.

Movements in these years such as Technocracy, the Utopian society, Share-the-Wealth, Townsend, E.P.I.C. also took their toll. Upton Sinclair's experience was an important case in point. After twenty-five years of untiring socialist evangelism, the veteran propagandist decided that socialism was alien to the middle-class mentality of America. In September 1933 he joined the Democratic Party and wrote two pamphlets, *I, Governor of California*, and *How I Ended Poverty in California*. In these two tracts he sketched a simple scheme for putting the unemployed to

[286] *New Leader*, Sept. 30, 1933, pp. 5-6. Just nine months before, Blanshard, in a speech to the Student League for Industrial Democracy, had vividly sketched a picture of *Socialopia* on the day after the revolution. The picture, as reported in *Time*: "An international government, speaking an international language would control all battleships, airplanes, munitions and currency. In the U.S. state lines would vanish and the President and Congress would be replaced by a national Socialist planning board. . . . The State would enforce birth control. Working mothers would leave their young in a communal nursery in each apartment house." *Time*, Jan. 9, 1933.

[287] Private communication from Norman Thomas to Maslow, White, and Rosner, Dec. 19, 1933.

work in cooperative self-help units, and outlined an appealing reform program which included tax exemption for the small homeowner and $50 a month for the aged over sixty. The ideas caught on like wildfire and Sinclair suddenly found himself heading a political crusade, E.P.I.C., whose initials were drawn from the title of his second tract. Within six months the astonished pamphleteer found that he had won the Democratic nomination for governor (with 436,000 votes over George Creel's 288,000) and was being touted for victory in November. The frightened movie industry, banks, and railroads in full fury opened a vicious smear campaign. Advertisements mocked Sinclair's faddism, faked newsreels showed "widows" trembling over their loss of savings if Sinclair won, movie stars were pressured to speak out against him, the studios threatened to leave the state. After one of the dirtiest political campaigns on record Sinclair was beaten. But he had rolled up an astounding 879,000 (against Governor Merriam's 1,138,000). Sinclair's quick and spectacular rise, like that of the Non-Partisan League before him, showed that socialists could utilize the primary system to great political advantage. But the lesson went unheeded. The socialists denounced him for replacing orthodox socialism with panaceas, and for wrecking the party in California.[288]

But the Militants and the young intellectuals around Norman Thomas had no eye for the American scene. To them, these shapeless movements of discontent were tokens, like the flight of swallows before a storm, of the panic of the petty bourgeoisie. Their attention was riveted on Europe, because, as Marxist theory foretold, the fate of capitalism there foreshadowed the course of capitalism here.

The European events, particularly the collapse of German social democracy, pushed the Militants to the left. The movement of Bebel and Kautsky had been the shining example for right-wing socialism everywhere. Its membership was in the millions, its trade unions and cooperative societies mighty and wealthy, it exuded the air of solidity and strength. Yet it surrendered to Hitler without a shot. The lessons, said the youngsters, were clear. The German socialist movement failed because it did not disturb the economic power of the old capitalist class and it had failed to uproot the deeply embedded cultural and ideological traditions of junkerism and Prussian authoritarianism.

The rise of Hitler heightened anxieties that the rise of a mass Fascist movement here was only a matter of time.[289] Even if capitalist America

[288] Oliver Carlson, *A Mirror for Californians* (Indianapolis, 1941), pp. 291-302.
[289] See, for example, the symposium, "Will Fascism Come to America?" by Stuart Chase, Charles A. Beard, Theodore Dreiser, Norman Thomas, Horace M. Kallen, Waldo Frank, V. F. Calverton, in the *Modern Monthly*, Sept. 1934. Said Thomas: "No one can doubt that the raw material of Fascist construction or destruction lies all around in America. It simply lacks the occasion and the man to put together the

did not go Fascist, it would plunge into another war in order to escape its "contradictions" and "economic crisis." In order to stave off or combat these threats, the Militants also demanded united action with the communists. The "activism" of the communists, their tough-minded discussions of "seizing power," their learned quotations from Lenin on "tactics," their dogmatic predictions about the "course of history" had impressed many of the younger socialists. (In fact, at one point the national chairman of the Young People's Socialist League and a large segment of its national executive committee resigned *en bloc* and announced their allegiance to the Young Communist League.) But the main impulse behind the demand was the lesson of disunity in Germany and the ease with which Hitler had destroyed both communists and socialists. The united front issue came up in April 1933 when the national executive committee of the Socialist Party barely defeated, by a vote of six to five, a motion to set up a committee to meet with the Communist Party. In arguing for the motion Norman Thomas declared: "I cannot too strongly urge the adoption of this proposal. I have recently been traveling rather extensively in New England and elsewhere and know that in our own party and outside of it we shall suffer very considerable harm if we can be made to appear to be blocking any kind of united action. Frankly I am skeptical whether the Communists will undertake united action on honorable terms. But for the sake of our own members, especially our younger people, it must be made obvious that it is they who sabotage our united front, not we who disdainfully reject it."[290]

Yet if any single event served to crystallize a revolutionary wing (or two or three) in the Socialist Party, it was the Dollfuss *Putsch* in February 1934. Red Vienna, with its great municipal socialist housing projects, had long been the pride of world socialism. And "Austro-Marxism," whose great theoretician was Otto Bauer, was the inspiration of revolutionary socialism the world over. The Austrian Socialist Party, unlike its slothful German sibling, had been a vigorous party of action. Its powerful youth movement, whose symbol was the three arrows, was a model for socialist youth organizations everywhere. Its trained military corps, the *Schutzbund*, was a citizens' militia, ready to fight. But the sudden onslaught by

---

pieces of the Fascist picture. . . . The reason why . . . there has been no strong Fascist movement as yet in the United States is the fact that neither the dominant owning class [n]or its lower middle class allies and dupes have as yet felt the necessity of using Fascism to protect for a little while longer their profit system and their property rights" (p. 462).

[290] Letter to the members of the national executive committee on April 13, 1933, from Clarence Senior, the national secretary, reporting on results of the mail ballot on the motion, together with the comments by various members. Although formal action was rejected, the Socialist Party shortly afterward officially joined the Communist Party in the "United States Congress against War" and worked with it for several months until vitriolic attacks by the communists forced it to withdraw.

the *Heimwehr*, supplied with arms and mortars by Mussolini, caught the socialists off guard. In a week the *Heimwehr* was able to isolate and cut up the socialist detachments.

The gallant Austrian struggle stirred the American socialists. This was atonement for the feckless surrender of German social democracy; this was the answer to the communists who had mocked the socialist reformists. To hail their Austrian comrades during the Vienna fighting, the socialists called a mass meeting in Madison Square Garden. But to the consternation and disgust of the entire radical movement, the communists, in "third-period" style, stormed the Garden, threw chairs from the balcony, and completely disrupted the meeting. Thus, for a while, ended the united front.

Following the Austrian events the left wing opened a drive to capture control of the party. The Militants, for the first time, outlined a set of organizational and programmatic goals. They called for a "disciplined, centralized organization that can control its membership and its institutions"; by this they meant a party-owned press, direct control of the state organizations, and jurisdiction over local election campaigns. They demanded that "socialist fractions" be set up in unions in order to work for party-outlined policies. More sharply than ever before their program was etched with revolutionary acid. They called, with thundering phrases, for turning the imperialist war into a civil war; they declared their readiness, if necessary, to use extraparliamentary means to win power; they warned that a "workers dictatorship" might be needed to defend socialist victories.[291]

Even this program, however, was not sufficiently "left" for a new group that called itself the Revolutionary Policy Committee. In a resolution on the "Road to Power," the R.P.C. declared: "We make no fetish of legality . . . no institution or instrument set up by the capitalist class [i.e., parliamentary democracy] can be depended upon to establish the Workers Republic. Therefore the working-class state will be an entirely new type

[291] In May 1934 the revised Militant program declared: "The National Executive Committee should intensify the work of the party in the unions (particularly in the war, chemical and transportation industries) in order to induce them *to call a general strike in case of war* . . . the struggle against war is part of the struggle to overthrow capitalism, *and . . . if an imperialist war does break out we should make every effort to turn it into a class war.*" See *Towards a Militant Program for the Socialist Party of America*, pamphlet, May 1934, p. 35, italics in the original. This was the sharp mood engendered by the rise of fascism in Europe and the fear of its emergence here. Within the short space of four years, the views of almost all the Militants changed completely: the reactionary character of the Soviet regime revealed itself more fully in the subsequent "confession trials" and purges; at the same time, the American socialists began to appreciate more fully the democratic resiliency and traditions of American society. By 1939 the rash and adolescent rhetoric had been repudiated completely.

of state based on workers' councils, historically suited to serve as the organs of liberation."[292]

Actually the R.P.C. was a weird mélange of revolutionary romanticists and secret Lovestoneite agents. Its first head was that irresponsible adventurer J. B. Matthews; its secretary, a former theological student, Francis Henson. For a while the R.P.C. functioned as a party within a party. It had a national executive committee, maintained an R.P.C. magazine, met regularly in caucus, etc.

Despite the European events, the old guard's position had not changed. In its theory, the old guard had never been "revisionist"—that is, it had never held the gradualist, evolutionary socialist doctrines of the German Eduard Bernstein. Instead, it subscribed to Kautsky's orthodox doctrine that armed force might be necessary to defend the state power won by a legitimately achieved socialist majority. In practice, however, the old guard had completely abandoned any ideas of revolution and shied away from doctrines of force. Its European counterparts had entered "coalition" governments with bourgeois parties; it believed almost entirely in reform and slow, peaceful means as the road to socialism.[293] But the old guard was at serious disadvantage. The "tides of history" were running against it. Equally damaging was the death in October 1933 of Morris Hillquit. Hillquit was the last major link with the American socialist past and with European socialist thought. While Debs had been the voice and Berger the windmill of action, Hillquit had been the intellectual nestor of American socialism. In a party which was tossed constantly by the winds of passing theoretical fads, he was one of the few who anchored their doctrine in a solid knowledge of Marxist thought. In a movement subsisting largely on emotion, his forte was logic. His oratory, never flamboyant or rhetorical, won his audiences by the clear-cut schematism of his well-ordered mind. But his dryness of wit, his coolness of temper, his reserve of manner kept most of the membership at a distance. He was a man who among most inspired respect rather than love; the obverse, in this regard, of Debs.

Hillquit's heirs were Algernon Lee and Louis Waldman. Lee, born in Dubuque, Iowa, in 1873, and the director of the Rand School since 1909, became the party theoretician. A cultivated personality and a precise thinker (a Yankee talmudist, Ben Stolberg called him), he was a colorless speaker—a great handicap in a movement with so high a premium on oratory—and a man of procrastinating habits. On the other hand, Wald-

[292] *An Appeal to the Membership of the Socialist Party*, Mar. 1934, a pamphlet issued by the Revolutionary Policy Committee.

[293] In the fall of 1933, in fact, Abraham Cahan, the editor of the *Jewish Daily Forward*, speaking at the dressmakers' victory celebration in Madison Square Garden, extended an invitation to Roosevelt to join the Socialist Party.

man, one of the five socialist assemblymen expelled from Albany, was a dynamic speaker and a highly charged personality, but his explosive ego made him the special target of left-wing attacks. Neither of the two had Hillquit's great gifts as a compromiser, Hillquit's magnetism or his personal authority, both within and without the party. Although competent individually, the two together proved an old theorem that the sum of the parts was not equal to the whole.

The showdown came at Detroit in 1934. While Thomas was not one of the Militants, he joined with them to rewrite the party's declaration of principles. The new version was written largely by Devere Allen, a Gandhian pacifist. Yet it incorporated most of the flaming phrase-mongering of Militant rhetoric. The Socialist Party, stated the declaration, "will meet war and the detailed plans for war already mapped out by the war-making arms of the government by massed war resistance. . . . It unhesitatingly applies itself to the task of replacing the bogus democracy of capitalist parliamentarianism by a genuine workers' democracy. . . . If the capitalist system should collapse in a general chaos and confusion, which cannot permit of orderly procedure, the Socialist Party, whether or not in such case it is a majority, will not shrink from the responsibility of organizing and maintaining a government under the workers' rule."[294]

The old guard stood aghast. This was the communist incubus emerging full-size. "Anarchistic, illegal, Communist," Waldman cried. The debate continued on a heated, exaggerated plane. Devere Allen retorted, "To remain legal [in the next war] would be to brand forever the socialist movement with the mark of shame." He declared that once the new declaration was adopted, the workers of the nation would flock into the Socialist Party. "Do we want to abandon the democratic method in the attempt to gain power in the United States?" asked Jacob Panken. "We know the workers are on the march," shouted Andrew Biemiller. "We do not agree with Comrade Waldman," he continued, "that the workers are playing a slow and steady game. That is no longer true. Each week brings us fresh evidence. It is upon this general philosophy that this [drafting] committee proceeded."[295]

After three hours of heated debate in this vein, the left wing carried the day 99 to 47 (by weighted membership 10,822 to 6,512). It also swept into office a coalition national executive committee and named Leo Krzycki, a vice-president of the Amalgamated Clothing Workers, as national chairman. The fissure in the party had widened.

In retrospect, it is difficult to understand what the declaration exactly

[294] "Declaration of Principles," on p. 6 of special supplement, *American Socialist Quarterly*, July 1934, containing full stenographic report of the debate on the declaration.

[295] *Ibid.*, pp. 9, 16, 47, 53.

meant. Less than a month after the convention Thomas began backing away from the shrill phrases. "It neither says nor implies that American capitalist democracy is as yet equivalent to Fascism," he declared, and he ascribed the old guard's opposition as a "rationalization of [its] bitter disappointment . . . at losing to a large degree [its] control over Party machinery."[296] In later years Thomas regretted much of the wording, especially the phrase "bogus democracy."[297] Because some panicky party members feared that the wording of the revolutionary declaration might result in jail sentences, as predicted by Waldman, the declaration was submitted to a picked committee of lawyers to find out whether it was legal to be a revolutionist. They replied that it was.

The passage of the Detroit declaration unloosed a civil war in the Socialist Party and many members welcomed the party strife. "Capitalism," after all, was an abstract enemy, speaking on street corners was dull, arguing with unconvinced workers, tedious. Here the struggle was real, the enemy tangible, and most important, victory promised organizational power. For a year and a half guerrilla warfare raged in the party to the exclusion of almost all other problems. Meetings of the branches and of the city central committees became battles planned weeks in advance. Letters, telegrams, and communiqués would call members to caucuses; debates at meetings would rage fiercely for hours and spill over into the neighboring cafeterias until the small hours of the morning. Youngsters boned up eagerly on Marx, Lenin, Kautsky, and tirelessly locked phrases over long windy resolutions on "the road to power." All world history was ransacked for glittering metaphors, while in the corridors petty gossip would zestfully circulate regarding one or another party leader. Spies were planted in the opposing ranks and membership lists were packed. The barricades of Petrograd were being repeated in New York, especially one evening when the old guard abruptly raided the Yipsel offices in the Rand School and snapped new locks on the doors. Nor was this a mimetic combat. Capitalism was doomed; the only problem at hand was to capture the Socialist Party, issue the correct manifestoes, and victory would be assured.

The old guard came alive with a vigor that surprised even itself. It set up two factional newspapers[298] and issued a stream of pamphlets, booklets, and monographs. The Militants responded by issuing the *Socialist Call*, and setting up a *Call* Educational Institute to rival the Rand School.

[296] Norman Thomas, "What Happened at Detroit," *World Tomorrow*, June 28, 1934, p. 321.

[297] *Hammer and Tongs*, supplement to the *Call*, April 23, 1947, p. 9.

[298] The *Socialist Sentinel*, published by the Interstate Conference, and the *Socialist Voice*, published by the Committee for the Preservation of the Socialist Party.

Although the Detroit declaration had carried by a referendum vote of 5,933 to 4,872,[299] the conflict did not end.

Each side pointed to the 1936 convention. The old guard threatened a split if it lost. But the Militants were light-hearted. They felt that with the old guard barnacles scraped away, the ship of socialism would move more lightly, swiftly. The strike wave of 1934—the San Francisco general strike, the pitched battles in Toledo, the fifteen-state walkout in textiles, the citywide truck drivers' strike in Minneapolis—"has no near parallel in American labor history," declared a Militant leader.[300] Reinhold Niebuhr, from his *bénitier*, invoked a philosophy of history: "The right wing of our party . . . has not . . . learned a single lesson from events. . . . It meets the genuine disillusionment of young and vigorous elements in the party merely by repression and mouths the old platitudes about democracy. Its insistence that socialists must always remain within the bounds of legality is a perfect revelation of spiritual decay in socialism. No revolutionary group of whatever kind in history has ever made obedience to law an absolute obligation. . . . The touching devotion of right-wing socialism to legality and the constitution is proof either of inability or unwillingness to profit from the clear lessons of recent history or it is merely a convenient ideological tool for suppressing new life in the party."[301]

Outside party activity was almost at a complete standstill. (In 1934 Thomas received 129,000 votes for United States senator and Charles Solomon 79,000 for governor in New York City, a sharp drop of 30 per cent.) Many left the party in disgust. In New York alone, more than one thousand persons dropped out, and in the period from September 1934 to September 1935 membership dropped over the country from 22,943 to 16,270.[302]

"I find myself having less and less desire to attend the Cleveland convention," wrote James D. Graham, president of the Montana State Federation of Labor and a member of the national executive committee; ". . . this quarreling and bickering among ourselves is very depressing."[303] Similar sentiments were expressed by Dan Hoan. Neither of the two was a Militant; they had both gone along on the feeling against New York, and now felt dismayed.

The 1936 convention of the Socialist Party opened on June 1 in Cleve-

[299] *New Leader*, Oct. 27, 1934.

[300] Paul Porter, "The Meaning of the Labor Upsurge," *American Socialist Quarterly*, Dec. 1934, p. 3.

[301] Reinhold Niebuhr, "The Revolutionary Moment," *ibid.*, June 1935, p. 9.

[302] Figures computed from national office reports. Since the first total was probably inflated by purchase of extra dues stamps by both sides in order to increase convention strength, the loss in real members was probably not so high. Since party membership records were based only on the number of dues stamps sold, the figures at any point must be taken with caution.

[303] Letter to Norman Thomas, May 6, 1936.

land's gargantuan Municipal Auditorium. Giant pictures of Marx, Debs, Berger, and Hillquit decorated the hall, but most visible was the thick pall of "split." Waldman had warned a few weeks before the convention that if the Detroit declaration were not rescinded, the right wing would form a new party. But Thomas was prepared. "Personally I do not believe that a mere defection of Old Guard groups in New York, Massachusetts or even Pennsylvania or Connecticut is so terribly serious," he wrote in a private memorandum to his aides. "To some extent it may help us. Our great loss will come anyway on account of the Roosevelt sentiment and many of the votes that our right-wing friends think they can control would have gone to Roosevelt anyway. . . . It will be our own fault if we do not play up Waldman's announcement before and during the convention to our own help."[304]

On the first day both a left-wing and a right-wing delegation from New York appeared and demanded to be seated. The convention voted immediately to seat the Militants. Someone struck up the *Internationale* and the delegates rose and sang. A delegate pointed to Waldman and Lee. The two rightists had remained seated. A howl of rage broke from the convention. Amid the general uproar, few heard Waldman's tight-lipped answer: "I will not rise to sing a song of solidarity with a group that has just expelled us and split the Socialist Party."

For a second time since 1901 a major division had run its course in the American Socialist Party. With the New York old guard went the Connecticut organization of Jasper McLevy, large blocs in Massachusetts and Pennsylvania (although the Reading organization remained), the Finnish Socialist Federation, the largest of the foreign-language blocs, and the Jewish socialists—in all about 40 per cent of the membership. The old guard retained, too, the party institutions, such as the powerful Workmen's Circle, one of the financial mainstays of the party, the *Jewish Daily Forward*, radio station W.E.V.D., the Rand School, the *New Leader*, and various summer camps. More important, the trade-union officialdom in the International Ladies' Garment Workers, the Millinery Workers, and the Amalgamated Clothing Workers went with the right wing. Dan Hoan, who had fought a split, reluctantly remained with the official Socialist Party.

Yet many socialists were quite optimistic. "Many friendly critics of the party think that this split will destroy whatever prospects of future usefulness the party may have had," wrote Reinhold Niebuhr. "They are in error. . . . The vital forces of the party are not with the [old guard]. . . . In New York there is already a remarkable burst of new energy in the

[304] Letter dated May 11, 1936.

party since the hand of the Old Guard has been removed from the wheel of power."[305]

Mr. Niebuhr probably mistook the glare for the heat; it was not new energy, but new fireworks and noise. In late 1935 Norman Thomas had proclaimed the doctrine of the "all-inclusive party." He invited into the Socialist Party all independent, unaffiliated, affiliated, and dependent radical homeless, the splinter groups, factions, fractions, droplets, and kibitzers. He hoped in this fashion to achieve a "unity" of left-wing forces against fascism. Gitlowites, Zamites, Fieldites, Trotskyites, Lovestoneites all streamed into the party, and each group of intellectual pitchmen set up its own stand. A host of previously isolated one-ring circuses was now operating under one huge billowing tent. And the result was bedlam.

In the next three years, the Socialist Party was torn apart in as many directions as there are on the compass. Some fragments moved toward the communists. In the spring of 1936 exploratory talks were held between spokesmen for the Socialist and Communist parties. Present at these private sessions were Earl Browder and Jack Stachel for the communists, and Norman Thomas, Max Delson, Jack Altman, and Frank Trager for the socialists. They discussed a common ticket in the 1936 elections and "joint fraction work" in the trade unions.[306] Although the first never materialized, the second did. Jack Stachel and Rose Wortis for the communists, and Frank Trager and Herbert Zam for the socialists, worked out a merger of a communist and a socialist-led union in the white-collar field which produced the United Office and Professional Workers Union. In the unemployed field the socialist-communist alliance gave rise to the Workers Alliance, headed by the socialist David Lasser; in the colleges previous moves toward unity produced the American Student Union, headed by socialist Joe Lash. (In these, as well as other organizations, the socialists eventually either were forced out or, like Lasser and Lash, remained for the time being as captives of the communists.) United-front demonstrations on the Spanish issue were held with the communists in July 1936, and later the two groups worked together for a while in the North American Committee to Aid Spanish Democracy. Shortly before the 1936 party convention, Browder proposed a joint presidential ticket of Thomas and Browder. It is doubtful whether the idea would have been accepted; in any event, the tempo of the "Popular Front" soon pushed the communists over toward covert support of Roosevelt.[306a]

[305] Editorial, "The Conflict in the Socialist Party," *Radical Religion* (later *Christianity and Society*), Winter 1936.

[306] No "minutes" of these negotiations were ever kept. Their existence was vouched for to the writer by a participant.

[306a] The united front, it should be emphasized, was a sincere effort of the socialists

Roosevelt too made serious inroads. The New Deal had rescued a number of unions which had been on the rocks. It had given encouragement to the nascent C.I.O., particularly in its organizing campaign against big steel. Labor sought to repay that aid in the 1936 campaign. In New York, Roosevelt strategists, particularly Frances Perkins, wanted to capture 100,000 socialist and needle-trade voters who traditionally avoided the old-party lines. Hillman and Dubinsky wanted to vote for Roosevelt, but not on the Democratic ticket. Together with Waldman they launched in New York State the American Labor Party.

The A.L.P. put the Socialist Party in a dilemma. One group of socialists headed by Jack Altman feared that the right wing had pulled a coup and that the Socialist Party would be isolated. Many socialists in the C.I.O. felt that a campaign by Thomas would compromise their activity in the unions. Powers Hapgood and Franz Daniel, two members of the national executive committee—once extreme leftists, but both now C.I.O. officials—privately urged that the 1936 campaign be soft-pedaled. As the campaign developed, some of the leading Militants defected and joined the American Labor Party.

Organizationally, the party was weak. In 1936, for the first time since its growth in 1929, the party publicly admitted a sharp net loss of members.[307] In the 1936 campaign, Thomas centered his fire completely on Roosevelt. "The 'New Deal' like the 'Old Deal' has failed," the 1936 national platform declared. "Under the New Deal, more vicious attacks have been made on our civil liberties than at any period since the days immediately following the World War. . . . big business has been given almost unheard-of powers. . . . Twelve million men and women are still jobless. Hunger and destitution stalk the land. . . . Under both the 'Old Deal' and the 'New Deal' America has drifted toward insecurity and war—the logical results of capitalism."[308] The talk fell on deaf ears. The Thomas vote nationally plummeted to 187,500; in New York State he received 86,000 votes while the American Labor Party rolled up 238,000.

---

to create wide anti-Fascist unity. For the communists, as the socialists later learned to their sorrow, it was only a tactic to gain eventual control of united-front organizations.

[307] "No single explanation can be found for the loss," reported national secretary Clarence Senior. "In some states there was desertion to some of the patent-medicine remedies, Long, Coughlin or Sinclair. . . . In one, the type of evangelistic campaign put on in 1934 brought in droves of new members who did not realize what they were doing and soon dropped out. . . . Difficulties in the relationship with the Farmer-Labor Party caused a fall in Minnesota. . . . Oregon withdrew from the party for fear members would run afoul of the criminal syndicalist law." Mimeographed report to the national convention, May 23, 1936.

[308] *For a Socialist America* (1936), National Platform, Socialist Party leaflet.

In June 1936 there were two factions in the Socialist Party. One was expelled and then there were three: the old Militant group, the Clarity caucus, and the Appeal group; the last of which was a thinly woven scrim for the Trotskyites who entered the Socialist Party *en bloc* in June.

The old Militant group, the balding Young Turks of yesteryear, had opposed the right wing because of the latter's lethargy. They had hoped that, with the sources of inertia removed, the party would leap swiftly ahead. Now they found themselves isolated. In New York, an American Labor Party had been formed. The Wisconsin socialists were entering the Farmer-Labor Political Federation, a combination in that state of the La Follette progressives and the Milwaukee socialists. In Illinois and Detroit municipal labor parties were being organized. The old Militants wanted to move in that direction. They favored a mass labor party, cautiously approved of the Popular Front, and haltingly endorsed collective security as against any kind of revolutionary defeatism. The old Militants were led by Jack Altman, the party secretary in New York, a past master of factional infighting, and Paul Porter of Wisconsin, a serious-minded student of socialism who had sought, in proposals like the commonwealth plan, to break away from the old stereotypes of socialist planning.

The Clarity group, composed in part of the Militant caucus, the Revolutionary Policy Committee[309] and the driftwood of the left, repeated the clichés of revolution. ("The backbone of the capitalist state is made up of the army and burocracy. . . . These instruments of permanent reaction make a purely peaceful transition to power extremely unlikely. . . . A parliamentary majority for the working-class is improbable, and in America almost impossible. . . . [These] parliamentary campaigns must be part of a general preparation of the masses for revolutionary struggles on the extra-parliamentary front.")[310] The Clarity group, in Leninist fashion, counterposed a "revolutionary vanguard" party to a mass labor party, opposed the Popular Front and damned collective security as "merely leading the working class into support of a new imperialist war." The leaders of the Clarity group were Herbert Zam, a sectarian field marshal with a worker's baton in his knapsack, Gus Tyler, a brilliant but mercurial dialectician, and the Delson brothers, Max and Robert, two intense young lawyers.

The Trotskyites were the Pharisees of the revolution. Expelled from the Communist Party in 1928, they wandered in the wilderness for five years, almost in unconscious imitation of what Toynbee called the etherialization of leadership—the group suffers privation and the leader

[309] The rest of the Revolutionary Policy Committee withdrew and followed Lovestone in seeking to infiltrate the American Labor Party and the C.I.O.

[310] "Where We Stand," editorial statement in *Socialist Clarity*, Mar. 1, 1937, p. 3.

withdraws to return renewed in strength. After its expulsion, the Trotskyite group had decided to remain a faction within communism rather than "turn its face to the masses" and seek new recruits. "Let us not delude ourselves with the idea we can go to the great unschooled mass now," wrote James P. Cannon, the historic leader of American Trotskyism. "The road to the masses leads through the vanguard and not over its head." In 1933, the revolutionary moment arrived. Their ranks weeded of the impatient, the dilettante, and the unstable, the Trotskyites stood in the crucible, ready for the fire. "By the end of 1933," Cannon wrote, "we felt confident that we were on the way to the reconstitution of a genuine Communist Party in this country. We were sure that the future belonged to us. A lot of struggles were yet ahead of us but we felt that we were over the hill, that we were on our way. History has proved that we were right in those assumptions. Thereafter things moved very rapidly and continually in our favor. Our progress from that time on has been practically uninterrupted."[311]

Whatever "progress" the group did make was largely by cannibalism. The first victim was the American Workers Party, a small but promising indigenous radical group led by a Dutch-born preacher named A. J. Muste. In the tradition of the proletarian preacher Muste had gone among the workers, and after ten years of pastorates emerged in 1919 as the leader of the famous Lawrence, Massachusetts, textile strike. Thereafter, he devoted himself full time to the labor movement, becoming in 1921 dean of Brookwood Labor College at Katonah, New York, the seed bed for many of the top labor organizers in the United States today. Muste gathered around him a group of brilliant labor intellectuals like David Saposs, the economist, and J. B. S. Hardman, former leader of the Jewish socialists. In 1929, these men formed the Conference for Progressive Labor Action in order to stimulate labor thinking.

With the depression, the emphasis of this group turned to action. In a few cities, notably Toledo, Allentown, and other industrial centers in the Ohio Valley area, they organized unemployed leagues with notable success. The group gained national attention when in the spring of 1934 it led the spectacular Auto-Lite strike in Toledo, one of the first of the new-style militant strikes which flashed through the Ohio Valley in the next five years.

In 1933, the C.P.L.A., in response to the industrial ferment, decided to organize the American Workers Party. In its nondogmatic approach to the American worker, the party attracted a number of quixotic and independent spirits including, besides Muste and Hardman, Sidney Hook, James Burnham, Ludwig Lore, and Louis Budenz. The responsibility of being a radical party, however, turned their attention to the need of

[311] James P. Cannon, op.cit., p. 117.

"theory." The theme of "unity" was also in the air. Trotsky's analysis of the criminal nature of the "social fascist" theory struck many as acute. So when the Trotskyites proposed unification of the two groups, a majority of the American Workers Party agreed. Hardman opposed the move and retired from active politics; Budenz also opposed unity, but he reentered the Communist Party.[312] In 1934 the two groups fused and formed the Workers Party. Although the Muste group was larger, the Trotskyites were more compact and soon played the dominant role.

Under Trotsky's orders, the Workers Party soon sought entry into the Socialist Party (the tactic known in radical history as the "French turn" in honor of the first infiltration maneuver into the French Socialist Party). A number of Trotskyites, feeling this to be a dilution of revolutionary purity, bolted the Workers Party and formed the Revolutionary Workers League. Muste, exhausted by these gyrations, simply retired from political activity.[313]

The Trotskyites entered the Socialist Party, as Cannon stated candidly, in order to supply leadership to the confused and leftward moving masses. The socialists, however, were somewhat unappreciative of the honor. In his elegant prose, Commissar Cannon told of the reception and voiced his complaints:

"The negotiations with these *papier-mâché* heroes were a spectacle for gods and men. I will never forget them. I believe that in all my long and . . . checkered experience, which has ranged from the sublime to the ridiculous, and vice versa, I never encountered anything so fabulous and fantastic as the negotiations with the chiefs of the 'Militants' caucus in the Socialist Party. They were all transient figures, important for a day. But they didn't know it. They saw themselves in a distorting mirror, and for a brief period imagined themselves to be revolutionary leaders. Outside their own imagination there was hardly any basis whatever for their assumption that they were at all qualified to lead anything or anybody, least of all a revolutionary party which requires qualities and traits of character somewhat different from the leadership of other movements. They were inexperienced and untested. They were ignorant, untalented, petty-minded, weak, cowardly, treacherous and vain. And they had other faults too. . . . Our problem was to make an agreement with this rabble to admit us to the Socialist Party. In order to do that we had to negotiate. It was a difficult and sticky job, very disagreeable. But that did not deter

---

[312] Where subsequently he became managing editor of the *Daily Worker*, and in 1945 a returnee to his Catholic faith and one of the chief witnesses in the government's indictment in 1950 of the American Communist Party.

[313] A few years later he renounced Marxism and became the executive director of the Fellowship of Reconciliation, a pacifistic Christian socialist organization which preached Tolstoyan love and Gandhian *satyagraha*.

us. A Trotskyist will do anything for the party, even if he has to crawl on his belly in the mud. We got them into negotiations and eventually gained admission by all sorts of devices and at a heavy cost. . . . We received no welcome, no friendly salute, no notice in the press of the Socialist Party. Nothing was offered to us. Not one of the leaders of our party was offered so much as a post as branch organizer by these cheapskates—not one. . . . If we had been subjective people standing on our honor, we might have said, 'To hell with it!' and walked away. . . . [But] we just said to ourselves: that is blackmail we are paying for the privilege of carrying out an historically important . . . task. . . . When, a little later, the leaders of the Socialist Party began to repent of the whole business; wishing they had never heard the name of Trotskyism . . . it was already too late. Our people were already inside the Socialist Party and beginning their work of integrating themselves in the local organizations."[314]

Having integrated themselves, the Trotskyites dialectically proceeded to the task of disintegration. They took over the *Socialist Appeal*, a paper published by a small band of Trotskyite scouts who had cased the terrain before the full invasion; they also set up a newspaper in California, arranged for meetings of the Trotskyite "plenums" and, in short, set up shop as a fullfledged faction.

The tumult of the earlier years was a thin-throated noise compared to the din that now ensued. Mimeograph machines clicked overtime. Meetings of fractions, caucuses, committees, blocs, splintlets took place every day and night in the week. By this time, the only ones left to debate were the party "pros" (party officials, functionaries of allied organizations such as the Workers Defense League, Workers Alliance, etc.), some remaining union officers, a sprinkling of teachers and lawyers, and the students; these debates became the substance of their days. Other party members dropped away like leaves in the October wind.

The chief issues in dispute were the labor party and Spain. For the Trotskyites a "correct" policy on Spain was the *sine qua non* of the revolutionary policy; there the "road to power" was being laid. All arguments were refracted through the experiences of the Bolsheviks in the days between February and October. Should one be a "defeatist" (i.e., place the social revolution above the civil war and set the defeat of the "bourgeois and Popular-Front" coalition as the first task), or be a "defensist" (i.e., place defeat of the enemy as the first order)? The Trotskyites wanted to set up Spanish soviets as the only means of rallying the people. They argued that Socialist Party aid should not go to the Loyalist government—as it was doing in part, through participation in the North American Committee to Aid Spanish Democracy—but to left-wing forces such as the Catalan P.O.U.M. which had a social revolutionary program.

[314] Cannon, *op.cit.*, pp. 224-26, 232.

The old Militants favored support of Largo Caballero, the leader of the socialist left wing and then the premier of the government. The Clarity group, however, carried the day by committing the party to a resolution which "advanced the notion of a social program simultaneously with a civil war." "Here for the first time," wrote Gus Tyler, "the party comes out in favor of workers', soldiers' and peasants' committees as the basis of a Socialist government."[315]

This program was not good enough, however, for the Trotskyites. Moreover, it was time to leave. Trotsky now felt that, as the German debacle had discredited the Second and Third Internationals, the defeat of the Loyalists would show the need for a Fourth International which could carry the banner of revolution across Europe. The Spanish P.O.U.M., the small Independent Labor Party of England, the dissident communist Brandler-Thalheimer group of émigré German communists were all moving in that direction. The Trotskyites wanted to get there first and, since the American group was the biggest Trotskyite faction in the world, the new line was to break loose from embarrassing "centrist" entanglements. Consequently, the Trotskyites began a series of provocations. Finally in August 1937, little more than a year after they had entered the Socialist Party, they were expelled. Soon afterward, they organized the Socialist Workers Party. The Trotskyites had gained measurably by their infiltration.

They came in with a few hundred members and walked out with more than a thousand. They had the entire socialist youth organization in tow; they had made marked gains in New York, disrupted the Illinois party, and left the California organization a shambles. If the Trotskyite experience left any positive results within the Socialist Party, these were, first, a complete political inoculation against the communists, and second, the end of the witless policy of an all-inclusive party.

Following this violent emetic, the Socialist Party was viscerally weak. The stolid and respectable Pennsylvania Dutch socialists of Reading, unable to stomach the factional diet, had joined the Social Democratic Federation. The Wisconsin socialists, hoping to build a national farmer-labor movement through their alliance with the La Follettes, talked of leaving. Only the New York and Michigan organizations maintained any degree of viable political strength.

The question of the labor party, however, disrupted the New York and Michigan socialists. In New York, the Altman-Laidler bloc, representing the trade-union and middle-class reform elements still in the party, argued for support of the American Labor Party. Thomas was inclined to go along. He was the Socialist Party's nominee for mayor of New York, but withdrew in November 1937, although the party did not publicly support

[315] Gus Tyler, *Save the Socialist Party from the Wreckers*, mimeographed statement (1937, but undated).

La Guardia. (The American Labor Party received 480,000 votes that year in New York City.) By a narrow vote of eight to seven, the national executive committee endorsed this policy. The Clarity forces were bitter. "The real forces behind this narrow victory for the opponents of the National Convention line," they charged, "was [sic!] the irresponsible bullying of Thomas. His constant implied threat in the open, and much more in private, to make this party decision one as between him or his loss gave some NEC members the choice of ratifying a fait accompli, or losing Thomas. The real blackjack for the petty trade union burocracy in the party was Norman Thomas."[316]

The labor-party issue dominated the 1938 convention of the Socialist Party, which opened in April, in Kenosha, Wisconsin. By this time the party membership had sunk to 7,000, or a plunge of 66 per cent from the high-water mark of 21,000 in 1934; it was even below the all-time low of 7,800 reached in 1928. Of this 1938 membership, two-thirds were concentrated in Wisconsin, New York, and Pennsylvania.[317]

Although reduced to this tiny number, the convention majority tenaciously refused, against the urgings of Thomas and Hoan, to endorse the outright entry of the Socialist Party into labor parties, such as the A.L.P. in New York and the Farmer-Labor Political Federation in Wisconsin. The majority, led by Maynard Kreuger of the University of Chicago, argued that unless the socialists affiliated as a federated bloc and retained the "right to run Socialist Party candidates against any capitalist candidates" endorsed by the labor groups, the party would lose its identity. After about five hours of vociferous debate, the majority won by a weighted membership vote of 3,414 to 3,163. On foreign policy, the socialists condemned collective security, charged that the New Deal was making war plans which would "fasten on American life a virtual fascist dictatorship," and urged the lifting of the embargo on Loyalist Spain. The line, shaped by Thomas, called for "people's boycotts" and qualified support of neutrality legislation. This was the first beginning of the "isolationist" line in Socialist Party foreign policy. (No attention was paid to the fact that this policy contradicted the party's attitude toward the application of the neutrality laws in the case of Spain.)

After the 1938 convention, the influence of the Socialist Party in the labor movement—aside from some strength among the auto workers—sank to almost zero. Leading socialists who held C.I.O. posts found themselves absorbed by trade-union problems to the exclusion of all others, and, out of political necessity, committed to the support of Roosevelt and the New Deal. Important figures such as Leo Krzycki, the former na-

[316] *The Struggle for Revolutionary Socialism Must Go On!* mimeographed statement of the Clarity group on the present situation in the party (1937, but undated), p. 3.
[317] National office report to the national convention, April 21, 1938, mimeographed.

tional chairman, Powers Hapgood and Franz Daniel, former members of the national executive committee, John Green, president of the shipyard workers, and a host of minor C.I.O. functionaries, quietly dropped away. Only one enclave of socialist strength remained, Michigan, but this too was shattered by New Deal pressure, C.I.O. discipline, and factional union politics.

Within the United Auto Workers, a showdown was shaping between president Homer Martin on the one hand and a "Unity" caucus on the other. Martin (a former Missouri Baptist minister with an other-worldly fervor, but a this-worldly, erratic, and unstable temperament) was tutored by Jay Lovestone, and surrounded by Lovestone's assistants, Francis Henson and Irving Brown (both of whom had been leaders of the socialist Revolutionary Policy Committee). The "Unity" caucus was a strange mélange of communists, aggressive union politicians, and for a while, Walter Reuther, who, nominally a socialist, was acting on his own. Their trump card was the John L. Lewis and communist alliance and the confidence that the national C.I.O. would back them.

The Socialist Party was in a dilemma. On ideological grounds, particularly because of his antiwar stand, Thomas tended to favor Homer Martin. The Michigan socialists, for union reasons—charging that Martin was a poor union leader who maintained unsavory alliances with reactionary southern know-nothing elements in the union—opposed him; but they were unhappy about allying themselves with the communists. As a logical move, the socialists approached Martin to form a harmony caucus which would fight both the communists and the reactionary elements. Martin was willing, but the scheme was finessed by Lovestone. Reuther, to the joy of the socialists, finally broke with the communists and launched an independent caucus. Hillman and Lewis, not averse to building balances of power, privately encouraged him. As a price, however, they insisted he resign from the Socialist Party. They pointed out that Frank Murphy needed full labor support for reelection as governor of Michigan, and Reuther would have to support Murphy.[318]

The Murphy issue symbolized the full dilemma of the Socialist Party in relation to the unions and the New Deal. In a letter to Norman Thomas,

[318] This was not the first time that such exactions were levied. In 1936 the auto workers convention, prodded by the socialists and with the mute consent of the communists, defeated a proposal to endorse Roosevelt for reelection. When Lewis' representative, Adolph Germer (the wartime national secretary of the party), heard this he raged: "Communists and socialists have taken over the convention, and are voting not as auto workers, but according to their political views." Lewis informed the delegates, after being prodded by a perturbed White House, that unless they supported Roosevelt a mine-workers contribution of $100,000 for organizing would be withheld. With this pistol at its head the U.A.W.—in the five minutes before adjournment—voted unanimously to support Roosevelt. See Irving Howe and B. J. Widick, *The U.A.W. and Walter Reuther* (New York, 1949), pp. 52-53.

George Edwards, the Socialist Party caucus leader in the auto union (and later president of the Detroit City Council), summed up the issue that had been wracking the party for two months: "We are now faced with a very difficult situation on the political field. Our party here is growing in the unions in membership and influence. But our progress is jeopardized by the complex situation in the current political campaign. Some of the leading unionists cannot refrain from giving some support to Murphy without sacrificing their own positions. This handicaps the party's campaign and even endangers the party organization at a time when there is a splendid chance to build the party and draw in many new elements from the entire labor movement here."[319]

The socialists in Michigan also proposed that Walter Reuther be allowed a "friendly resignation" from the party (i.e., without public notice or blast). The idea disturbed Thomas. Said he, ". . . the more I think of it, the less I like it. It will not be understood as completely friendly. It will lessen our influence and prestige and the only reason that you now seem to think it necessary is that he may have to support Murphy in some fashion. Aren't we going to be in some serious position if we have to let go every good union man who, according to your own doctrines, is obliged to support a non-Socialist candidate?"[320]

The Michigan socialists worked out a typical compromise. As union men and within the union they supported Murphy; among the socialists they supported Socialist Party candidates. This double bookkeeping was censured by the national party, and the Michigan socialists finally ran a candidate for governor against Murphy. Their candidate's vote was feeble, and the party suffered.

In New York, too, that year the socialists ran a gubernatorial candidate, despite the pleas of many union men to endorse Herbert Lehman. One reason was the refusal of the American Labor Party to admit the socialists on other than an individual membership basis. An important secondary consideration was that the party's place on the ballot depended, according to electoral law, on the vote for governor. Not only would the socialists have had to agree not to run a socialist but they would have had to endorse the A.L.P.'s "old-party" capitalist candidate; this the party would not do. Thus, the doctrinaire stand on the election issues of 1938 completed the socialist isolation from the labor movement.

By the spring of 1939, the Socialist Party was collapsing. There was almost no functioning national office, whole branches dropped away because of the continued factionalism, the party dues-paying membership in New York was averaging only 150, while only 300 persons had reg-

[319] Letter from George Edwards to Norman Thomas, Sept. 24, 1938.
[320] Letter from Norman Thomas to Ben [Fischer] and Tucker [P. Smith], Aug. 19, 1938.

istered.[321] But the old battles were still being fought. The right wing, to the extent that there still was an organized grouping, had returned to a viewpoint in no way different from that of traditional social democracy. Its spokesman, Paul Porter, rejected the Leninist conception of the party, and the role of disciplined cadres which had dominated left-wing thinking for a decade. He argued that socialists could function within "the present democratic system" and that the Socialist Party had no future in independent electoral action. Unity negotiations were opened with the Social Democratic Federation and continued in desultory fashion. But unity was impossible because of differences on the war question. The Reading, Pennsylvania, organization, because it was pacifist by inclination, did rejoin the Socialist Party.

The outbreak of war completed the destruction of the Socialist Party as a political entity. When Hitler's armies marched across Poland the party declared that "our first duty to the ideal of democracy, as well as to the interests of 130,000,000 men, women and children, is to keep America out of war. . . . Only in an America at peace can the masses make democracy work so well that it can inspire our brethren in the rest of the world to new faith in it."[322] But there was no prescription this time, as so readily in the past, on how the Polish proletariat or the French workers or British labor should act.

World War II exposed socialist thinking as the politics of irresponsibility. The socialists wanted Hitler to lose, and the Allies to win, but "it was not our job to say so," as one leading member declared. The effort to escape the dilemma of "in but not of" the world reached the most absurd heights in the party discussion on the Finnish issue. There was full sympathy for Finland in her efforts to defend herself against Russia, but concern lest any support aid the Allies or Hitler. At the meeting of the national executive committee in December 1939, these were the motions discussed and acted upon:

"We support sending of money and supplies from working class organizations here to working class organizations in Finland. (Carried)

"We support cancellation of the Finnish debt. (Carried)

"We do not raise the slogan of 'Arms to Finland.' (Carried)

"We oppose withdrawal under present conditions of [the] American ambassador to [the] U.S.S.R. (Carried)

"No reference to government policy in [the] statement. (Motion withdrawn because of actions above.)

"Full moral, financial and material support to Finnish workers." (De-

[321] Letter from Arthur G. McDowell, acting executive secretary, to Jack Altman, April 4, 1939.
[322] Socialist Party statement, released Sept. 11, 1939.

feated after Allard, in reply to questions, said that "material" included arms.)

Robert Delson, a member of the national executive committee, stated: "I vote for the motion as a whole with very serious misgivings as to whether there is any group in Finland to which we can give aid, since there is no evidence that the working class is carrying on an independent struggle."[323]

The 1940 Socialist Party convention, which opened in Washington on April 6, continued this tortuous line of reasoning. Its statement on war declared that "the fact that Hitler is the opponent does not make the Allied war a fight for democracy." It maintained that the defeat of Hitler would have meaning only if a working-class revolution followed, and charged that the Allies were discussing the "restoration of the monarchy or removal of Hitler with maintenance of domestic fascism in the Reich." In the logic of this analysis it declared: "The American working class . . . must aid the working class in the warring powers and particularly the heroic underground movements that have carried on for years despite the terror. It can render that aid only if it remains free from dictatorship itself—by keeping America out of war and out of the conditions that create dictatorship." The heart of the resolution declared that America's entry into the war would mean a dictatorship at home. It centered its fire, therefore, on military defense measures and affirmatively called for "the continuance of independent working class action through the medium of the workers' boycott of German and Japanese goods." It declared for economic neutrality and said "we condemn America's economic partici- pation on the side of the Allies just as we condemn Russia's economic participation on the side of Nazi Germany."[324]

This resolution had not been adopted without much pulling and haul- ing. A "sizable" pacifist group had developed in the Socialist Party, the remnants of the revolutionary wing were still shrill, the right-wing group wanted limited aid to the Allies. Only the personal authority of Thomas held the pieces of wreckage together.

Soon after the convention, however, Hitler began his invasion of Nor- way and his blitzkrieg across France. For many, the politics of irre- sponsibility were shed. They had never expected Hitler to win and the terrifying realization that he might do so forced them to dispense with the luxury of their illusions. One prominent left-winger, who in a letter of May 1939 had stated: "In case of war . . . I am for an underground movement especially among those who remain in key industrial areas," now urged "all-out effort" to help the Allies. Half of the *Call* editorial

[323] Minutes, national executive committee, Milwaukee meeting, Dec. 9, 1939.
[324] *Proceedings, National Convention of the Socialist Party, April 6-8, 1940*, mimeographed (Washington, D.C.), pp. 3-6.

board spoke out for full economic aid to Hitler's opponents. The Wisconsin state convention voted overwhelmingly to ask the party to reconsider its stand. Altman and the right-wing group in New York joined the Committee to Defend America by Aiding the Allies. Thomas pleaded that these men leave the party quietly, rather than make a fight for their point of view, since any new factional struggle would end the party and leave no antiwar voice in America.[325]

The quickening pace of the war hastened the disintegration of the Socialist Party. When Norman Thomas testified against the bill for lend-lease aid to Britain, a group of socialists, including Reinhold Niebuhr, Alfred Baker Lewis, Jack Altman, and Gus Tyler released a statement opposing him.[326] Little more than a month later, three members of the national executive committee, Paul Porter of Wisconsin, Leonard Woodcock, party secretary in Michigan, and Arthur McDowell, former labor secretary, resigned, charging they had been gagged. Both the leaders of the Militants as well as of the Clarity group were now prowar. Only Thomas remained. Although his own position was probably at this time in the minority, Thomas was able to keep control of the party and steer it on an isolationist course because of the inability of a scattered opposition to organize. Instead they resigned.

Probably the low point of party influence was reached in May 1941 when Norman Thomas, his moral opposition to the war so complete, joined Charles Lindbergh and Burton K. Wheeler at an America First Committee rally at Madison Square Garden. Until this point there had been the ludicrous dilemma of exempting oneself from all public-policy responsibility by calling for "workers action" instead of capitalist government action, and seeking to mobilize public opinion on government policy. Now Thomas spoke out solely in terms of affecting government policy. He argued that the possibility of a "complete Anglo-American victory . . . [is] exceedingly slim," and "if we are to talk negotiated peace, why not begin a peace offensive now?" But when he spoke, Thomas spoke alone; behind him lay only the charnel house of American socialism.

XIII. The Days of Sere and Yellow Leaf

Among the radical, as among the religious minded, there are the once born and the twice born.[327] The former is the enthusiast, the "sky-blue healthy-minded moralist" to whom sin and evil—the "soul's mumps and measles and whooping coughs," in Emerson's phrase—are merely transient episodes to be glanced at and ignored in the cheerful saunter of

[325] Letter from Norman Thomas to Jack Altman, June 5, 1940.
[326] New York Times, Jan. 23, 1941.
[327] I use the distinction coined by Francis W. Newman and elaborated by William James in his The Varieties of Religious Experience.

life. To the twice born, the world is "a double-storied mystery" which shrouds the evil and renders false the good; and in order to find truth, one must lift the veil and look Medusa in the face.

The trauma of the twice born, like the regenerative rites of Demeter, is a phase in the cycle of self-consciousness. Every political generation has expressed this anguish, from Milton's *Ready and Easy Way*, the disillusioned outcry of his loss of faith in Cromwell by one of the greatest of all Christian humanists, to Dostoevsky's *The Possessed* whose biting picture of Shigalovism is the most savage prophecy of the fate of egalitarian movements. The generation of the 1930's passed through the looking glass of illusions in the years from the Moscow trials to the Nazi-Soviet pact. "What is the opposition?" asks Silone's Uliva in *Bread and Wine*. "Another bureaucracy that aspires to totalitarian domination in its turn. . . . a totalitarian orthodoxy which will use every means, from cinema to terrorism, to extirpate heresy and tyrannize over individual thought."

The Nazi-Soviet pact, which exposed the moral pretensions of the communists, was a winter blast shattering the "sky-blue" optimism of the once-born enthusiasts. The *Nation* and the *New Republic*, two of the chief supporters of the Popular Front, recoiled in genteel horror. Vincent Sheean, the latter-day John Reed of communist romanticism, published a series of articles denouncing Stalinism as the "Thermidor," the counter-revolution that betrayed "October." Louis Fischer voiced the doubts that he had suppressed for years. Granville Hicks resigned rather than parrot the stupid explanations given him. Heywood Broun, the day after the pact, wrote, "the masquerade is over." In England, Harold Laski, John Strachey, Victor Gollancz, and others stepped out of the parade. The communist hacks answered back. "Why do many intellectuals retreat at sharp turns in history?" asked V. J. Jerome, the party's cultural commissar. They are, he said, "impotent subjectivists . . . Don Quixotes. . . ."[328] Chief hatchetman Mike Gold, never very happy amidst the bourgeois respectability of the Popular Front, unloosed his scatalogical adjectives: ". . . these Mumfords, MacLeishes and Franks," he shouted, "may go on spouting endlessly their torrents of 'spirituality,' all the large, facile, greasy abstract words that bookmen, like confidence men, are so perfect in producing. [But] . . . Where are they going after rejecting liberalism? Not to Communism surely, but toward the other pole, toward fascism." "Intellectuals," said Gold, recalling an earlier essay of 1937, "are peculiarly susceptible to Trotskyism, a nay-saying trend."[329]

Some communists retreated to a theory of class morality. "History"

[328] V. J. Jerome, *Intellectuals and the War* (pamphlet, New York, 1940), pp. 16, 23.
[329] Michael Gold, *The Hollow Men* (New York, 1941), pp. 73, 122.

was the final arbiter and all values were sacrificed to the expediency of the party in fulfilling its "tasks." Others, less hard-bitten, secretly cherished the hope that the Soviet Union "really" was anti-Fascist, but biding its time. Events quickly disproved that illusion. All over the world, communists began sabotaging the war against Hitler. In September of 1940, during the dangerous days of the buzz bombs over the channel, the communists called a "peace conference" in London. In the United States communists pulled crippling strikes in the tank-producing Allis-Chalmers plant at Milwaukee and the plane-producing North American Aviation factory in Inglewood, California. The Communist Party declared in its election program that ". . . the Roosevelt Government . . . shares the responsibility for inciting war in Europe, in Scandinavia and in the Baltic."[330]

The party fronts were quickly transformed. The League for Peace and Democracy became the American Peace Mobilization, and it raised as its slogan, "The Yanks Are Not Coming."[331] Around the gates of the White House the communists began a "perpetual peace vigil." On the morning of June 22, 1941, it magically vanished.

After the Nazi invasion of Russia, the communists became the exemplars of patriotism. They eagerly adopted a no-strike pledge and actively sought to discourage other unions from striking (as when Harry Bridges kept his local Montgomery-Ward warehousemen on the job when other mail-order workers walked out in Chicago). They soft-pedaled the Negro issue, called for speedup in the factories, and mobilized their entire propaganda apparatus to exert pressure for a second front in Europe. By 1944, following the conferences of great powers at Teheran, the communists dissolved the Communist Party and became the "educational" American Communist Political Association.[332] But Browder, in his enthusiasm for the new capitalism, had stepped a little too far. Little more than a year later, in April 1945, he was denounced by Jacques Duclos, leader of the French Communist Party, for a "notorious revision

[330] *Party News*, Pre-Convention Number. Issued by the National Committee, Communist Party, for Members of the Communist Party (April 1940), p. 7.

[331] On Memorial Day, May 30, 1941, Vito Marcantonio, the vice-chairman of the American Peace Mobilization, spoke over a nation-wide radio hook-up. He began: "As a member of the United States House of Representatives, I have fought the Administration's imperialist program of armaments, conscription, war and dictatorship from the very beginning. At times I have had to vote alone. I have not opposed it partially. I have opposed it in its entirety. Therefore, I now make answer to the President's fireside speech of last Tuesday night, which proclaimed the shooting and bloodshedding and dictatorship phases of the Wall Street-Downing Street Axis scheme for war, empire and dictatorship." Reprinted as *Marcantonio Answers F.D.R.* (June 1941), a pamphlet published by the American Peace Mobilization.

[332] "Teheran and America," statement of the National Committee Plenary Meeting Issue, *Communist*, Feb. 1944, pp. 99-101.

of Marxism,"[333] and shortly after, reviled and scorned, he was cast from the party. The communists now tacked sharply toward the "third-period" line.[334] When the Russians began stirring up the Greek guerrilla E.A.M. in what had tacitly been acknowledged at Teheran as a British sphere of influence, the communists began their cry against Anglo-American imperialism. Following the rejection of the Marshall Plan and the communist coup in Czechoslovakia in February 1948, the cold war was on in earnest.

Since 1946 communist influence in the United States has diminished, although tardy public understanding of the past history of communist penetration has been whipped into almost a panic by Senator McCarthy and other right-wing Republicans. By 1950 the decline in communist influence was so huge that the total membership of party-controlled unions was less than 5 per cent of the numerical strength of organized labor. Except for the battered United Electrical Workers and the west-coast longshoremen, none of these unions were in vital defense areas; on the other hand, the communists had been beaten decisively and cleaned out of the auto workers, the maritime unions, the transport workers, and strategical areas of industrial concentration. In the political field, the communist effort to build a new political party behind Henry Wallace failed miserably when the Progressive Party obtained little more than 1,000,000 votes in 1948; shortly after the outbreak of communist aggression in Korea, Wallace, O. John Rogge, and other noncommunist progressives repudiated the communists, leaving them, for the first time in fifteen years, with no major political or labor figure to front for them. In the intellectual field the only figures who remained were Howard Fast, a writer of slick historical novels,[335] and Paul Robeson, the Negro singer. The government's indictment and conviction of the eleven-man party "politburo" on the grounds of sedition sent the party reeling even further. The membership base of the party, which from 1935 on was largely middle class, began to disintegrate.

[333] *Daily Worker*, May 24, 1945.

[334] But not sharply enough for an inveterate group of revolutionists who had growled at Browder's cozying up to the National Association of Manufacturers. They too were expelled. In the Communist Party being "premature" about a change in the party line is as fatal as being too late. The communist "purge" of 1945 was the first since 1929 and rivaled in numbers the expulsions of the twenties, although it achieved little prominence because no factional bloc was involved. Among those expelled: writer Ruth McKenney and her husband Bruce Minton, Harrison George, editor of the west-coast *People's World*, Max Bedacht, former general secretary of the party, William F. Dunne, former editor of the *Daily Worker*, Bella Dodd, New York State legislative representative, Sam Darcy, district organizer of Philadelphia, and a top group of officers of the National Maritime Union.

[335] One of which, *The American*, a fictionalized version of the life of John Peter Altgeld, was charged by Harry Barnard as infringing on his biography, *Eagle Forgotten*. Fast settled out of court for an undisclosed sum while Fast's publishers reprinted the Barnard book.

In 1950 the communist movement stood revealed before the American people not as a political party but as a conspiracy, and that conspiracy was being driven out of American life, not always with scrupulous regard for civil liberties.[336] Its operations had revealed to easygoing Americans the meaning of an expansionist ideological force of a magnitude previously unknown in history. To the twentieth-century political experience it had contributed two notable innovations: the "front technique," one of the great political inventions for manipulation in the mass society; and the creation of a disciplined political army, in mufti, stirring disaffection from within.

Withal, there remains the problem of explaining the tremendous emotional hold that communism has on tens of thousands of persons (and the curious liberal mentality which regards with understanding a conversion to communism yet views with disdain the ex-communist, seeing him as a pariah, or as Koestler strikingly put it, as the defrocked priest). The answer lies, perhaps, on a mythopoeic and psychological level. For the convert to communism there is the seductive myth "of humanity's salvation through the rebellion" and "the triumph of the unfortunate," and beyond that, "acquiescence in the mysterious and imperative law of history, resignation to a future deemed even more inevitable than glorious, subservience to the masters of the world."[337] These frame, for the average communist, a set of satisfactions: those that arise from a life of dedication and submission to discipline; a sense of conspiracy and

[336] For a detailed description of the conspiratorial nature of American communism and its complete subordination not only to the Russian political line but to Moscow's espionage demands, see Louis F. Budenz, *Men without Faces* (New York, 1950); Hede Massing, *This Deception* (New York, 1951); and Whittaker Chambers, *Witness* (New York, 1952).

[337] Raymond Aron, "Politics and the French Intellectual," *Partisan Review*, July-Aug. 1950, pp. 588-99. See too a fascinating psychoanalysis of a communist by Dr. Henry Lowenfeld, "Some Aspects of a Compulsion Neurosis," *Psychoanalytic Quarterly*, Jan. 1944. "At about the age of eighteen he joined the Communist Party," Dr. Lowenfeld writes (on. p. 9), "and made it the focal point of his life, serving it with a self-sacrificing faithfulness which contrasted sharply with his otherwise oversceptical, defensive attitude. In his conviction of the scientifically unquestionable correctness of the theory he found an inner security in the chaos of reality. He became a part of a great and powerful movement to which he could abandon himself in complete devotion. In identifying himself with the proletariat, the small and the weak, now large and powerful, he found a tremendous prop for his ego. . . . At the same time he considered himself a member of a modern intellectual aristocracy, with a feeling comparable to that of the religious zealots or the nobility in other periods, which further relieved his sense of smallness [his basic anxiety].

"This extensive sublimation performed the same function of preventing anxiety as did the oceanic feeling or religious faith in other individuals and in other cultural periods. . . . The end of the great figures of the Russian Revolution during the Moscow trials played an important rôle in his loss of faith. Thus his political theories no longer gave him assurance and security in the chaos but instead led him into new conflicts which finally contributed decisively to the outbreak of his neurosis."

martyrdom; an identification with "names" who espouse party causes; an air of being "informed," because one has a set of answers and a fund of organized information (drilled in incessantly at party meetings and through party literature) which one's friends do not possess; a feeling of "purpose" in a world where most people's energies are dissipated in a set of violent but aimless quests. As Ortega y Gasset said in a remarkably prescient passage twenty years ago: "Whatever the content of Bolshevism be, it represents a gigantic human enterprise. In it, men have resolutely embraced a purpose of reform, and live tensely under the discipline that such a faith instils into them. . . . If Europe, in the meantime, persists in the ignoble vegetative existence of these last years, its muscles flabby for want of exercise, without any plan of a new life, how will it be able to resist the contaminating influence of such an astounding enterprise? It is simply a misunderstanding of the European to expect that he can hear unmoved that call to new *action* when he has no standard of a cause as great to unfurl in opposition."[338]

The Socialist Party in the past decade has been alive only because of Norman Thomas. Much as he would have liked to lay down the party burdens (he once sought to build Maynard Kreuger as the party spokesman), he could not; the identification was too complete. As the character of a social movement is often symbolized in its patristic surrogates, so Norman Thomas amazingly sums up the many contradictions of the Socialist Party. A communist critic once sneered at Norman Thomas for entitling his study of poverty in the United States as *Human Exploitation* rather than *Capitalist Exploitation*. The critic had a point, for what arouses Thomas is the emotional and ethical, not the analytical and sociological. Intellectually Thomas knows that "the system" is to blame; but such abstractions have rarely held meaning for him. His interest has always been the personal *fact* of injustice, committed by people; and while socialism might remove the impersonal "basic" causes, he was always happiest when he could *act* where the problem was immediate and personal. In courageously speaking out against the sharecropper terror in Birdsong, Arkansas; in combating martial law in Terre Haute, Indiana; in exposing the Klan in Tampa, Florida; in uncovering the municipal corruption of Jimmy Walker's New York; in defying the anti-free-speech ordinances of Jersey's Boss Hague—in all these instances, Thomas' voice has rung out with the eloquent wrath of an Elijah Lovejoy or a William Lloyd Garrison.

These impulses came naturally to Norman Mattoon Thomas. Religion, orthodox Presbyterianism, was the center of his boyhood home. His father

[338] José Ortega y Gasset, *The Revolt of the Masses* (New York, 1932), pp. 199-200.

was a minister, as was his Welsh-born grandfather. He was raised in a strict Sabbatarian code, but the harshness of his ancestral Calvinism was modified by the kindness of his parents. "My father who believed theoretically in eternal damnation," wrote Thomas, "would never say of any one that he was damned."[339]

Thomas, born in Marion, Ohio, in 1884, was a sickly little boy who grew tall too fast, became an awkward, skinny kid, shy with his peers and talkative with his elders, and who found his main satisfaction in reading.[340] Norman was the eldest of six children and the family was busy always with household chores and other activities of small-town middle-class life. Of the parents Emma Mattoon was the more outstanding personality and "father was content to have it so." In thinking back on his boyhood in the small Ohio town, Thomas remarked: "What a set-up for the modern psychologically-minded biographer or novelist. A study in revolt born of reaction from Presbyterian orthodoxy and the Victorian brand of Puritanism in a midwest setting. The only trouble is that this isn't what happened."

With the financial help of an uncle, Thomas satisfied a boyhood dream and entered Princeton, graduating in 1905 as class valedictorian. Entering the ministry was a more or less destined fact. But in the age of genteel faith in progress, acceptance of the old orthodoxies seemed out of place. As with many socially-minded ministers of the day, the modernist and liberal gospel of Walter Rauschenbusch had its appeal. But it was the filth and poverty of the cold-water flats of the Spring Street slums on New York's west side that turned Thomas actively to social reform. And it was World War I and the influence of the Fellowship of Reconciliation, a religious pacifist organization, that made him a socialist. "God, I felt, was certainly not the 'God and Father of Our Lord Jesus Christ' if his servants could only serve him and the cause of righteousness by the diabolic means of war." Thomas' stand took him from the ministry into politics and journalism. (Rather than endanger the financial support his church received, he resigned the pastorate.) A tall handsome man with strongly-etched patrician features, rich resonant voice, and fine American credentials, he quickly became an outstanding leader in a party depleted of public figures. In 1924 he was nominated for governor of New

---

[339] Thomas has made some autobiographical references in his *As I See It* (New York, 1932). The above quotation as well as some description of Thomas' beliefs are from an unpublished memoir which Thomas wrote for his family in 1944 and to which this author had access.

[340] "I was naturally left-handed," Thomas writes, "but I had to learn to write with my right hand. Father even tried to make me throw a ball with my right arm. Nowadays, all sorts of psychic disturbances are supposed to result from this insistence on right-handedness. As far as I know I escaped. I don't think the faulty process was even responsible for my socialism. But I do suppose it added to my lack of manual skill."

York; four years later—because the two veteran party leaders, Morris Hillquit and Victor Berger, were European-born and because Dan Hoan was busy being mayor of Milwaukee—Thomas was nominated for the presidency.

As a party leader, Thomas had two serious flaws. For one, he strikingly distrusted his own generation and surrounded himself almost entirely with considerably younger men who stood in an admiring and uncritical relation to him. The other was a profound fear of being manipulated, so that every political attack was taken personally. Thomas was intent on being party leader. Often a situation would develop—particularly in the late thirties—when, if party policy tended in a direction other than his, Thomas would threaten to resign (otherwise how could he speak on an issue with pure conscience?). Yet many of Thomas' decisions were made not with an eye to the political results but to the moral consequences, as he saw them. Moreover, by background and temperament, Thomas was concerned largely with issues rather than ideas. In a party whose main preoccupation has been the refinement of "theory" at the cost, even, of interminable factional divisions—Thomas' interest in specific issues often meant shifting alliances with different factions while maintaining aloofness from the jesuitical debates that gave rise to these groups. Thus in the late thirties, Thomas was with the right wing on the labor-party issue, and shifted to the pacifist and left wing on the war problem. Thomas was probably most unhappy during the early and middle thirties when, as a professed non-Marxist, he was involved in the conflicts of fifty-seven varieties of claims to revolutionary orthodoxy.

As a man whose instincts are primarily ethical, Thomas has been the genuine moral man in the immoral society. But as a political man he has been caught inextricably in the dilemmas of expediency, the relevant alternatives, and the lesser evil. As a sophisticated modern man, Thomas has been acutely aware of his ambiguous role, and feels he has made the political choice. "One is obliged," he wrote in 1947, "to weigh one's actions in terms of relative social consequences . . . and the tragedy is that no choice can be positively good. . . . Positively [the pacifists] had nothing to offer in the problem of stopping Nazism before its triumph could not only enslave but corrupt the world. Nothing that is, except for a religious faith in the power of God, a faith stronger if it could include a belief in immortality. It was something but not enough to affirm that the method of war was self-defeating for good ends. It was not enough to say 'if all Americans would act like Gandhi' we should more surely defeat avowed fascism. Possibly, but since almost no Americans would thus act the question remained of the lesser evil." Thomas did learn the lesson of the lesser evil: instead of being an absolute pacifist, however, he became an indecisive one. When the Franco rebellion broke out, Thomas gave up his religious pacifism, but was led to an ambiguous distinction whereby he supported the right of individuals to volunteer and fight, but not "American official intervention by war which would involve conscription." After Pearl Harbor, Thomas came out in "critical support" of the United States government, a position which consisted in the first years largely of ignoring foreign policy and speaking out against injustices on the home front. The Socialist Party itself adopted a formula sufficiently elastic and ambiguous to permit pacifists, antiwar socialists, and prowar socialists to continue together inside the party.[341]

In 1944, the party almost touched bottom, with Thomas receiving only 80,000 votes. The death of Roosevelt in 1945 and the severe New Deal congressional setback in 1946 raised the hopes of some socialists that labor would form a third party. A few individuals began trickling back into the Socialist Party and in 1948 some socialists hoped that a large Thomas vote would stimulate new left-wing political activity. But labor could not afford the luxury of "protest" voting and Thomas received a disappointing 140,000 votes. In 1949, the socialist vote in the New York mayoralty elections fell to an unbelievable low of under 5,000. By 1950, Thomas was ready to give up the political ghost. At the Socialist Party national convention he urged that the party give up all electoral activity and become an educational organization. But a combination of pacifists, left-wingers, and municipal isolationists from Reading and Bridgeport combined to defeat the motion. Shortly afterward the Connecticut state organization left the party when Jasper McLevy was censured for accepting the electoral support of the outspokenly reactionary businesswoman Vivien Kellems. Although some socialists believed, almost to the extent of a faith, that a correct resolution would set the party aright, even such a faith could not, as once before in history, raise this Lazarus from the dead.

After fifty years what had the Socialist Party accomplished in America? It had ruled many American cities, and three of them, Milwaukee, Reading, and Bridgeport, carry an indelible socialist stamp.[342] Many generations

[341] A situation which provoked the comment from Dwight Macdonald: "This failure to split on the war issue has always seemed to me an indication of a certain lack of political seriousness in all the S.P. factions." "Why I Will Not Support Norman Thomas," *Politics*, Oct. 1944, p. 279.

[342] Why was socialism more successful in these cities than others? In the first two, there was an identity of leadership of the labor movement and the Socialist Party. More important, there was a basic ethnic homogeneity which allowed the socialist movement, whose leaders were of similar ethnic backgrounds, to develop. "James Maurer, and most of his colleagues," reports an historian of the Reading movement, "were Pennsylvania-Germans and were conversant with the prejudices, the 'stubbornness,' the virtues, and weaknesses of this group." (See Henry G. Stetler, *The Socialist Movement in Reading, Pennsylvania* [Storrs, Conn., 1943], p. 144.) Of

had been influenced by its ideas. In the last twenty years a depression-matured generation, without profession and hope, had received a schooling in the socialist movement which permitted them to achieve high place as trade-union leaders and staff technicians, government administrators, political scientists, and propagandists. The "progressive" unions in American life, the garment workers, clothing workers, auto workers, textile workers, and many others, had a leadership that in a general way was socialist in spirit. The socialists who had left the party during the war were instrumental in creating the Union for Democratic Action and later the Americans for Democratic Action, which in 1950 had become the leading political voice of liberalism in America. Many of these quondam socialists (almost the entire leadership of the Wisconsin socialists, for example) had entered the Democratic Party, and several of them, such as Andrew Biemiller of Milwaukee and George Rhodes of Reading, had been elected to Congress. These have been the "organizational" fruits. In the form of a set of ideas, socialism has, as a pale tint, suffused into the texture of American life and subtly changed its shadings.

In 1885, an optimistic Andrew Carnegie could, in "A Talk to Young Men," advise how surely to become a success: "There is one sure mark of the coming partner, the future millionaire; his revenues always exceed his expenditures. He begins to save early. . . . A rare chance will soon present itself for investment. The little you saved will prove the basis for an amount of credit utterly surprising to you. . . . [What your] seniors require . . . is the man who has proved that he has the business habits which create capital, and to create it in the best of all possible ways, as far as self-discipline is concerned, . . . by adjusting his habits to his means. Gentlemen, it is the first hundred dollars saved which tells. Begin at once to lay up something. The bee predominates in the future millionaire."

Sixty-five years after his talk, the Carnegie Mansion, one of the last remaining large private mansions on Fifth Avenue, became the new center for Columbia University's School for Social Work. How does one

---

Milwaukee, the story is told of the 1932 election where the socialists won three out of four city-wide offices. When asked to explain the loss of the fourth, an old German socialist explained: "You see, our candidate's name was Bennowicz. If we had had someone with a good American name like Schemmelpfennig we could have won." In Milwaukee and in Bridgeport, however, many of the party's successes are due to the characters of Dan Hoan and Jasper McLevy. Milwaukee actually has never been completely socialist. In the election years that span the period of socialist rule, 1910 to 1940, although Dan Hoan was elected to office fifteen times (three as city attorney and twelve as mayor) the city invariably elected a council that was more than half nonsocialist. (See J. T. Salter, The Pattern of Politics [New York, 1940], pp. 135-59.) Both Dan Hoan and Jasper McLevy have been able city executives who after elections often found their greatest support in the good-government and upper-class wards of the city.

measure the contribution of a specific social movement to so great a change? Certainly, the Malthusian morality, with its insistence that social welfare robs the individual of his moral fibre, has an archaic flavor today. "As a Socialist candidate for Mayor of New York in 1925, I advocated a municipal housing program," Norman Thomas recently stated, "but in those days I would not have tried to get the kind of federal housing subsidy that Senator Taft proposed two decades later. The housing program that has been carried out in recent years would have been considered utopian in 1925."[343] Nor did Thomas dream that many of the planks in his first presidential platform, in the campaign of 1928, would have become law or accepted party policy within two decades. Among them were extension of public works, old-age pensions, public unemployment insurance, a shorter work day, government insurance against weather damage to crops, adequate flood control, the right to organize, Puerto Rican autonomy, Philippine independence, and recognition of Russia. In other words "to the considerable extent that capitalism has delivered more than seemed possible a generation ago," Thomas concluded, "it has done so by accepting things it used to denounce as Socialism."

And yet these welfare concepts, also, grew out of the American soil. It was only because we placed so high a premium on individual worth that we began to accept the idea—reminiscent of frontier communal responsibility—of the social obligations to the individual. (What is social *insurance* if not the sharing of risk and reward?) In this sense the welfare ideals of America in the middle of the twentieth century certainly differed from the collectivization tendencies in other parts of the globe which subordinated the individual and deified *group* concepts.

American society at the middle of the twentieth century was evolving in a far different direction from that predicted by Marxist sociology. There were not in America an "Army," "Church," "Large Landowners," "Bureaucracy," "Bourgeoisie," "Petty Bourgeoisie," and "Proletariat"— the staple ingredients of European social politics which in different combination accounted for the social forms of Germany, Spain, France, and Britain. How could one apply standard political categories to explain the "social role" of a Franklin D. Roosevelt? Should he be called a Tiberius Gracchus who deserted his class to become a people's tribune; an Athenian Solon whose political reforms deflected the revolutionary surge of a propertyless mass; a Louis Napoleon, manipulating first one class and then another while straddling all in order to assure his own Bonapartist rule? Or how does one define the actual political reality presented by the contrast images of industry and labor in that the one proclaims

[343] "Norman Thomas Re-Examines U.S. Capitalism," *Fortune*, Sept. 1950, p. 76.

that this is a "laboristic" society and that "Washington" is leading us off to socialism, the other declares that businessmen are running the administration and labor has no voice.

The old simplistic theories no longer hold. We seem to be evolving toward some form of technical-military-administrative state, especially as the pressures of a permanent war economy bring into focus a priority of needs which are national in character and override the demands of any particular interest group. The growth of a federal budget from four billion in 1930 to more than forty billion in 1950 (apart from the wartime peak budget of over ninety billion in 1944) was an unplanned and crescive fact, and yet these new enormous magnitudes are of decisive import in shaping the economy. Along the way, the nascent state capitalism has had to enlarge its social budgets and provide for the welfare of large masses; quondam socialists, now in high positions in labor and government, have tended to instill a sense of social responsibility. But it is not primarily a social welfare state which has developed. In the dimly-emerging social structure, new power sources are being created and new social divisions are being formed. Whatever the character of that new social structure may be—whether state capitalism, managerial society, or corporative capitalism—by 1950 American socialism as a political and social fact had become simply a notation in the archives of history.

If a cenotaph ever were to be raised for American socialism, I would nominate for inscription one story and one remark which sum up the adventures of the Socialist Party as an American political movement:

The Rabbi of Zans used to tell this story about himself:

In my youth when I was fired with the love of God, I thought I would convert the whole world to God. But soon I discovered that it would be quite enough to convert the people who lived in my town, and I tried for a long time, but did not succeed. Then I realized that my program was too ambitious, and I concentrated on the persons in my own household. But I could not convert them either. Finally it dawned upon me: I must work upon myself, so that I may give true service to God. But I did not accomplish even this.

Hasidic Tale

He who seeks the salvation of souls, his own as well as others, should not seek it along the avenue of politics.

Max Weber

193

Bibliographical Essay*

The standard bibliographical source for material on American social-ism before 1952 is Volume II of *Socialism and American Life* (Princeton, 1952), compiled by T. D. Bassett. Since then, a number of bibliographical essays, principally on the Socialist movement before 1919, have been published. The study by Ira Kipnis, *The American Socialist Movement, 1897-1913* (Columbia, 1952), lists a large periodical literature. Henry F. Bedford's *Socialism and the Workers in Massachusetts, 1886-1912* (Mas-sachusetts, 1966) surveys various collections. Gerald Friedberg's "Source for the Study of Socialism in America, 1901-1919," in *Labor History* (Vol. VI, No. 2, Spring 1965), annotates existing collections. *Labor History*, published by the Tamiment Institute, regularly publishes a section on "Problems and Sources," and its studies of the holdings of various research libraries, as well as bibliographies and articles, are a necessary source for students of American socialism and the labor movement. Walter Goldwater's "Radical Periodicals in America, 1890-1950: A Bib-liography with Brief Notes," in the Yale University Library Gazette (Vol. 34, No. 4, April 1963), lists nearly three hundred titles. Regrettably, no bibliographies or sources have been compiled on the Socialist Party since 1919.

The literature on the communist movement is vast, but except for the *Bibliography* published by the Fund for the Republic in 1955, there is no full compilation of materials. That bibliography itself was sketchy, and it has been revised and brought up to date by Professor Joel Seidman of the University of Chicago and his students, and is scheduled to be published by the M.I.T. Press in 1968.

The following notes are not meant to be comprehensive. They do not include memoirs or histories written as personal documents, or the huge collection of materials assembled by the House Un-American Activities Committee and the Senate Subcommittee on Internal Security, sources which must be used with care. My list, with brief comments, covers only scholarly works written in the last fifteen years.

On American Socialism

The Forging of American Socialism, by Howard Quint (South Caro-lina, 1953; reprinted by Bobbs-Merrill, 1964) is a competent history of the period between 1865 and 1901. Its value lies in its emphasis on the

* I am indebted to Professor Gerald Friedberg of the University of California at Davis, and Mrs. Dorothy Swanson of the Tamiment Institute Library at New York University, for suggestions.

non-Marxist elements in the background of American socialism, principally the Nationalists (Bellamy), Populists, Christian Socialists, and Communitarians. A straightforward narrative, it lacks any interpretative scheme. David Shannon's *The Socialist Party of America* (Macmillan, 1955), written in tandem with Quint, brings the history of the Socialist Party up to World War I. It is a detailed and meticulous account, but is written within a narrow and conventional framework. Thus it neglects the nature of ideology, the roles of social status and generational differences, and other variables which sociological thinking has introduced into historical discourse. For Shannon, the pre-World War I Socialist Party was "just like" the Democratic and Republican Parties. Political parties in the United States, he says, "are famous for bunking strangers together, even incompatible strangers, and the Socialists until World War I were above all a political party." But this is precisely what the Socialist Party was not. It was a social movement held together by an ideology and a loose organizational structure. Because of its structure it was subject to interminable factional struggles, and because of its ideology it could never achieve the flexibility necessary for adapting to the changing American scene.

The American Socialist Movement, 1897-1912, by Ira Kipnis (Columbia, 1953), is a running history of the internal factional battles of the Socialist Party. But Kipnis arbitrarily constructs a set of positions labelled "left" and "right" without ever probing into the changing meanings of these labels, and his argument that the Socialist Party would have succeeded if it had only adopted a more "militant" posture is simply wishful thinking about history. Since Mr. Kipnis ends his account at 1912, he escapes the burden of explaining why the right-wing leaders of the Socialist Party, Morris Hillquit and Victor Berger, maintained an anti-war position in 1917, while almost the entire left-wing intellectual leadership of the party (William English Walling, J. G. Phelps Stokes, Frank Bohn, and Jack London) supported the war.

Since 1952, two biographies of Norman Thomas have appeared. One of them, Murray Seidler's *Norman Thomas* (Syracuse, 1961), is a straightforward but pedestrian effort. The second, Harry Fleischman's *Norman Thomas* (W. W. Norton, 1964), has more personal detail and is warmly admiring, but it is largely uncritical.

For a movement as varied as the Socialist Party, there have been few "local" histories scrutinizing in detail the structure of the party and its vicissitudes. To the two such histories written before 1952—Marvin Wachman's on Milwaukee and Henry Stetler's on Reading—there has been added a very good book by Henry F. Bedford, *Socialism and the Workers in Massachusetts, 1886-1912* (Massachusetts, 1966). At the turn of the century, the Socialist Party of Massachusetts was thriving. It elected in Haverhill the first Socialist Mayor in the United States, John C. Chase. But it was beset by factional and ideological squabbles, and the Socialists of Massachusetts could never decide whether theirs was a political party or not. Mr. Bedford builds his interpretative scheme around the fate of the Reverend Mr. Roland D. Sawyer, who was the party's candidate for governor in 1912 but who was expelled from the party a year later because of his "reformism"—that is to say, he wanted the party to actively engage in day-to-day politics. Mr. Bedford's conclusions are harsh but just. He writes that by 1913, "The party had reached a point where it always saw risks, never opportunities. Like the S.L.P., it could react decisively to expel, not to attract. It would not be revolutionary and had no capacity to reform. It was not a cell, nor a sect, and certainly not a political party. It was not significant enough to discuss, or worry about, or even laugh at. It was dead, and lacked the dignity to lie still."

Since 1952, a considerable number of Ph.D. theses have been written on the socialist movement, particularly studies of individual figures. Except for the dissertation of Martin Diamond, *Socialism and the Decline of the American Socialist Party* (Chicago, 1956), few of the doctoral theses attempt any interpretations of American socialism. Mr. Diamond, who has been influenced by the theories of the political philosopher Leo Strauss, holds that American socialism failed not for any sociological reasons but because its political doctrines were in error, and the party was therefore bound to go under. The major prewar figures of American socialism have been examined in some detail. Robert W. Iverson has written *Morris Hillquit: American Social Democrat* (Iowa, 1951); Gerald Friedberg has used the career of John Spargo to explore the political experience of socialism in its heyday, in *Marxism in the United States: John Spargo and the Socialist Party of America* (Harvard, 1964); Edward J. Muzik has written *Victor Berger: A Biography* (Northwestern, 1960), though not all the Berger papers are as yet completely available; Robert A. Huston has discussed *A. M. Simons and the American Socialist Movement* (Wisconsin, 1965); Herbert R. Dietrich has entitled his study *Patterns of Dissent: The Reform Ideas and Activities of George D. Herron* (New Mexico, 1958).

The Duke University collection has been used by William C. Seyler for his dissertation *The Rise and Decline of the Socialist Party of the United States* (Duke, 1952); Frederick I. Olson has studied *The Milwaukee Socialists, 1897-1941* (Harvard, 1952); Robert E. Doherty has opened up the largely unexplored area of *The American Socialist Party and the Roman Catholic Church* (Teachers College, Columbia, 1959).

The Socialist Labor Party and Daniel De Leon have provided the subject of an excellent dissertation by Don McKee, *The Intellectual and*

Historical Influences Shaping the Political Theory of Daniel De Leon (Columbia, 1955); they have also been studied by Charles M. White in *The Socialist Labor Party in America, 1890-1903* (Southern California, 1959).

There have been few detailed studies of the relationship between the Socialist Party and the trade-union movement. The dissertation by Howard M. Gittleman, *Attempts to Unify the American Labor Movement, 1865-1900* (Wisconsin, 1960), has a chapter on the De Leonite Socialist Trade. John H. M. Laslett has attempted a comprehensive analysis of the early years in an Oxford D.Phil. thesis, *Socialism and the American Federation of Labor, 1886-1903* (1962).

There has been a large and discursive periodical literature on American socialism, but the scope of this note makes it impossible to list the major articles. Two important sources in recent years have been *Labor History* (where sections of the dissertations by McKee, Laslett, Doherty, and Bedford have been printed), and *Studies on the Left*, where James Weinstein has been publishing his explorations in American socialist history. Mr. Weinstein's argument, which I find debatable, is that the decline of the American Socialist Party can be explained not by the split on the syndicalist and sabotage issue in 1912, but by Government repressions during the First World War. I find his evidence of the Socialist Party's vitality during World War I unconvincing, but his studies are serious and have to be taken into account. A book by Mr. Weinstein, *The Decline of American Socialism, 1912-1925*, is scheduled to be published in the winter of 1967-1968.

Curiously, in all that has been written on American socialism, there are no studies of the Party during the period from the 1930's to the 1950's, other than in this book.

On American Communism

The literature on American communism since 1952 has been of three kinds: exposés, memoirs and confessions, and serious academic studies. Very few of the exposés have any merit. Many of them (e.g. Angela Calomiris', Herbert Philbrick's) are accounts of single incidents or experiences which are then generalized into sweeping statements about the nature of communism. An especially weird book which reveals the murky "Dostoevskian" nature of the times is *False Witness*, by Harvey Matusow (Cameron and Kahn, 1955). Mr. Matusow, a former activist in the Young Communist League, testified before several Congressional committees against his former comrades. Then, repenting of these acts, he repudiated that testimony in a book which attacked the F.B.I. and was published by a left-wing firm. J. Edgar Hoover's *Masters of Deceit* (Holt, 1958) brings all the stereotypes about communism together in one volume, and it is useful, perhaps for that omnibus achievement. James Burnham's *The Web of Subversion* (John Day, 1954) is a more sophisticated rendering of the "military" nature of communist conspiracy.

The memoirs and confessions are of a different nature, and they often provide invaluable raw material for the serious student of the subject. But the *parti pris* or simply the biased point of view of the writer introduces distortion. The successive works of a single writer can serve to illustrate the process. Louis Budenz' *This is My Story* (Whittlesey House, 1947) is a valuable record of his experiences as the editor of the *Daily Worker*. But his later books, such as *Men Without Faces* (Harper, 1950) or *The Techniques of Communism* (Regnery, 1954), reweave Budenz' personal experiences for the purpose of political exposé.

On the crucial question of espionage and the extent of communist penetration in Washington, the major memoirs are Whittaker Chambers' *Witness* (Random House, 1952), Elizabeth Bentley's *Out of Bondage* (Devin-Adair, 1951), and Hede Massing's *This Deception* (Duell, Sloan and Pearce, 1951). A critical discussion of their testimony before various Congressional committees can be found in Herbert Packer's *Ex-Communist Witnesses* (Stanford, 1962).

Of the various individuals who held a high rank in the communist movement, the following have written memoirs that are significant for historians: H. M. Wicks (an early leader of the underground Communist Party), *Eclipse of October* (Challenge Publishers, 1957); Granville Hicks, *Where We Came Out* (Viking, 1954), an account of the communist literary world of the 1930's; Bella V. Dodd, *School of Darkness* (Kenedy, 1954), emphasizing teacher activities in New York; Howard Fast, *The Naked God: The Writer and the Communist Party* (Praeger, 1957), useful mostly for its discussion of the psychology of "self-deception"; John Gates, *The Story of an American Communist* (Nelson, 1958), especially valuable for material on the decision of the Communist Party to go underground in the 1950's, and on the effect of the Khrushchev disclosures and the Hungarian events of 1956. Earl Browder, expelled from the Communist Party in 1946, has never written any "intimate" memoirs. His book *Marx and America* (Duell, Sloan and Pearce, 1958) is an exposition of his "revisionist" point of view. Mr. Browder has written an unpublished autobiography which deals largely with his public life.

One of the best studies of the 1930's and 1940's, told through the personal lives of "representative men," is Murray Kempton's *Part of Our Time* (Simon & Schuster, 1955), a book which avoids sentimentality by its blend of poignant and astringent writing.

The academic study of American communism in the past fifteen years has produced some brilliant accounts. But they have often been regrettably marred by a psychological or sociological "reductionism" which sees the communist in one-dimensional terms, and fails to understand the variety of individuals, the many different kinds of motivation, and the schwärmerei and grubbiness of the communist world. Thus Gabriel Almond's *The Appeals of Communism* (Princeton, 1954), based on interviews with a sample of ex-communists, argues that certain specific personality types are attracted into the communist movement. Philip Selznick, in his valuable *The Organizational Weapon* (Free Press, 1960), at times mistakes "intentions" for reality and attributes to the communist movement a political success which was due not to organizational flexibility but to historical circumstances. Frank S. Meyer, in *The Moulding of Communists* (Harcourt, 1961), provides a mechanistic and over deterministic account of the way cadres are "moulded" by the Communist Party, a view which allows little room for explanation of the large-scale defections of individuals from the Communist Party. And Earl Latham, in his disinterested evaluation of communist influence in government, *The Communist Controversy in Washington* (Harvard, 1966), makes the mistake, for example, of taking a key Communist Party text, J. Peters' *Manual on Organization*, as a blueprint of actual party structure and behavior. What these analytical efforts show is that there can be no substitute for the detailed and difficult reconstruction of the actual events and actions which, in the first instance, is the task of the painstaking historian.

The best study of American communism is to be found in Theodore Draper's books, *The Roots of American Communism* (Viking, 1957) and *American Communism and Soviet Russia* (Viking, 1960). These are models of patient exploration, of separating fact from hearsay, and are the closest approximation we shall probably have to a definitive study of the first decade of American communism. Mr. Draper's first volume is devoted mainly to the emergence of the Communist Party out of the tangled factional struggles within the Socialist movement, and the murky periods spent underground by the different communist sects. It succeeds in reestablishing the place of Louis Fraina (who later wrote under the name of Lewis Corey) as the central figure of those early years. The second volume deals with the relationship of the American Communist Party to Moscow, and shows in explicit detail how the American party came under Soviet direction. It is exemplary for the study not only of the American party but of the relation of any communist party to the Comintern.

Draper's two volumes are part of a series, "Communism in American Life," which was directed by Clinton Rossiter as a project of the Fund for the Republic. It was the intention of this series to set down a clear historical record of the role and influence of the Communist Party at a time when McCarthyite excesses and journalistic hysteria were creating a distorted picture. And the series succeeded admirably. The Rossiter project brought together a number of able scholars and provided them with research and consultative help, particularly that of Earl Browder, who cooperated with Draper and a number of the other authors. The project built up a comprehensive library of communist documents, including rare archive material such as the minutes of the Central Committee of the Communist Party in the 1920's and other important source material. This collection was donated to the Tamiment Institute Library, which is now a division of New York University.

The "Communism in American Life" series also includes the following books: Robert W. Iverson, *The Communists and the Schools* (Harcourt, 1959), concludes that the communists left little impression on educational methods and that their influence extended, for a brief time, to certain key locals of the American Federation of Teachers; Nathan Glazer, *The Social Basis of American Communism* (Harcourt, 1961), explores the sources of membership support of the Party, particularly among minority groups, and concludes that "there seemed to be no precise relationship between the general economic and social position [of the ethnic group] and their response to the party"; Ralph Roy, *Communism and the Churches* (Harcourt, 1960) is an effort to set the record straight against the reckless charges, made by J. B. Matthews and others, that the Protestant churches in the United States had been heavily influenced by the Communist Party; Daniel Aaron, *Writers on the Left* (Harcourt, 1961), is a study of the appeals of radicalism and the literary wars of the 1930's, focusing mainly on the careers of a few key figures such as Max Eastman, V. F. Calverton, Malcolm Cowley, and Joseph Freeman: Frank S. Meyer, *The Moulding of Communists* (Harcourt, 1961), is best read as a literary portrait of the Bolshevik *imago* rather than as a case study of any real-life situations—in fact, since the discussion is so abstract, it is unfortunately never clear which countries or what time periods are covered; Earl Latham, *The Communist Controversy in Washington* (Harvard, 1966), is central to the discussion of McCarthyism, and is, in fact, as much an inquiry into the nature of that phenomenon as it is a patient evaluation of the extent of communist infiltration into the American government in the 1930's and 1940's; Latham concludes that "the public record supports the finding that there was considerable activity, and that it was not negligible, even if exaggerations are discounted"; David A. Shannon, *The Decline of American Communism* (Harcourt, 1959), is a history of the party since 1945: it is very useful on such phenomena as the Progressive Party, but it lacks, necessarily, any account of the "underground" phase of the party in the 1950's—a forthcoming work by Joseph Starobin (at Columbia University), who has access to sources unavailable to Shannon, will probably fill in the details for this period; Clinton Rossiter, *Marxism: The View From America* (Harcourt, 1960), while not a history, is an effort to survey the Marxist views which influenced the American radical parties, and to contrast these ideas with the "American Tradition" in an effort to see why Marxist theory failed to take root in the United States.

Few of the other serious studies of American communism measure up to the level of the volumes in the Rossiter series. *The American Communist Party*, by Irving Howe and Lewis Coser (Beacon, 1957), has the virtues of being well-written and of covering the entire history of the party—the only book which provides a synoptic view; but it is drawn almost entirely from secondary sources, few of the party leaders were interviewed, and it is inferior in detail to the studies of Draper and Shannon. *The Communists versus the C.I.O.*, by Max Kampelman (Praeger, 1957), draws its material almost entirely from the trial record of the communist unions tried before the C.I.O. in 1946-47, and it is superficial. *Communism in American Unions*, by David Saposs (McGraw-Hill, 1959), is an effort to update his classic *Left-Wing Unionism*, written more than a quarter of a century earlier; but it suffers from seeing communist policy in monolithic terms and failing to understand the tensions between the communist leaders of several unions and the party. *Race and Radicalism*, by Wilson Record (Cornell, 1964), is a competent study of the effort of the Communist Party to influence the N.A.A.C.P. *Liberals and Communism*, by Frank A. Warren III (Indiana, 1966), is an effort, fifteen years later, to check the conclusions of Eugene Lyons' *The Red Decade*. While Warren indicates that some of Lyons' conclusions were exaggerated, his study is flawed by the fact that he bases his discussion almost entirely upon a review of the periodical literature of the 1930's; the book provides no "feel," as Daniel Aaron's book does, of the literary politics of the time.

The American radical movements have never been in the mainstream of American life, though, like powerful dyes, they have suffused it through their influence in the labor movement, the literary intelligentsia and the university world. The major interpretative history of American radicalism still remains to be written, but its intrinsic fascination is bound to attract its chronicler someday. The materials of a great and tragic story, now shards and detritus, await its archeological historian.

Index

Abendblatt, 47n, 98
Abramovitch, Raphael, 150
Acton, John, 5, 7
Adams, Brooks, 56
Adams, Henry, 56
Agar, Herbert, 152n
Agitprop, 142, 143
Agrarian League, 18
Alinsky, Saul, 140n
Allen, Devere, 158, 159n, 166
Allen, Frederick Lewis, 135n
Altgeld, John, 50
Altman, Jack, 159, 170, 171, 172, 180n, 182
Alvarez del Vayo, Julio, 150
Amalgamated Clothing Workers, 98, 117, 169
America First Committee, 182
American Alliance for Labor & Democracy, 101
American Fabian, 59
American Fabian Society, 59
American Federation of Labor, 11, 30, 31, 33, 36, 44, 59, 63, 64, 73, 74, 119, 121, 145, 161; and socialism, 40-44
American Federationist, 40, 41
American Labor Alliance, 126; *see also* United Communist Party (1920)
American Labor Party (1919-1920), 119
American Labor Party (N.Y.), 145, 171, 172, 172n, 176-177, 179
American Labor Union, 42, 64, 65
American League for Peace and Democracy, 148
American Peace Mobilization, 184
American Plan, 118
American Railway Union, 48, 49, 51, 93
American Socialist, 103, 104
American Socialist Quarterly, 159n
American Student Union, 148, 148n, 170
American Workers Party, 173-174
American Youth Congress, 148, 149
Americans for Democratic Action, 191
Ameringer, Oscar, 88, 94n, 95
Amter, Israel, 157n
Anabaptism, 6
Anarchism, 7, 21, 25-26
Anderson, Sherwood, 142, 152n, 153
Anvil, 142
Appeal Group (Socialist Party), 172
Appeal to Reason, 47, 58, 101
Araquistain, Luis, 150n

Aron, Raymond, 11, 186n
Arvin, Newton, 142

Babel, Isaac, 143n
Baker, Charles, 104
Baker, Ray Stannard, 60
Bakunin, Mikhail, 7, 21-22, 23
Barbusse, Henri, 147
Barmine, Alexander, 151n
Barnes, J. Mahlon, 40, 69
Baron, Murray, 159n
Barton, Bruce, 135
Bauer, Otto, 163
Beard, Charles A., 56, 162n
Bebel, August, 162
Beck, F., 151n
Becker, Carl, 152n
Becker, Lazar, 154
Bedacht, Max, 133, 133n, 185
Bellamy, Edward, 8, 17, 48, 50, 52n, 57-59
Benham, G. B., 82
Bennett, William F., 103
Benson, Allan, 99, 100
Bentley, Elizabeth, 146n
Benton, Thomas H., 152n
Berger, Victor, 32, 49, 51, 52, 65, 66, 71, 73, 75, 81, 82, 84, 84n, 94n, 95, 99, 101n, 104, 105, 111, 114, 158n, 165, 189
Berkman, Alexander, 27n, 76n, 104
Bernieri, Camillo, 150
Bernstein, Eduard, 165
Berry, George, 121
Beveridge, Albert, 54
Biemiller, Andrew J., 159n, 166, 191
Bilbo, Theodore, 79
Billings, Warren K., 104
Bimba, Anthony, 146
Bittleman, Alexander, 133n-134n
Black International, *see* International Working People's Association (Anarchist)
Blanc, Louis, 19
Blanshard, Paul, 157, 159, 159n, 161
Blast, 104, 142
Blatchford, Robert, 50
Bliss, William D. P., 52n, 59
Blitzstein, Marc, 151
Bloor, Ella Reeve, 133
Bohn, Frank, 83, 101
Bolshevik Revolution, 106-107
Bolshevism, 106, 115, 123; political theory, 13-16

Bordiga, Amadeo, 155
Bouck, William, 121
Boudin, Louis B., 78, 108, 123
Brandeis, Louis D., 56
Brenan, Gerald, 150n
Brenner, Anita, 150n
Bridges, Harry, 145, 184
Bridgman, Percy, 152n
Briefs, Goetz A., 4n
Brissenden, Paul, 67, 68n
Brookhart, Smith W., 95
Brooks, Van Wyck, 77
Brookwood Labor College, 173
Brophy, John, 140n
Brotherhood of Locomotive Firemen, 48
Brotherhood of the Co-operative Commonwealth, 48, 51
Broun, Heywood, 159, 183
Browder, Earl, 128, 129, 133, 133n, 137-138, 144, 145n, 146, 170, 184-185
Brown, Irving, 178
Bruce, Andrew A., 91n
Bryan, William Jennings, 31, 50, 55, 70
Budenz, Louis F., 146n, 146-147, 186n
Bukharin, Nikolai, 107, 133, 150; in U.S., 108
Bullard, Arthur, 101
Burke, Fielding, 142
Burnham, James, 173
Bush, Charles D., 95n

C.I.O., 145-146, 171, 172n, 177-178
C.I.O. News, 145
Caballero, Francisco Largo, see Largo Caballero, Francisco
Cabell, Branch, 135
Cadman, S. Parkes, 135
Cahan, Abraham, 98, 165n
Caldwell, Erskine, 142
Calhoun, Arthur W., 79n
Calverton, Victor F., 162n
Cannon, James P., 126, 128, 129, 132, 133n-134n, 154, 154n, 173, 174-176
Cantwell, Robert, 142
Carey, Henry C., 27
Carey, James F., 45, 62, 71n
Carlson, Oliver, 162n
Carr, Edward H., 22n
Chamberlain, John, 59, 151n, 152n
Chambers, Whittaker, 146n, 186n
Chase, Stuart, 162n
Chicago Daily Socialist, 70, 87, 100
Christensen, Parley, 119
Christian Commonwealth colony, 52n
Christian socialism, 51, 58, 100
Claflin, Tennessee, 22

Clarity group (Socialist Party), 172, 176, 177, 182
Class struggle, 69, 75
Class Struggle, 108, 110
Clayton Act, 90
Cleveland Citizen, 66
Coates, Robert, 151
Coeur d'Alene strike, 30, 49
Coldwell, Joseph, 112
Coleman, McAlister, 50, 140n, 159n
Colonization, 47, 51, 59
Coming Nation, 47, 58
Comintern, see International, Third (Communist)
Commission to inquire into the charges made against Leon Trotsky in the Moscow trials, see Dewey Commission
Committee for a Third International, 126
Committee for Cultural Freedom, 152
Committee for Industrial Organization, see C.I.O.
Committee on Un-American Activities, see United States, Congress, House, Committee on Un-American Activities
Common Sense, 150
Communism, and democratic society, 13-16; political tactics of, 13-16; see also Socialism
Communism (Russian), N.E.P., 138n; see also Bolshevism
Communism (U.S.), 99; factionalism, 122-133; front technique, 119, 147-149; and government agencies, 145-146; history, 122-133; and labor unions, 140, 145; Popular Front tactics, 143-149; splinter groups, 153-157; "third period" tactics, 138-143; see also Communist Party (U.S.)
Communist Club (N.Y.), 22
Communist International, see International, Third (Communist)
Communist International, 138n
Communist Labor Party (1919), 112, 123
Communist League of Struggle, 154
Communist Manifesto, 123
Communist Party (Russian), Zinoviev-Stalin faction, 131; see also Bolshevism; Communism (Russian)
Communist Party (U.S.), 82, 112, 122, 125, 163, 172; front technique, 131; history, 126-133, 138-153; and labor unions, 185; organization, 112; recent period, 183-187; unity negotiations

with Socialist Party, 170; *see also* Communism (U.S.)

Communist Party Opposition, 133

Communist Political Association, 184

Communist World, 122

Comrade, 100

Comte, Auguste, 57

Conciliators (Communist Party), 128

Conference for Progressive Labor Action, 173

Conference for Progressive Political Action, 86, 115, 120-121

Congress of Industrial Organizations, *see* C.I.O.

Conroy, Jack, 142

Continental Congress of Workers and Farmers, 160

Cooke, Alistair, 146n

Coolidge, Calvin, 117, 120

Cooper, Peter, 20, 24

Cooperative movement, 18; consumers', 53; producers', 19, 53

Corey, Lewis (before 1925 known as Louis Fraina), 108, 109, 112, 122, 134n

Coughlin, Charles E., 93, 171n

Counts, George S., 152n

Cowley, Malcolm, 142, 151

Cox, Jesse, 82

Coxey, Jacob, 31

Coxey's army, 49

Croly, Herbert, 56, 80, 101

Cumbie, Tad, 94

Cunningham, William, 95n

Curran, Joe, 145

Czolgosz, Leon, 27n

Daily Worker, 132, 134n, 146n, 174n, 185n

Daniel, Franz, 159n, 171, 178

Darcy, Sam, 185n

Darrow, Clarence, 50, 101

Davis, Elmer, 152n

Davis, John W., 120

Davis, Stuart, 151

Debo, Angie, 94n

Debs, Eugene V., 8, 32, 34, 45, 47, 63, 64, 65, 76, 81, 82, 86, 94, 96, 99, 158, 165; and Bellamy, 58; and Bolshevism, 114-115; death, 122; early career, 48-51; and I.W.W., 42, 66-68; on 1900 campaign, 55; on Socialist Party tactics, 72-73; on working class affiliation, 82-83; on World War I, 104-105; personal characteristics, 87-90; presidential campaigns, 62, 66, 68-70, 76-77, 114, 119; and Social Democratic Party, 52; views on labor party, 70-71

Debs, Kate (Mrs. E. V.), 88n, 104

Debs, Theodore, 52n

De Caux, Len, 145

De Leon, Daniel, 29, 30, 31, 40, 45, 46, 53, 61; career, 32-33; dual unionism, 41; and I.W.W., 66-68; Nationalist affiliation, 58; theories, 34-36

Dell, Floyd, 104

Delson, Max, 170, 172

Delson, Robert, 158n, 172

Democratic centralism, 15

Democratic Party, 55, 79, 92, 123, 145, 161, 191

Dewey, John, 101, 151, 151n, 152, 157

Dewey Commission, 151

Dial, 117

Dies, Martin, 148n

Dimitrov, Georgi, 144, 144n

Dittmann, Wilhelm, 116

Dodd, Bella, 185n

Dombrowski, James, 48n, 52n, 58

Donnelly, Ignatius, 31

Dorfman, Joseph, 53n, 61

Dos Passos, John, 88, 135, 136, 142, 142n, 150, 152n, 153

Douglas, Paul, 103, 157

Dreiser, Theodore, 89, 162n

Dual unionism, 41-42, 140

Dubinsky, David, 160, 171

Duclos, Jacques, 134n, 184

Dunne, William F., 113n-144n, 127, 185n

Duranty, Walter, 143n

Dutt, R. Palme, 139n

Dynamo, 142

E.P.I.C. movement, 92, 161

Eastman, Max, 78, 84, 100, 101n, 104, 126, 143n, 152n

Eberlein, Hugo, 111

Ebert, Friedrich, 116

Edman, Irwin, 152n

Edwards, A. S., 82

Edwards, George, 179

Edwards, George S., 148n

Eisler, Gerhart, 134n

Ely, Richard T., 58

End Poverty in California, *see* E.P.I.C. movement

Engdahl, J. Louis, 104, 114, 126

Engels, Friedrich, 39, 83n; on American prospects, 3; on factionalism in U.S., 32; on isolation of S.L.P., 36; *see also* Marxism

Epstein, Melech, 98n

Equalitarian Society, 156n
Ercoli, M. (Togliatti), 144n
Ernst, Morris L., 152n
Esenin, Sergei A., 143n
Evangelical revivalism, 94
Evans, George Henry, 18, 27

Faris, Ellsworth, 122n
Farmer-Labor Party (1920), 119
Farmer-Labor Party (1924), 119-120, 121
Farmer-Labor Party (Minnesota), 119, 171n
Farmer-Labor Political Federation (Wisconsin), 172, 177
Farmer-Labor Reconstruction League, 95
Farrell, James T., 142n, 153
Fascism, 138, 143
Fast, Howard, 185
Feigenbaum, Benjamin, 82
Fellowship of Reconciliation, 174, 188
Field, B. J., 154-155
Fighting Worker, 155n
Fine, Nathan, 46n
Fischer, Louis, 183
Fischer, Ruth, 114n, 144n
Fisher, Dorothy Canfield, 152n
Fitzgerald, F. Scott, 135, 136
Fitzpatrick, John J., 119
Foner, Philip, 83
Foster, William Z., 121, 128, 129-133, 141-143
Fourier, Charles, 3
Fourth International, 155n
Fraenkel, Osmund K., 78
Fraina, Louis, *see* Corey, Lewis
Frank, Waldo, 142, 149, 151, 162n
Frazier, Lynn, 91, 93, 95
Freeman, Joseph, 108n
Freese, Arnold, 159n
Freiheit, 27n
"French turn," 155, 174
Furriers Union, 98
Furuseth, Andrew, 90

Gary, Elbert, 117
Gaylord, W. R., 100
General German Labor Association (N.Y.), 22
General strike, 7
George, Harrison, 134n, 185n
George, Henry, 27-29
Gerber, Julius, 112
Germer, Adolph, 104, 178n
Ghent, William J., 84, 100, 122
Gideonse, Harry D., 152n
Ginger, Ray, 48n, 50

Gitlow, Benjamin, 78n, 110, 112, 121, 123, 126, 128n, 133, 133n, 154; on internal struggles in Communist Party, 126-128
Glassberg, Benjamin, 113
Godin, W., 151n
Goebel, George, 71n, 75, 82
Gold, Michael, 142, 183
Goldman, Emma, 27n, 76n
Gollancz, Victor, 183
Gompers, Samuel, 11, 17, 22, 36-44, 58, 63, 67, 121; career, 37-38; pure and simple unionism, 39
Goose Caucus (Communist Party), 127-129
Graham, James D., 168
Green, John, 178
Green Corn Rebellion, 93-96
Greenback Labor Party, 24
Greenback Party, 20
Greenberg, Hayim, 3n
Gridley affair, 85-86
Gronlund, Laurence, 17, 47, 48, 50, 58
Grosse, Edward, 38
Group Theatre, 142
Gusev, S., 139

Haase, Hugo, 116
Haile, Margaret, 82
Hallgren, Mauritz, 135n
Halper, Albert, 142
Halperin, S. William, 139n
Hanford, Ben, 66
Hapgood, Powers, 140n, 171, 178
Hardie, Keir, 49
Harding, Warren G., 134
Hardman, Jacob B. S., 117n, 173, 174
Hardy, Jack, 146
Harriman, Job, 33, 61, 62, 74, 75, 82
Hayes, Max S., 42, 61, 66, 82, 119
Haymarket affair, 26
Haywood, William D., 45, 66-68, 73, 75, 76, 77, 78, 83n, 86, 104
Hearst, William Randolph, 59, 99, 103
Heath, Frederic, 52, 59, 82
Heiden, Konrad, 143n
Heinzen, Karl, 27n
Hemingway, Ernest, 149, 150n
Henderson Bay community, 53n
Hendrick, Burton J., 60
Henson, Francis, 165, 178
Herron, George D., 45, 52n, 61, 100
Herzen, Alexander, 21
Hewitt, Abram S., 29
Hickey, Tom, 75
Hicks, Granville, 136n, 138, 142, 183
Hilferding, Rudolf, 44, 114n, 116

Hillman, Sidney, 160, 171, 178
Hillquit, Morris, 17, 32, 32n, 33, 45, 46, 61, 63, 70, 73, 82, 85, 85n, 99, 102, 105, 105n, 111, 113, 114n, 120, 157, 158, 189; and A.F.L., 42; death, 165; N.Y. mayoralty campaign, 102-103, 107; on propaganda tactics, 72; opposition to, in Socialist Party, 159-160; theoretical orthodoxy, 115-116; views on labor party, 71
Hindus, Maurice, 143n
Hirsch, David, 37
Hiss, Alger, 146n
Hitler, Adolf, 9, 16n
Hoan, Dan, 159, 168, 169, 189, 191n
Homestead strike, 30
Hook, Sidney, 10n, 139n-140n, 142, 152, 173
Howard, Sidney, 142, 152n
Howe, Irving, 178n
Howell, Robert B., 95
Howells, William Dean, 58
Hughan, Jessie Wallace, 71n
Hughes, Charles Evans, 118
Hughes, Langston, 142
Hunter, Robert, 70, 85n, 100
Hutcheson, William, 121
Hylan, John F., 102-103

I.W.W., 42, 64, 66-68, 73, 77, 104; Chicago faction, 68; Detroit faction, 68
Immediate demands, 8, 62, 75; De Leon on, 35
Industrial Communists (1919), 125
Industrial Workers of the World, see I.W.W.
Ingerman, Sergius, 107
Intercollegiate Socialist Society, 100
International, First, 21; in U.S., 22-23
International, Second (Socialist), 36, 115
International, Third (Communist), 107, 111, 113, 114, 116, 133; shifts in tactics, 1919-1945, 138n; 7th world congress, 143-144
International, Fourth (Trotskyist), 176
International Ladies' Garment Workers' Union, 98, 161, 169
International News, 155n
International Socialist Review, 70, 76, 84, 86-87, 103, 107
International Trade Union Educational League, 129
International Working Men's Association (1864-1878), see International, First
International Working People's Association (Anarchist), 25
Isaacs, William, 157n

Iskra, 156
Italian Left Fraction of Communism, 155

Jakira, Abraham, 127n
Jefferson, Thomas, 146
Jerome, Victor J., 183
Jewish Daily Forward, 66, 98, 103, 157, 159, 165n, 169
Johnson, Magnus, 95
Jonas, Alexander, 82
Jones, Ellis O., 100
Jones, (Mother) Mary, 100
Jones Family, 94
Josephson, Matthew, 142

Kallen, Horace M., 162n
Kamenev, Lev B., 150
Karsner, David, 50n, 122
Katterfeld, L. E., 127n
Kautsky, Karl, 3, 50, 114n, 115, 162, 167
Kazin, Alfred, 135n
Kearny, Denis, 24n
Keep, Arthur, 46, 47n
Keinard, Benjamin F., 47n
Keller, Helen, 78
Keracher, John, 123
Kilpatrick, William H., 152n
Knights of Labor, 24, 26, 33; Journal, 33
Koestler, Arthur, 150n, 186
Kollontay, Alexandra, 108
Kreuger, Maynard, 159n, 177, 187
Kriege, Herman, 18-19, 28
Kruse, William F., 104
Krzycki, Leo, 166, 177
Kuczynski, Jurgen, 4n

Labor exchange bank, 19
Labour Party (British), 120
Labriola, Antonio, 3
La Follette, Robert M., 95, 120-122
La Follette seamen's act, 90
La Guardia, Fiorello, 161
Land reform, 19, 27-29, 37
Langer, William, 93
Largo Caballero, Francisco, 150, 176
Larkin, James, 110, 112
Lash, Joseph P., 148n, 170
Laski, Harold J., 183
Lasky, Victor, 146n
Lassalle, Ferdinand, 21
Lassalleanism, 38
Lasser, David, 170
Lasswell, Harold, 88n
Laurrell, Karl Ferdinand, 38
Lawson, Thomas, 60

League for a Revolutionary Workers Party, 155
League for Independent Political Action, 157
League for Industrial Democracy, 158
League for Peace and Democracy, 184
League of American Writers, 149
League of Professional Groups for Foster and Ford, 152n
Lee, Algernon, 82, 102, 158, 165-166, 169
Left, 142
Left Front, 142
Left Review, 142
Lehman, Herbert, 179
Lemke, William, 93
Lenin, Vladimir I., 21-24, 34, 81, 83n, 107, 167; Bolshevik Revolution, 106-107; and De Leon, 34n; 1918 letter to American workers, 110-111; on political tactics, 14-16; united front tactic, 131
Leninist League, 156
Lens, Sidney, 140n
Leo Frank case, 89
LeSeur, Arthur, 91n
Lewis, Alfred Baker, 182
Lewis, John L., 37, 117, 121, 140n, 161, 178
Lewis, Lena Morrow, 71n
Lewis, Sinclair, 152n
Liberator, 110
Liebknecht, Karl, 106
Lincoln, Abraham, 146
Lindbergh, Charles, 182
Lindeman, E. C., 143n
Lindgren, Edward I., 110, 127n
Lippmann, Walter, 78, 80, 101
Liquidators (Communist Party), 127-128
Lloyd, Henry Demarest, 50, 59-60, 86
Lloyd, William Bross, 84n
Locomotive Firemen's Magazine, 49
London, Jack, 45, 83, 100
London, Meyer, 45, 45n, 82, 99, 105, 158n
Long, Huey, 171n
Longuet, Jean, 114n
Lore, Ludwig, 108, 123, 131, 132, 133n-134n, 173
Los Angeles Times, 68n, 73
Lovestone, Jay, 127, 128, 129, 132, 133, 133n, 172n, 178
Lovestoneites, *see* Communist Party Opposition
Lowenfeld, Henry, 186n
Lumpkin, Grace, 142
Lundberg, Ferdinand, 152n

Lunn, George R., 80
Lusk committee, 112
Luxemburg, Rosa, 14, 107, 111
Lyons, Eugene, 141n, 147, 152n

McAdoo, William G., 120
McBride, John, 40
McCarthy, Joseph R., 185
McCartney, Frederic O., 82
McClure, Samuel S., 60
McClure's Magazine, 60
MacDonald, Duncan, 119, 121
MacDonald, Dwight, 190n
MacDonald, J. Ramsay, 96, 114n
McDowell, Arthur, 180n, 182
McGlynn, Edward, 29
McGuire, P. J., 37, 40, 58
McKay, David, 120n
McKenney, Ruth, 185n
McKinley, William, 55
MacLeish, Archibald, 149
McLevy, Jasper, 169, 190, 191n
McNamara case, 73
Manuilsky, Dmitri Z., 139
Marcantonio, Vito, 184n
Marlen, George (pseud. of George Spiro), 156n
Martin, Homer, 178
Marty, André, 150
Marx, Karl, 10, 19, 83n, 167; class theories, 11n; on American prospects, 3; on single tax, 28
Marxism, and American intellectuals, 136-138; Austro-Marxism, 163-164; De Leon's contribution, 34-36; introduction to America, 19, 21-23
Marxist, 155n
Marxist Workers League, 156
Masses, 77-78, 100, 101n, 103, 104, 110
Massing, Hede, 134n, 168n
Masters, Edgar Lee, 89
Matles, James, 145
Matthews, Joseph B., 147-148, 159n, 165
Maurer, James, 190n
Maxwell, S. A., 91n
Mayakovsky, Vladimir V., 143n
Melville, Herman, 56
Mencken, Henry L., 68n
Mensheviks, 106
Merriam, Frank F., 162
Mienov, Karl, 156
Militants (Socialist Party), 158-159, 162-164, 166-172, 174-176, 182
Millennialism, 6
Miller, Louis, 82
Millinery Workers Union, 98, 169
Mills, Walter Thomas, 91n, 94

Milwaukee Leader, 97, 103
Milwaukee Vorwärts, 51
Minor, Robert, 133
Minton, Bruce, 185n
Mitchell, John Purroy, 103
Mitchell, Wesley Clair, 152n
Modern Quarterly, 150
Modigliani, Giuseppe E., 114n
Molly Maguires, 23
Monetary reform, 19, 37, 50
Mooney, Tom, 104
Morgan, Thomas J., 40, 70n, 82
Morris, William, 8
Moscow trials, 149, 150-152
Most, Johann, 26, 27n
Moyer-Haywood-Pettibone case, 66-67
Muckrakers, 59-60
Münzenberg, Willi, 147
Murphy, Frank, 178-179
Murray, William, 96
Muste, A. J., 173-174
Myers, Gustavus, 56

Nation, 117, 183
National Labor Union, 20, 22
National Maritime Union, 185n
National Miners Union, 140n
National Party, *see* Greenback Labor Party
National Rip-Saw, see *Social Revolution*
National Youth Administration, 149
Nazi-Soviet pact, *see* Soviet-German pact
Nazism, 151, 162-164
Nechayev, Sergei, 22
Negrete, Rosario, 155
Negrín, Juan, 150
Neue Zeit, 107
New Appeal, see *Appeal to Reason*
New Dance, 142
New Deal, 9, 53, 160, 171, 178
New Democracy, 22
New International (Socialist Propaganda League), 108
New Leader, 77n, 150, 169
New Republic, 80, 101, 117, 183
New Theatre, 142
New York Call, 71, 83n, 97, 99, 101, 103
New York Tribune, 49
New Yorker Volkszeitung, 31, 46
Newhouse, Edward, 142
Niebuhr, Reinhold, 168, 169-170, 182
Nin, Andrés, 150
Non-Partisan League, 80, 91-93
Norris, George W., 95, 157
North American Committee to Aid Spanish Democracy, 175
Nye, Gerald, 93, 95

Odets, Clifford, 142
Oehler, Hugo, 155
O'Hare, Kate Richards, 94, 111
Olney, Richard, 49
One Big Union Club, 156n
Oneal, James, 77, 84, 107, 113, 158n, 159
Ortega y Gasset, José, 187
Otis, Harrison Grey, 68n
Overstreet, Harry A., 152n
Owen, Robert, 18, 19

Page, Kirby, 158
Page, Myra, 142
Paine, Thomas, 146
Palmer, A. Mitchell, 118
Palmer raids, 118
Panken, Jacob, 166
Parrington, Vernon L., Jr., 17
Parsons, Albert R., 24, 26
Parsons, Lucy, 66
Partisan Review, 142
Party Builder, 77
Party Organizer, 141
Patterson, Joseph Medill, 45n, 84n
People, 45, 46
People's World, 185n
Pepper, John, 129, 131, 133n
Perkins, Frances, 171
Perlman, Selig, 4, 64n
Perry, Ralph Barton, 152n
Pieck, Wilhelm, 144, 144n
Pilnyak, Boris, 143n
Pinchot, Amos, 119
Political Action Committee, 92, 123
Poole, Ernest, 100
Popular Front, 138n, 142-143
Populism, 33, 50, 79
Porter, Paul, 168n, 172, 180, 182
Powderly, Terence V., 33, 58
Poyntz, Juliet Stuart, 133n-134n
Pressman, Lee, 145, 146n
Profintern, 130
Progressive Labor Party (N.Y.), 29
Progressive Party, 185
Proletarian Party (1920), 123, 126
Proletarian Socialist Party, *see* Industrial Communists (1919)
Proletarischer Magid, 98
Proletcult, 142-143
Pullman strike, 30, 49

Quill, Michael, 145

Radek, Karl, 150
Railway Times, 50
Rand, Carrie, 100

Rand School, 100, 113, 167
Rauschenbusch, Walter, 188
Reed, John, 84, 100, 111, 112, 123
Reed, Louis S., 40n
Reese, Maria, 144n
Rein, Mark, 150
Religious socialism, see Christian socialism; Utopian socialism
Republican Party, 55, 92
Reuther, Walter, 178-179
Revolutionary Age, 108
Revolutionary Policy Committee, 164-165, 172, 178
Revolutionary Workers League, 155-156, 174
Rhodes, George, 191
Rieve, Emil, 160
Robeson, Paul, 185
Robinson, Reid, 145
Rochester, Anna, 140n
Rockefeller, John D., 50
Rogers, Kathryn, 88n
Rogge, O. John, 185
Rolland, Romain, 147
Rollins, William, 142
Roosevelt, Eleanor (Mrs. F. D.), 149
Roosevelt, Franklin D., 9, 144, 145, 160, 169, 171, 177, 178n
Roosevelt, Theodore, 29, 59, 76, 103
Roosevelt, Theodore, Jr., 121
Rorty, James, 142, 152n
Rosenberg, Harold, 10n
Ross, Edward Alsworth, 151n
Rummager, 126
Rummagers' League, see Industrial Communists (1919)
Ruskin Community, 47
Russell, Charles Edward, 60, 76, 91n, 100, 101n, 102
Russo-German pact, see Soviet-German pact
Ruthenberg, Charles, 102, 104, 109, 112, 128, 129, 130-132, 133n
Rykov, Aleksei I., 150

Sacco, Nicola, 118
St. John, Vincent, 67
Salter, John T., 191n
Sanger, Margaret, 78
Sanial, Lucien, 39, 46n, 101
Saposs, David J., 38n, 173
Scheidemann, Philipp, 116
Scheler, Max, 86, 90
Schlüter, Hermann, 82
Schneider, David, 140n
Schumpeter, Joseph A., 136
Schurz, Carl, 97

Seaver, Edwin, 142
Seidel, Emil, 76
Seidman, Joel, 140n
Senior, Clarence, 158n, 163n, 171n
Serge, Victor, 150n
Shachtman, Max, 132, 154n, 156
Shapiro, Theodore, 158n
Share-the-Wealth movement, 161
Shaw, George Bernard, 43
Sheean, Vincent, 149, 183
Shipkov, Michael, 150n
Shipstead, Hendrik, 95
Shuster, George N., 152n
Simons, Algie M., 62, 68, 70, 100
Simpson, Herman, 46n
Sinclair, Upton, 60, 92, 100, 149, 159n, 161-162, 171n
Single tax, 27-28
Sissman, Peter, 82
Skidmore, Thomas, 18
Slobodkin, Henry, 100
Smith, Alfred E., 121
Smith, Edwin S., 146, 146n
Smith, J. Allen, 56
Smith Act, 134n
Social Democracy of America, 32, 45, 48, 51
Social Democracy Red Book, 59
Social Democratic Federation, 176, 180
Social Democratic Herald, 66, 82
Social Democratic Party of America, 17, 46, 52-55, 59, 62; immediate demands, 53-54
Social Democratic Party of North America, 23
Social Gospel, 52n
Social Legislation, 90
Social Party of New York, 22
Social Reform Association, 19
Social Revolution (formerly National Rip-Saw), 103
Socialism; and art, see Art and socialism; causes of failure, 5-16; see also Christian socialism; Communism; Utopian socialism
Socialism (U.S.): and agrarian radicalism, 91-96; evaluation, 190-193; its peak in U.S., 55-56; and unionism, 11-13; utopian spirit, 3-5
Socialist Appeal, 175
Socialist Call, 167
Socialist International, see International, Second (Socialist)
Socialist Labor Party, 39, 40, 41, 45, 46n, 51, 53, 62, 81, 125n-126n, 156-157; early history, 24-37; factions, 31-32; Kangaroos, 33-34, 46

Socialist Labor Party (Cincinnati), 32
Socialist Party (New York), 121
Socialist Party (U.S.), 34, 36, 45, 54; causes of decline, 79-81; commercialism, 86-87; and communism, 107-115; decline, 90-116; factionalism, 61-66, 157-170, 172-176; foreign language federations, 96-99, 109, 111, 115; formation, 45; history, 61-66; immediate demands, 160; internal problems, 81-90; its dilemma, 8-10; labor party issue, 176-177; and labor unions, 177-179; and Nazism, 181-182; 1920 nomination, 119; Popular Front, 172; recent history, 157-172, 174-182, 187-190; unity negotiations with Communist Party, 170; wooed by communists, 144; and World War I, 96-97, 99-106; and World War II, 180-182
Socialist Propaganda League, 107, 108
Socialist Sentinel, 167n
Socialist Trades and Labor Alliance, 33, 41
Socialist Voice, 167n
Socialist Workers Party, 134n, 176
Socialistic Labor Party, *see* Socialist Labor Party
Solomon, Charles, 168
Sombart, Werner, 3-5
Sorel, Georges, 7
Sorge, Friedrich, 22, 23, 28, 36, 39
Soviet-German pact, 138n; its effect on American communists, 183-184
Spanish Civil War, 149-150, 175-176
Spargo, John, 70, 74, 85n, 100
Spark, 156
Spartacism, 124
Spencer, Herbert, 57
Stachel, Jack, 133, 133n-134n, 170
Stalin, Joseph, 83n, 106; address on unionism, 140; consolidation of power, 133, 138; "troika," 150
Stamm, Tom, 155
Stearns, Harold, 135
Stedman, Seymour, 82, 112
Steffens, Lincoln, 60, 136
Stephens, Uriah, 24
Stetler, Henry G., 190n
Steunenberg, Frank, 67
Stewart, Donald Ogden, 149
Stokes, J. G. Phelps, 45n, 78, 83, 101
Stokes, Rose Pastor, 101
Stolberg, Benjamin, 145n, 151n
Stone, Irving, 88n
Stone, Nahum, I., 40n, 82
Strachey, John, 183
Strand, Paul, 151

Strasser, Adolph, 23, 37, 40
Strong, Anna Louise, 143n
Sylvis, William, 20
Syndicalism, 7, 21, 64, 68
Syndicalist League of North America, 129

Taft, M. H. 82
Taft, Philip, 64n
Tarbell, Ida, 60
Technocracy, 161
Thälmann, Ernst, 139n
Thalheimer, August, 124
Theatre Collective, 142
Theatre of Action, 142
Theatre Union, 142
Thomas, Norman, 13n, 121, 122, 152n, 157-163, 170, 176-177, 182, 187-190
Thompson, Carl D., 100
Thompson, Dorothy, 152n
Toledano, Ralph de, 146n
Tom Watson's Magazine, 89
Torgler, Ernst, 144n
Townley, Arthur C., 91-92
Townsend movement, 161
Toynbee, Arnold J., 81
Trachtenberg, Alexander, 78n, 113
Trade Union Educational League, 130
Trade Union Unity League, 140
Trade unionism, 74; and politics, 120-121; *see also* entries under specific unions
Trager, Frank, 170
Trautmann, William, 67
Tresca, Carlo, 134n, 151n
Trevellick, Richard, 24
Trilling, Lionel, 136n
Trotsky, Leon, 3, 83n, 107; Dewey commission, 151; in U.S. 108, 107n-108n; on democratic centralism, 15; on Hillquit, 107; on Moscow trials, 151; supported by Cannon and Shachtman, 132; supported by L. Lore, 131
Trotskyism (U.S.), 154, 172-176
Tucker, Irwin St. John, 104
Tukhachevsky, Mikhail N., 151
Turati, Filippo, 114n
Turner, Frederick Jackson, 31n
Tyler, Gus, 172, 176, 182

United Auto Workers, 123, 178
United Communist Party (1920), 124, 126
United Electrical Workers, 185
United Hebrew Trades, 32
United Labor Party, 27-29
United Labor Party of Chicago, 27

United Mine Workers, 96, 119, 140n
United Office and Professional Workers Union, 170
United States, Congress, House, Committee on Un-American Activities, 146n, 148n
United Toilers of America (1922), 126, 127
Untermann, Ernest, 87, 100
Utopian socialism, later influence of, 17-19
Utopian Society, 161
Utopianism, 17

Van Doren, Carl, 149
Van Patten, Philip, 25
Vanzetti, Bartolomeo, 118
Vayo, Julio Alvarez del, see Alvarez del Vayo, Julio
Veblen, Thorstein, 56
Villard, Oswald Garrison, 157
Vladeck, B. Charney, 159
Vogt, Hugo, 46, 46n
Vorwärts, 45, 46n

Wadleigh, Julian, 146n
Wagenknecht, Alfred, 104, 109, 127n
Waite, David H. ("Bloody Bridles"), 31
Waldman, Louis, 158, 165-166, 167, 169
Wallace, Henry, 185
Walling, William English, 70, 78, 83, 99, 100
Walton, J. C., 95
Ward, Harry F., 143n, 148
Ward, Lester F., 57
Waton, Harry, 112
Watson, Tom, 89
Wayland, Julius A., 47-48, 58
Weatherwax, Clara, 142
Weaver, James B., 31, 33, 55
Weber, Max, 6, 13n, 193
Wechsler, James, 148n
Weisbord, Albert, 154, 155
Weitling, Wilhelm, 19, 28
Western Federation of Miners, 42, 64, 66, 67, 96
Western Labor Union, 42, 64
Weydemeyer, Joseph, 19
Weyl, Walter, 56, 101
Wheeler, Burton K., 182

White, Harry D., 146n
Wicks, Harry M., 127
Widick, B. J., 178n
Wilshire, Gaylord, 87
Wilshire's Magazine, 87
Wilson, Edmund, 106n, 137, 142, 142n, 153
Wilson, J. Stitt, 86, 100-101
Wilson, William, 90
Wilson, Woodrow, 56, 76, 79, 80, 90, 99, 100, 101n, 104, 105, 117
Witt, Nathan, 146
Wolfe, Bertram D., 112
Wolman, Leo, 118n
Woodcock, Leonard, 182
Woodhull, Victoria, 22
Woodrow Wilson Independent League, 100
Woodward, C. Vann, 89n
Work, John M., 62n
Workers Alliance, 170
Workers Challenge, 127
Workers Communist League, 154
Workers Council, 126
Workers Defense Conference of New England, 126; see also United Toilers of America
Workers Laboratory Theatre, 142
Workers League, 126
Workers Party (Communist), 121, 126-129; see also Communist Party (U.S.)
Workers Party (Trotskyist), 155-174
Working Class Union, 94
Workingmen's Party of New York, 18
Workingmen's Party of the United States, 24
Workmen's Circle, 98
World Tomorrow, 158
Wortis, Rose, 170
Wright, Chester M., 101
Wright, Richard, 142n, 153

Young Communist League, 163
Young People's Socialist League, 104, 163

Zack, Joseph (Kornfeder), 156n
Zam, Herbert, 170, 172
Zinoviev, Grigory, 114, 124, 125, 138n, 150